"This pioneering anthology further paves the path for a deeper understanding of 'religion–urbanism–heritage' reciprocity and interaction, illustrated with several case studies from South Asia that emphasise the distinct role of religion in urban development and the making of historical cities. This collection will help scholars, planners and administrators in making urban policies more rational and viable."
– *Rana P.B. Singh, Professor of Cultural Geography and Heritage Studies, Banaras Hindu University, India*

"This is an interesting and original treatment of the relations between religion, space and heritage in South Asia. It brings sustainability into the forefront of interdisciplinary scholarship and focuses on connections between urban planning and important belief systems that are still not well understood."
– *Michael Redclift, Emeritus Professor of International Environmental Policy, King's College, London*

"These deeply researched essays grow from the idea that the religious needs of cities have been overlooked by scholars and planners, as have the contributions that religious belief and practice make to urban life. Dealing with urban questions in Afghanistan, Pakistan, India and Sri Lanka, this book offer readers new perspectives on the ways in which religious practice has helped to shape twenty-first century cities. The writers argue that sustainable, tolerable futures for South Asian cities will only result from processes that take account of the daily reality of religious belief and custom."
– *Robin Jeffrey, Visiting Research Professor, Institute of South Asian Studies, National University of Singapore*

"This book shows that religion has made a structuring impact over the city in South Asia. Not only because shrines and processions give it a sacred flavor – bringing devotees of different denominations together, sometimes –, but also because ethno-religious nationalisms have all crystallized in an urban space and because communal riots have been an urban speciality. Besides, ghettoization among sectarian lines is much more pronounced in urban settings than in the rural context. This multifaceted book explores all these topics in depth."
– *Christophe Jaffrelot, Professor of Indian Politics and Sociology, King's College London*

Religion and Urbanism

Conceptions of 'sustainable cities' in the pluralistic and multireligious urban settlements of developing nations need to develop out of local cultural, religious and historical contexts to be inclusive and accurately respond to the needs of the poor, ethnic and religious minorities, and women.

Religion and Urbanism contributes to an expanded understanding of 'sustainable cities' in South Asia by demonstrating the multiple, and often conflicting ways in which religion enables or challenges socially equitable and ecologically sustainable urbanisation in the region. In particular, this collection focuses on two aspects that must inform the sustainable cities discourse in South Asia: the intersections of religion and urban heritage, and religion and various aspects of informality.

This book makes a much-needed contribution to the nexus between religion and urban planning for researchers, postgraduate students and policy makers in Sustainable Development, Development Studies, Urban Studies, Religious Studies, Asian Studies, Heritage Studies and Urban and Religious Geography.

Yamini Narayanan is a Lecturer in International and Community Development at Deakin University, Melbourne, Australia.

Routledge Research in Religion and Development

The *Routledge Research in Religion and Development* series focuses on the diverse ways in which religious values, teachings and practices interact with international development.

While religious traditions and faith-based movements have long served as forces for social innovation, it has only been within the last ten years that researchers have begun to seriously explore the religious dimensions of international development. However, recognising and analysing the role of religion in the development domain is vital for a nuanced understanding of this field. This interdisciplinary series examines the intersection between these two areas, focusing on a range of contexts and religious traditions.

Series Editors:
Matthew Clarke, Deakin University, Australia
Emma Tomalin, University of Leeds, UK
Nathan Loewen, Vanier College, Canada

Editorial board:
Carole Rakodi, University of Birmingham, UK
Gurharpal Singh, School of Oriental and African Studies, University of London, UK
Jörg Haustein, School of Oriental and African Studies, University of London, UK
Christopher Duncanson-Hales, Saint Paul University, Canada

Religion, Heritage and the Sustainable City
Hinduism and Urbanization in Jaipur
Yamini Narayanan

Religion and Urbanism
Reconceptualising sustainable cities for South Asia
Yamini Narayanan

Religion and Urbanism

Reconceptualising sustainable cities for South Asia

Edited by Yamini Narayanan

LONDON AND NEW YORK

First published 2016
by Routledge
2 Park Square, Milton Park, Abingdon, Oxon OX14 4RN

and by Routledge
711 Third Avenue, New York, NY 10017

First issued in paperback 2018

Routledge is an imprint of the Taylor & Francis Group, an informa business

© 2016 selection and editorial matter, Yamini Narayanan; individual chapters, the contributors

The right of the editor to be identified as the author of the editorial material, and of the authors for their individual chapters, has been asserted in accordance with sections 77 and 78 of the Copyright, Designs and Patents Act 1988.

All rights reserved. No part of this book may be reprinted or reproduced or utilised in any form or by any electronic, mechanical, or other means, now known or hereafter invented, including photocopying and recording, or in any information storage or retrieval system, without permission in writing from the publishers.

Trademark notice: Product or corporate names may be trademarks or registered trademarks, and are used only for identification and explanation without intent to infringe.

British Library Cataloguing-in-Publication Data
A catalogue record for this book is available from the British Library

Library of Congress Cataloging-in-Publication Data
Religion and urbanism : reconceptualising sustainable cities for South
    Asia / edited by Yamini Narayanan.
        pages cm. — (Routledge research in religion and development)
    1. Cities and towns—Religious aspects.   2. Cities and towns—South
Asia.   3. Sustainable urban development—South Asia.   4. Sustainable
development—Religious aspects.   5. South Asia—Religion.   I. Narayanan,
Yamini, editor.
    BL65.C57R45 2015
    200.954'091732—dc23
    2015022246

ISBN 13: 978-1-138-59785-3 (pbk)
ISBN 13: 978-0-415-74520-8 (hbk)

Typeset in Goudy
by Apex CoVantage, LLC

Contents

List of figures		ix
List of table		xi
Contributors		xii
Preface		xv

1	Religion, urbanism and sustainable cities in South Asia	1
	YAMINI NARAYANAN	

PART I
Urban history, religion and heritage 25

2	Origins of Buddhist nationalism in Myanmar/Burma: an urban history of religious space, social integration and marginalisation in colonial Rangoon after 1852	27
	ANTHONY WARE	

3	Religious heritage in the old city of Kabul	46
	STEPHANIE MATTI	

4	Revisiting planning for Indian cities: the pilgrim city of Amritsar	67
	SHIKHA JAIN	

5	Tradition versus urban public bureaucracy? Reshaping pilgrimage routes and religious heritage around contested space	80
	VERA LAZZARETTI	

6	Recognising the spatial and territorial nature of religious communities in Colombo, Sri Lanka	97
	ROHAN BASTIN	

viii *Contents*

PART II
Informality, marginalisation and violent exchange 115

7 Religious structures on traffic lanes: production of
informality in New Delhi 117
SURAJIT CHAKRAVARTY

8 Animals and urban informality in sacred spaces: bull-calf
trafficking in Simhachalam Temple, Visakhapatnam 143
YAMINI NARAYANAN

9 Karachi – a case study in religious and ethnic extremism:
implications for urban sustainability 162
CLAUDE RAKISITS

PART III
Reflections 181

10 Including religion as well as gender in Indian urban planning
policy: with reference to lessons from the United Kingdom 183
CLARA GREED

11 Religion and urban policy for South Asia: where next? 201
YAMINI NARAYANAN

Index 211

Figures

2.1	The Sule Pagoda in the heart of the central business district of Yangon. Adjacent buildings include: City Hall, Immanuel Baptist church, the former Supreme Court and the Bengali Sunni Jaime Mosque	29
2.2	Map of the downtown urban grid area of contemporary Yangon, highlighting the juxtaposition of some of the key religious buildings	30
3.1	The historic district of Murad Khani is situated at the centre of rapidly expanding Kabul	47
3.2	The traditional-style buildings of Murad Khani at sunrise	49
3.3	The private courtyard and inward-facing windows of Great Serai (recently restored by Turquoise Mountain) is typical of traditional buildings in Murad Khani	53
3.4	The Abu'l Fazl Shrine is at the centre of a large bazaar and economic hub	54
3.5	Decades of civil war and neglect left the physical structures of Murad Khani in ruins with much of the area buried under several metres of accumulated garbage	59
3.6	Together with the community, Turquoise Mountain has restored over 112 historic structures in the area	60
3.7	A large mosque is being constructed alongside the Abu'l Fazl Shrine	61
3.8	Members of the Murad Khani community come together to celebrate *Nawruz* (New Year)	63
7.1	Zabta Ganj Mosque on Rajpath	125
7.2	Picturesque setting of Zabta Ganj Mosque	126
7.3	Mosque not aligned with the orientation of the channel	126
7.4	Auliya Mosque, Connaught Circus	127
7.5	Auliya Mosque between the structure and the street	128
7.6	Parking space	128
7.7	Irwin Road Mosque, Baba Kharak Singh Marg	129
7.8	Sidewalk designed to ease the appearance of protrusion	129
7.9	Lost traffic lane reappears	130

x *Figures*

7.10	Colonial and post-independence interpretations of protecting religious structures	132
7.11	Temple on carriageway creates traffic bottleneck	133
7.12	Lost lane of traffic opens up after temple structure	134
7.13	Shrine on carriageway, one lane lost	135
8.1	A weeks-old donated male calf stands abandoned at the bottom of the 1000 steps to the Simhachalam Temple	151
8.2	The Simhachalam Temple and the peri-urban areas in Visakhapatnam district wherein the bull-calves are trafficked between the temple, livestock markets and slaughterhouses	152
9.1	Karachi's ethnic neighbourhoods	168

Table

6.1 Population census data for district and division according
to ethnicity   99

Contributors

Rohan Bastin teaches anthropology at Deakin University and specialises in the study of religious pluralism and ethnic conflict in Sri Lanka. He is author of a monograph on a major multireligious temple, as well as numerous articles on religious interaction, the impact of development policies and practice on ethnic conflict, and is currently writing a study of the Sri Lankan civil war.

Surajit Chakravarty is an assistant professor of Urban Planning at Alhosn University, Abu Dhabi. He holds a PhD in Urban Planning from the University of Southern California. His research focuses on community planning, housing, informality and civic engagement in multicultural societies.

Clara Greed is Emerita Professor of Inclusive Urban Planning at the University of the West of England, Bristol, United Kingdom. She is a chartered town planner, and her main interests are in the social aspects of planning, urban design, accessibility, equality issues, including gender and religion. She has published more than 12 books and many journal articles on planning and other built-environment issues. Research activities include work on creating accessible, equitable and sustainable cities, and as a result, she has worked on mainstreaming gender into planning policy, the role of public toilets in creating accessible city centres, and currently on the relationship between faith and place, with particular reference to the difficult relationship between planning authorities and Pentecostal mega-churches seeking permission to build or expand. What all these social issues have in common is that they are often ignored by the planners, as they are 'beneath the radar' and therefore invisible to what is still a material, secular and land-use focused planning profession.

Shikha Jain has a doctorate in architecture with specialisation in preservation and community design. She heads the organization DRONAH (Development and Research Organisation for Nature, Arts and Heritage), India, and is Founder Trustee of the IHCN-F (Indian Heritage Cities Network Foundation). Her experience in cultural heritage ranges from steering conservation projects for various state governments in India to preparing conservation plans funded by the Getty Foundation, World Monuments Fund and Nomination Dossiers and Management Plans for World Heritage Sites in India. As a consultant to United Nations Educational, Scientific, and Cultural Organization (UNESCO), New Delhi, she has worked on the Cultural Heritage Toolkit for the Ministry of Urban Development. She is chief editor of the journal *Context: Built, Living and Natural* and has several published books and articles on cultural heritage of India to her credit. She is Visiting Faculty for Urban Conservation in the Department of Urban Planning, School of Planning and Architecture, New Delhi. She is also the State Convener of Indian National Trust for Art and Cultural Heritage (INTACH), Haryana Chapter and coordinator for the National Scientific Committee ICOFORT for ICOMOS India. She has been part of several Technical Committees on Heritage Conservation Projects for State and Central Government organizations in India. Since 2011, she is also the Member Secretary, Advisory Committee on World Heritage Matters (ACWHM) under the aegis of the Ministry of Culture, India.

Vera Lazzaretti holds a PhD in Euro-Asian Studies (Università degli Studi di Torino, 2013) and has a background in Indology and Anthropology. Her main research focuses are the transformations of sacred places and religious practices in contemporary urban contexts of North India, and her doctoral thesis investigated the phenomenon of spatial transposition of pan-Indian deities in Varanasi; in particular, it addressed the group of local 'replica' *jyotirlingas*, the construction of their traditions and the pilgrimage connected with them. Since 2013, she has been teaching a workshop series 'Paths in Indian sacred geography: places and traditions' at the Università degli Studi di Milano. Vera's current areas of research include local pilgrimages in the urban context, the negotiation of cultural and religious heritage, sacred water places and the anthropology of space and place.

Stephanie Matti is based in Pakistan where she works for the UN Office for the Coordination of Humanitarian Affairs. She has previously worked for various research institutes and non-government organisations including Turquoise Mountain – an urban heritage organisation – in Afghanistan, International Rescue Committee, and La Trobe University. Her recent publications include an edited volume entitled *Democratic Contestation on the Margins: Regimes in small African countries* and several peer-reviewed articles on humanitarian reform and African politics in *Disasters*, *Africa Today* and *Third World Quarterly*.

Yamini Narayanan is an Australian Research Council Discover Early Career Research Fellow at the Alfred Deakin Research Institute, Deakin University. Her research examines the nexus between god, gender and planning, arguing that religion has a vital role in inclusive urban planning in India especially as regards women and minorities. More recently, her work has also begun to explore trans-species feminist urban planning – examining the significant and yet invisible role of animals in city building, and the complicity of urban religion in enabling animal exploitation for urban development. Her book *Religion, Heritage and the Sustainable City: Hinduism and Urbanisation in Jaipur* (Routledge) was published in 2015.

xiv *Contributors*

Claude Rakisits who is based in Washington, DC, is a Senior Fellow at the School of Foreign Service at Georgetown University, as well as a Non-resident Senior Fellow at the Atlantic Council's South Asia Center. He is also an Honorary Associate Professor in Strategic Studies at Deakin University, Melbourne. Dr. Rakisits has had almost 20 years of experience in the Australian public sector, including in the Departments of Defence, Foreign Affairs and Trade, and the Prime Minister and Cabinet, and the Office of National Assessments. In 2010–2013, he was the academic adviser at the Centre for Strategic and Defence Studies, the senior staff college at the Australian Defence College in Canberra. Dr. Rakisits's doctoral thesis was on national integration in Pakistan, examining the role of religion, ethnicity and the external environment. His publications and media interviews can be viewed on his homepage at www.geopolitical-assessments.com.

Anthony Ware is a senior lecturer in International and Community Development at Deakin University, Australia. He has previously taught development studies at the University of Melbourne and worked in the development sector in Southeast Asia. His primary research interests include the impact of the sociopolitical background, political transition and conflict in Myanmar on development for the poor and marginalised.

Preface

Three major trajectories, whose roots lie in the last two decades of the 20th century, but which have spectacularly come to prominence in the 21st, shape the premise and thesis of the this ground-breaking volume. The first trajectory is the growth and intensification of *planetary urbanisation*. Planetary urbanisation (a term developed by Neil Brenner and Christian Schmid [2011]) not only refers to the quantity of urbanisation facing the world (i.e. that 70% of the world's population is estimated to be living in cities by 2050). It also refers to its all-pervasive quality, including new scales of urban conglomeration that will traverse regional and national boundaries, the disintegration of urban hinterlands in the expansion of industrial urbanisation or post-industrial urban networks, and the potential end of what is popularly imagined to be 'the wilderness' (p. 6). Planetary urbanisation is as much a new imaginary about what it is to be human and dwell on the earth as it is the ruthless integration of previous natural habitats into the 'rhythms of urbanisation' (p. 13). The focus on South Asian cities in this volume is therefore appropriate. It is this region, constituting Bangladesh, Bhutan, India, the Maldives, Nepal, Pakistan, Sri Lanka, Afghanistan and Myanmar, where planetary urbanisation is visceral and pronounced, producing intense strain on social, cultural environmental and political life as growing inequality and poverty vie with urban bling and neo-liberal boosterism.

The second trajectory is the growth of globalised religion that greatly complexifies what had hitherto been assumed to be an uncomplicated and linear teleology of secularisation upon which modern urban and economic planning had been predicated. The global picture of how and where religion impacts on the materialities of the urban is startling (at least from a Western perspective) if the latest projections from the Pew Research Centre on The Future of World Religions (2015) prove to be broadly accurate. Based on current trends for example, the United Kingdom will see a drop in those identifying as Christian from 64% in 2010 to 45% in 2050 whilst those identifying as Muslims will rise to 11%. The proportion of the population claiming no religion – or the unaffiliated – will have risen to 39%. The United Kingdom therefore will no longer be a majority 'Christian' country, and neither, according to the Pew Survey, will France, the Netherlands, Bosnia-Herzegovina, Australia or New Zealand.

xvi *Preface*

Globally however, because of population growth patterns in different regions of the world, the Pew report predicts that the unaffiliated will be a declining sector of the world's population – down from 16.4% to 13.2%. Christianity will retain its current share of the global citizen market at 31.4% (or just under 3 billion) as the decline of Christianity in some parts of Europe is offset by dramatic increases in sub Saharan Africa and more modest growth in Asia and the Pacific. Other religions stay broadly the same (with perhaps the exception of global Buddhist affiliation which is predicted to decline from 7.1% to 5.2%). Islam however is the exception, with its share of global affiliation set to rise exponentially from 23.2% to 29.7%. By 2070 it is likely to eclipse Christianity as the largest global population bloc.

This means that planetary urbanisation, at its most intense in regions like South Asia, is occurring within national and cultural contexts (i.e. nation states) in which religion is already pervasive and ubiquitous and is set to be even more so in the future. Leaving aside nations states where religious affiliation is almost 100% Muslim (i.e. Afghanistan and Pakistan) the profile of Sri Lanka (for example) in 2050 is 6% Christian, 12% Muslim, 14% Hindu and 68% Buddhist. Unaffiliated are less than 0.1%. Myanmar, it is projected, will be 8% Christian, 5% Muslim, 1.5% Hindu, 80% Buddhist, 5% folk religion and unaffiliated 0.5%. And so on.

The third trajectory is the increasing challenges to urban sustainability. Narayanan points out that such is the impact of planetary urbanisation on the globe, that sustainable development as defined by the Brundtland Commission in 1987 (namely '. . . development that meets the needs of the present without compromising the ability of future generations to meet their own needs') can only be addressed if urban poverty is addressed. As Kaika and Swyngedouw (2014) remind us, the inefficient management and planning of urban spaces is responsible for 80% of the world's resource use and generates most of the world's waste. This is due, they suggest, to the uncontrolled proliferation of interdependent physical and virtual networks that closer bind vital infrastructures such as water and sewage management to the demands of globalised capitalism (what they call 'the urban metabolism'). Under this unregulated growth in circulatory systems, the poorest sites of the city are where the most dangerous and toxic by-products of urban and technological waste are neutralised and recycled in (for example) 'the socio-ecologically dystopian geographies of Mumbai's or Dhaka's suburban informal wastelands' (2014).

This toxic and unsustainable urban future is reinforced, in their opinion, by what they label as 'the trap of nature fetishism or ecological determinism' (Kaika & Swyngedouw 2014). They argue that the inertia of the 'post-political consensus' that seeks only to manage decline, rather than confront the political and economic inequalities of the urban metabolism, is created by a mixture of fear and fatalism that is generated by inarticulate and sentimentalised appeals to Nature (with a capital N).

They call instead for a new vision of urban environmentalism that roots itself in a hard-headed analysis of the way cities replicate themselves via the urban metabolism, rather than a generalised and sentimentalised appeal to Nature.

Preface xvii

However this vision is far from developed. There are vague references to 'asking questions about what visions of Nature and what socio-environmental relations are being promoted; what quilting points are being used and how are they being stitched together; and who are promoting these visions and why'. There are the customary appeals to the radical voices of grassroots movements made up of the *indignados* who are demanding more inclusive democratic processes as to how cities are shaped in the future. But these movements are random and episodic lines of flight that are often more symbolic and rhetorical in their impact. They are not of sufficient institutional or embedded weight to leverage more mundane and deeply rooted circulations of affect and politics that can create a critical mass of change in both imaginary and practice.

Within the analysis of critical urban geographers such as Kaika and Swyngedouw, there is no mention of the role of religion as a potential source of practical resources and imaginaries by which to address the profound challenges to sustainable urban planning. This despite the figures quoted earlier highlighting the saturation of religion as a lived identity marker and embedded cultural and political reality within the very nation states in which planetary urbanisation is taking place. This absence of acknowledgement represents a traditional and ongoing blindspot within the post-Frankfurt school sociological tradition. But in an urbanised and increasingly religious globe, then the time is ripe to cultivate what Habermas has influentially (and controversially for some) called for: a postsecular imagination of the public sphere (or 'society as a whole') in which 'the vigorous continuation of religion in a continually secularising environment must be reckoned with' (Habermas 2005: 26). A postsecular sociological imagination, based on empirical realities, but also seeking a more open and dialectic political and intellectual engagement between the resources of both religious and secular worldviews, would take serious note of the resources that religious identities and imaginations bring to the urban sustainability and planning debate.

So what are these resources? Within the chapters of this volume, the following properties and attributes attached to religion emerge as powerful shapers of the urban environment. First, religion contributes a sense of place. Through its overlapping networks of ritual and membership faith communities help root urban spaces in what Vasquez refers to as 'face-to-face encounters'. It also locates peoples' lives within the context of 'storied place' – spaces where individual narratives are held within wider cosmic and national narratives. Within 'globalisation's relentless dialectic of de-territorialisation and re-territorialisation' (Vasquez 2011: 282) religious groups offer spaces of dwelling (or re-territorialisation) that not only communicate a sense of home and security to their members, but to the wider community as well. A sense of place is vital for the experience of well-being and flourishing, helping to foster an understanding of belonging (especially for religious and ethnic minorities) that is rooted in collective memories that go back beyond the immediate past and help contextualise the present, whilst also providing a normative narrative against which to weigh the future.

Second, religion provides a deep source of urban identity, that shapes other identity markers such as nationality, culture and ethnicity. It is conceptualised in

xviii *Preface*

this volume as a form of both tangible and intangible heritage (Narayanan 2015). Religion contributes built forms – monuments, sites, cultural landscapes etc. – as tangible heritage. But it also contributes *intangible* heritage in the guise of 'practices, representations, expressions, knowledge, skills of communities and groups, and individuals, as well as instruments, objects, artefacts and cultural spaces'. It is the dialectic interaction between these two expressions of heritage that help convey a deeper sense of identity, place and memory

Third, religious practice and theology can also foster an attitude of deep ecology within the structures of the city, which offer an alternative notion of urban metabolism to the hard-edged ones imagined by planners and some traditions of critical urban geography. Within some religious customs in South Asian cities, the dead, for example, are reverently offered back to nature in the form of cremation or natural decay in set apart sacred spaces. The passing of cosmic time and the cyclical seasons of the year are celebrated in public rituals of special food and communal pageant. These remind the wider city that secular time, with its focus on present and short-term realties, needs to be offset with longer timeframes and deeper trajectories of ethics and solidarity that emerge from sources beyond the immediately material. Meanwhile, religions like Hinduism, Buddhism and Shinto express a theological view that the created order is divine because it is suffused with the omnipresence of the supreme divinity. These insights lead to a deep respect for the balance and sustainability inherent within nature and its methods of self-regulation and growth.

Finally, there is the close link between religion and those who are the most poor and dispossessed in the urban ecology, who are forced to live in the 'gray' zones of informal planning – in other words the slums, shanty towns and other impromptu spaces of gathering and living (such as between railway lines or under flyovers). Here religious shrines and spaces of worship and ritual are physical expressions of the invisible codes norms and ethics of solidarity and hope by which these spaces are organised. Religious shrines and buildings often interrupt the linear assumptions of efficiency within modernist planning in many South Asian cities that are still shaped by colonial and neo-liberal mindsets. Surjit Chakravarty, in this volume, indicates how religious identities are wilfully misunderstood and ignored as irrational (in the hope that somehow they will go away). But they are also problematic entities that disrupt the smoothness of the secular imaginary, as these religiously framed and signposted areas of informality can also become spaces of political contestation and subversion. The production of space and relationships in these areas, so Chakravarty maintains, 'forces us to reimagine the global city and everyday life in terms of reference that are grounded in local realities'. These local realities are substantially grounded in religiously inspired ones that also create the networks of dense relationships and connectivity that help support the conditions upon which urban sustainability relies.

It would of course be wholly misguided to suggest that the social and physical impacts of religious practices and materialities are only progressive and serve the better interests of all. Many articles in this volume identify the visceral legacy of colonial planning and the brutal suppression of indigenous identity and ritualistic spaces it often entailed (usually as part of a policy of divide and rule). This served only to stoke up violence in later generations. As the grip of colonial power lessened in the 1930s, 1940s and 1950s, so religion often became the vehicle by which nationalistic, ethic and cultural wars were waged. A vicious cycle of violence going back decades has left many South Asian cities in the grip of religiously derived communalism and terror. For example, Claude Rakisits expertly unpicks the historical legacy of partition on the city of Karachi that has created what he calls the Fundamentalist City. This is the ghettoised city in which disparate ethic and religious groups (such as the Taliban) control their areas by strict and draconian enforcement of religio-political practices. They then reinforce their political control at municipal level through further practices of violence, extortion and terrorism.

Elsewhere, the innate conservatism of many religious traditions particularly in the areas of gender relations and human sexuality will often contribute to conditions of unacceptable stigmatisation, violence and control over women and sexual minorities in particular. Religion functions to legitimise other culturally conservative norms in society such as patriarchy and political hierarchy. However, I also want to broaden the concept of the Fundamentalist City by suggesting (in line with the thesis evident in several chapters in this book) that the religious Fundamentalist City often emerges as a direct counterpoint to the secular Fundamentalist city of high modernity and colonial exploitation. These planning and zoning practices often embodied a hubristic belief in the superiority of Western culture and education over the perceived regressive and simplistic world view of the religious and cultural Other.

In conclusion, Narayanan suggests that in order to counter both religious and secular expressions of fundamentalism we need to re-imagine religion as a 'progressive, liberal and postsecular construct'. This means developing awareness and understanding (including more empirical research) into the many ways religious practices and materialities not only sustain but also offer alternative imaginaries and strategies for managing urban sustainability and cohesion.

To my mind, this means expanding the tropes of heritage and informality with which this book theorises the relationship between religion and urbanisation, highly creative and illuminating as these are. There is a still a tendency from interdisciplinary social science and anthropology to view religion as a phenomenon inevitably tied to the past (as in the heritage discourse) or one that lies beyond the margins of the mainstream (as in the informality discourse). As the Pew Templeton research shows, but predicts with even more certainty, religious identity is mundane as well as remarkable. It is a pervasive, everyday, deeply embedded and intensely personal (and therefore often private) form of identity that nevertheless profoundly shapes the way that religious citizens engage in the public life of the *urbs* (i.e. the materiality of the city), as well as its *polis* (its politics and spirit). It is an active and dynamic reality, that doesn't simply filter into the present from the musty and exotic landscapes of the past. It is deeply embedded and increasingly at the forefront of urban justice movements and strategies of compassion and welfare that help humanise and balance the pressures of urban life.

xx *Preface*

In previous work, I have suggested that the value of the notion of the 'post-secular city' is best deployed as an heuristic device. It challenges all urban communities and citizens 'to recognise that the complexity and entrenched nature of the common problems facing urban societies (poverty, inequality, environmental degradation, terrorism, environmental threat) are beyond the skill and resources of either [religious or secular citizens] to meet on their own.' (Baker and Beaumont 2011: 259). I also ask whether we can see the postsecular city as a kind of laboratory, where we can be more open to understanding and encouraging the informal experimentation between people of different belief systems as they engage in the pragmatic search for practical and local solutions to entrenched forms of urban vicissitude. The growth of organic and informal 'geographies of postsecular rapprochement' (Cloke and Beaumont 2012) can complement and bring to life the more top-down planning initiatives that seek to create spaces and places of and for the common good.

The conversation about how we enact Habermas' challenge to reimagine the public square as a postsecular one within the context of sustainable urban planning has barely begun. Thankfully, this volume is an invaluable and important step in this direction.

Chris Baker
William Temple Professor of Religion and
Public Life, University of Chester

References

Baker, Christopher and Justin Beaumont. 2011. 'Afterword: Postsecular Cities'. In *Postsecular Cities – Space, Theory and Practice* (pp. 254–266), eds. J. Beaumont and C. Baker. London and New York: Continuum.

Brenner, Neil and Christian Schmid. 2011. 'Planetary Urbanisation'. In *Urban Constellations* (pp. 10–14), ed. Matthew Gandy. Berlin: Jovis.

Cloke, Paul and Justin Beaumont. 2012. Geographies of Postsecular Rapprochement in the City. *Progress in Human Geography* 37 (1): 27–51.

Habermas, Jürgen. 2005. Equal Treatment of cultures and the limits of postmodern liberalism. *Journal of Political Philosophy* 13 (1): 1–28.

Kaika, Maria and Eric Swyngedouw. 2014. Radical urban political-ecological imaginaries: planetary urbanization and politicizing nature. *Eurozine* (on-line article), www.eurozine.com/articles/2014-05-14-swyngedouw-en.html (retrieved June 12 2015).

Pew Research Center. 2015, 2 April. 'The Future of World Religions: Population Growth Projections, 2010–2050'.

Vasquez, Manuel. 2011. *More Than Belief: A Materialist Theory of Religion*. Oxford: Oxford University Press.

1 Religion, urbanism and sustainable cities in South Asia

Yamini Narayanan

Introduction

Sustainable urbanisation with its implications for climate change and socio-economic well-being is of global concern, but the combined importance of four trends that involve religion and/or sustainable development is largely neglected in the urban policymaking across South Asia. One, since 2006, the human population in cities has overtaken that of the rural regions worldwide. The pace of urbanisation in South Asia is fraught with environmental, socio-political and health risks for people as climatic catastrophes, population explosion, the growing scale of informal and slum developments, high consumption, and volatile identity politics involving religion and space threaten to overwhelm equitable growth.

Two, the last decade has noted problems associated with modernist planning in developing countries that 'have been imposed or borrowed from elsewhere' (UN Habitat 2009: 9). The zoning methods introduced by the British, for instance, prioritised motorised vehicles in heavily populated cities of the Indian colony, now India, Pakistan and Bangladesh. This introduced a system of socio-spatial segregation unknown even in caste-based Indian society (UN Habitat 2009). Modernist planning tends to assume a 'one-dimensional' view of civil society, while in fact, civil society is 'inspired more by religious movements' in developing cities (UN Habitat 2009:7).

Three, there are problems specifically with neglecting religion in urban planning policies, leading to 'flawed' planning. In the West, many planning theorists have argued that urban policy's lack of engagement with religion, spirituality and forms of the 'non-rational' (Sandercock 1998: 212) has created problems like marginalisation of particular groups, destruction of ecological resources and increased poverty. The neglect of religion in policy is similarly emerging as a problem in South Asian cities, as evidenced by increased ghettoisation and impoverishment of minority religious groups (Gayer and Jaffrelot 2012; Sachar Commission Report 2006).

Fourth, South Asia is home to nations going through extraordinary instability and volatility as they determine nationhood and national identities. Religion defines nation-building in South Asia, and nation-building occurs in the cities.

2 Yamini Narayanan

The newest member of the South Asian community, Afghanistan for instance – similar to Myanmar – has embarked on a project of reconstructing its beleaguered state through its cities. Indeed the recent upheavals have caused an increased rate of urbanisation as rural citizens migrate outwards for employment and security (UN-Habitat 2014). The capital Kabul alone contains more than 50 per cent of the nation's urban population (UN-Habitat 2014), a myriad mix of ethnicities and religions. It is ever more timely to foreground religion as a planning concern as national development becomes intimately intertwined with urban development.

The contributions in this volume address the idea that religion influences urbanisation and urban development in South Asian cities, and yet, religion's role remains a blind spot in mainstream urban planning. The need for South Asia to develop planning policies that are truly attuned to the specific needs of its cities is acute, and for this, consideration of religion is vital. Hancock and Srinivas (2008: 620) note, 'One of the persistently stubborn assumptions of so much of recent urban theory and policy seems to be that religion is external, incidental, or peripheral to the discussion of urban modernity or civic futures'. In particular, they note, this has most deeply impacted cities of Asia where the real and palpable influence on everyday urbanism has been treated as 'object lessons in a failed modernity or a modernity arriving by detours and hesitations, carnivalesque imitations and unavoidable tragedies' (620). Hancock and Srinivas (2008: 620) assert that these approaches have 'unintentionally pathologized the study of modern religion' but indeed the study of various dimensions of urbanisms as well. There is an urgent need for urban studies of South Asia to embrace the anthropological, sociological, and even the theological dimensions of religion to fully understand the cities of that region. Hancock and Srinivas (2008: 620) observe:

> Despite the depth and richness of the material and textual archives of urban religiosity, works within *urban studies* [authors' emphasis] focused on contemporary Asia and Africa, however, have been uneven in their self-conscious exploration of religion, particularly the ways in which it is imbricated [sic] with market economies, consumerism, migrations, mass media, informality or gentrification.

The planning and design of sustainable urban environments are by no means within the sole purview of urban planners and architects alone. This edited volume makes the plea that planning for sustainable urban development in South Asia must be regarded and approached as a multidisciplinary exercise. Conceptions and strategies for sustainability must necessarily comprise a range of worldviews. In his work on excavating the 'real' elements that comprise Old Delhi's sense of place, Indian anthropologist Ajay Gandhi (2011) emphasises the need for the 'anthropologist's gaze' from below to replace – or at the least, complement – the 'planner's gaze from the top'. In his analysis of sustainable development for the cities of the South, Bolay (2011: 85) notes, 'Each discipline, each profession, must partake in the shared endeavour to make sense of territorial and social complexities'.

To this end, nine experts from a variety of disciplines ranging from anthropology, sociology, politics, women's studies, sustainable development, religious studies and last but not the least – urban planning – come together in this edited volume to explore some critical questions related to religion, urbanism and sustainable cities in South Asia. How has religion physically and culturally structured and restructured urban spaces in South Asia? What do built artefacts of religion and the spaces that they organise tell us about how space is perceived, approached and utilised? How does religion privilege or control access to cityspaces in secular, multifaith postcolonial contexts in South Asia? How has religion differentially contributed to democratic and collective action in the Indian subcontinent? Aside from caste, are there other ways in which religion has contributed to socio-political inequalities in South Asian cities? How do these hierarchies determine how space is organised and utilised (Patel 2009)?

Two themes emerge in these chapters, often simultaneously, demonstrating the extent of the closely intricate relationships between the distinct forms and roles that religion takes on. Together, they also convey the case for religion to be factored in as a distinct planning concept, as it draws its forms and complexities from its anthropological conceptions. The first of these focus on urban histories and heritage with a focus on space, built form and living traditions. In order to pragmatically consider religion in policy without risking reductionism of this complex concept, the heritage discourse and the substantial body of work on heritage as a policy construct help to deconstruct religion as tangible and intangible heritage. This covers religion's 'physical, built, natural as well as its socio-cultural ritualistic and performative aspects, identities and values-based manifestations' (Narayanan 2015: 4).

The second theme focuses on the role of religion in delineating identities and the impact on the types of informal development, marginalisation and violence. Informality is not regarded merely as the illegal or the unplanned, such as unauthorised shanty towns and slums, but as a product of formal planning itself. Indeed, an overwhelming proportion of the activities that occur within the ambit of informal growth in developing nations is legal (Neuwirth 2011) and plays a irreplaceable role in sustaining developing cities.

As a final note, we recognise that 'South Asia' itself is far from a stable concept, and for this reason, we have deliberately chosen to refer to a looser and more inclusive list of countries that may also be regarded as South Asian. The political bloc SAARC (South Asian Association for Regional Cooperation) has a limited membership of eight countries, viz., Bangladesh, Bhutan, India, the Maldives, Nepal, Pakistan, Sri Lanka and, since 2006, Afghanistan. However, the shared experience of British colonial urbanism and the geographical proximity of urban nodes and transport routes is a useful framework for comparisons, and for that reason, India's other neighbours such as Myanmar may be safely and usefully regarded as South Asian, for the purposes of this study.

The city and religion in South Asia in the neoliberal age

More than two decades have passed since the demolition of the 500 year-old Babri Mosque by Hindu fundamentalists in Ayodhya city in north India on 6th December 1992. In the immediate aftermath of the destruction, repercussions were swift and equally violent in Dhaka and other major cities in Bangladesh where Hindu temples were burnt or broken, and minority communities were brutally persecuted. Through the story of the horrors faced by a Hindu family in her novel *Lajja* [Shame], exiled Bangladeshi feminist and writer Taslima Nasrin depicts how powerfully and intimately religion transcends national borders in South Asia, with the greatest intensity of consequences reserved for cities. Entire megapolises in South Asian nations go through complete upheaval as a result of religious fundamentalism in neighbouring countries. Interestingly, the events of 1992 are widely perceived to have had a more forceful and enduring impact than even the Partition holocaust of 1947. The Godhra carnage[1] in Ahmedabad in 2002 shows how large and small cities across South Asia continue to experience shockwaves and tremors that disrupt communities, physical sites and structures, ecologies and equity. Religious fundamentalism has since disrupted urban life in Ahmedabad, Jaipur, Karachi, Lahore, Varanasi, Peshawar among others, creating cities that are more spatially fragmented than before on sectarian lines.

The early 1990s marked a significant turning point for the nations of South Asia, marked by the dovetailing two megatrends of increased urbanisation and neoliberalism in the region, with a greater assertion of religion in public and political life. In 1991, India started its lurch towards neoliberal growth. In a radical departure from its conservative economic and foreign policies, the Indian government dismantled several of the restrictive regimes to its economic structures, and liberalised the economy in favour and pursuit of neoliberal growth. Cities are the springboard upon which neoliberal growth occurs, and it was notably then, that urban development and planning became explicitly a national priority in India. Previously, individual states determined their own urban development and growth trajectories (Narayanan 2015). In 1992, India implemented a 'National Urban Policy' for the first time when it became clear that the national growth engine depended centrally on the organisational efficiency and capacity of its cities. National prosperity became linked to urban prosperity.

India's liberalisation of its economy and the reshifting of its focus on its cities set the precedent for the refocussing of the national gaze from the villages to the cities throughout the Indian subcontinent, followed by an exponential urban population explosion. UN-Habitat's (2012: 25) *The State of the World's Cities* report notes that the yearly population rise in just six developing cities – four of which are in South Asia, viz. New Delhi and Mumbai (India), Karachi (Pakistan) and Dhaka (Bangladesh) – exceeds the entire per annum population growth of Europe. The speed and scale of urbanisation in India in particular is unprecedented almost anywhere in the world. By 2030, nearly 600 million Indians will live in cities where 70 per cent of the nation's employment and GDP will be generated (McKinsey Global Institute 2010). India (along with China

Sustainable cities in South Asia   5

and Nigeria) will contribute to 37 per cent of the total urban population between 2014 and 2050 (United Nations 2014).

The future of the urban scale in South Asia is quite simply staggering. Some of the largest megacities and the highest numbers of million-plus cities will be located in India, Pakistan and Bangladesh; indeed, with the exception of Sri Lanka, all South Asian nations report a rapid escalation of the size and numbers of their cities (United Nations 2014). More than 50 per cent of Pakistan's total population is expected to be urban by 2030 (Haider and Haider 2006). Even Nepal, one of the least urbanised nations in South Asia forecasts vital urban trends. At 6.6 per cent, Nepal's rate of urbanisation is the highest in the Indian subcontinent, and the Kathmandu Valley metropolitan region is the fastest growing in South Asia (UN-Habitat Nepal 2012). The face of such urban growth is almost consistently poor. In Dhaka, over 70 per cent of the population are poor and are squeezed into less than 20 per cent of the surface area of the megacity (Davis 2006: 95). Nearly 70 per cent of Indian urban citizens live in slums on about $1.80 a day (McKinsey Global Institute 2010).

During this time of rapid urban growth in recent decades, religion sat uneasily – but definitely – at the table reconfiguring urban spaces, and urbanisms or the ways of relating peoples and places. That urbanisation in South Asia was accompanied by a resurgence of sectarianism, and the greater visibility of religion in public spaces and debate should be entirely unsurprising; in her study of politics of growth and religious violence in Sri Lanka, Bulankulame (2013) notes that neoliberal development, especially in developing nations almost always occurs at the intersection of religion and devastating violence.

However communalism is not the only issue that makes the need for studies bringing religion and urban together in South Asia compelling. Indeed religion exerts a palpable influence on the very character and sense of South Asian cityscapes itself. Religion is a critical element that distinguishes place and sense of place in Indian cities, impacting urban design but also the relationship of the multifaith community with place (Narayanan 2015). Urban anthropologist Steven Parish (1997: 453) for instance documents the sheer diversity of Hindu religious built form, rituals, actions, values and belief systems that constitute the everyday in Bhaktapur city in Nepal and writes, 'The city is part what the Hindu pantheon makes it. Urban space, form, and action are shaped, known and experienced in terms of religious meanings'. If religion does not actually make the South Asian city, it certainly has a heavy-handed influence. Demonstrating the ways in which religion in both iconic and everyday forms is a *planning concern* in Jaipur city, I have argued that 'urban planning must be informed by anthropological language and concepts to stay close to the grounded realities of Indian urbanism, as it is *people* and their built environment that is being planned' (Narayanan 2015: 15).

Religion also collides with, and shapes several of the most significant of modernities in South Asia such as citizenship (Ring 2006), tourism (Bandyopadhyay et al. 2008), urban development and planning (Narayanan 2015) and even the growth of informal spaces (Roy 2005; Davis 2006). South Asian urban modernity has, in several ways, assumed similar forms as modern growth in cities

6 *Yamini Narayanan*

elsewhere – gentrification and ghettoisation, fortification and gated communal spaces; the growth of industrialised and manufacturing spaces alongside squatter settlements (Hancock and Srinivas 2008). However in each of these spaces, religion is a palpable force in the formation of an indigenous modernity (Hosagrahar 2005). Hancock and Srinivas (2008: 620) write, 'Far from withering away, religious spaces and practices have acquired heightened visibility in these settings'.

The 1990s also heralded the start of a third megatrend in South Asia – the increasing cooption of 'sustainable development' as a national development agenda. Along with concerns for poverty alleviation, renewable energies and ecological concerns, one of the most significant locus for conceptualising and implementing sustainable development has been in the cities. However development policymaking in the region has generally continued to rely on Euro-centric conceptions of sustainable development that emphasise the ecological dimensions of development (Patra 2009). While this is undoubtedly central to sustainable development, the risks that such approaches can lead to 'environmental racism' or 'environmental elitism' by disregarding the interests of the poor are real (Martinez-Alier 2002: 11), by strengthening existing social and political inequalities and/or creating new ones (Agyeman and McEntee 2012). 'Justice' must hence underpin approaches to sustainable urbanism (Agyeman and McEntee 2012), and the factors that determine justice are vital to the achievement of sustainable urban development itself. Harvey (1994: 53) emphasises the need 'to re-elaborate upon what it takes to create the values and institutions of a reasonably just society'. The consideration of religion, we suggest in this volume, is indispensible to the conception and development of sustainable, equitable cities in South Asia.

Religion, urbanism and sustainable cities: making the connections

Agenda for environmental and social development have generally been designed for areas outside of the city; however since the 1990s, there has been strong consensus that sustainable city planning has to be actively integrated in a global sustainability view, since cities arguably 'shape the world' (Newman and Kenworthy 1999: 6). In fact, Yanarella and Levine (1992) even propose that all other sustainability strategies should centrally revolve around designing and constructing sustainable cities. Beatley and Manning (1997) support this view. They write (1997: 56): 'Any sustainability strategy that is truly comprehensive requires concern about the condition and status of cities – whether older cities, inner cities or inner-ring suburbs'. In particular, they stress, 'the environmental agenda of sustainability must go hand in hand with a strong cities or urban agenda' (Beatley and Manning 1997: 56). The importance of the urban green agenda was evident in the Secretary-General's address to the Earth Summit in Rio de Janeiro in 1992: 'If sustainable development does not start in the cities, it will not go – cities have got to lead the way' (Brugmann 1996, in McGranahan et al. 2001: 9). This growing concern with city sustainability was prefigured in the Brundtland Commission report (1987: 279), which had noted that the new millennium would be the 'century of the "urban revolution"'.

More than two decades have passed since the acknowledgement of the indisputable role of cities in strategising and implementing sustainable development, and during this time, the centre stage of urbanisation has also decisively shifted to the rapidly urbanising, sprawling concentrations of the South. As South Asian cities experience historically unprecedented growth, as compared to the erstwhile focus on the development of its regions and villages, the focus on their *sustainable* development has also never been as urgent. Some of the greatest challenges for urban sustainable development are undoubtedly in the ecologically degraded cities of the Indian subcontinent where economic growth – without which social justice cannot be achieved – is a highly delicate and complicated task. South Asian cities are particularly vulnerable to two kinds of poverties identified by Stephens (2000: 101): 'physical poverties' such as food deprivation, water deprivation, land deprivation, inadequate or no access to health and sanitation, lack of shelter and transport poverty; as well as other standards of poverty, such as 'poverty of opportunity', which denies the poor employment and education, all vital to lift current and future generations out of endemic vulnerability. Haas's (2009: 7) concerns for the sustainability of the cities of the new millennium are possibly most resonant for the exploding cities and conurbations of South Asia:

> . . . [a] challenge that will shape the outcome of our cities is experienced through the waves of exploding population growth, transformation of networks, and economic disparity and prosperity that carry consequences for both the environment and the long-term social well-being of inhabitants.

The challenges for planning sustainable cities in South Asia are additionally vastly compounded by the sheer areal scale of the sites. In the Indian subcontinent, urban growth extends not merely to cities by any means, but ultimately, to the geographical nation-state itself through the industrialisation and/or commercialisation of its conurbations (Haas 2009). In the most populous South Asian nations like India, Pakistan and Bangladesh, the urban development authorities are responsible for not just the metropolitan areas of the city, but also the district and the region surrounding the city which can include smaller towns and cities, peri-urban and rural precincts. They are, in a sense, administrators of what Patrick Geddes terms 'conurbations' in his book *Cities in Evolution*: large urban regions that have developed through the merging of several kinds of urban spaces as well as population growth. Urbanisation is hardly a spatially bounded phenomenon by any means, but in South Asia, it now commonly occurs through the growth of conurbations, or the extended region surrounding megacities or other significant and usually large cities, which includes other smaller cities, towns and even peri-urban villages.

This areal mass now forms large continuous urban areas, and may be planned, but more often than not as in South Asia, is entirely unplanned. Rawalpindi and Islamabad cities in Pakistan for instance no longer remain distinct. They have merged completely into one gigantic city through growth of the populations as well as the physical sprawl of both cities, though they ostensibly are governed under two planning authorities. In fact, India, Pakistan and Bangladesh, which have particularly high population densities greatly under-estimate the size of urban populations as most population studies interpret 'urban' rigidly, excluding peri-urban areas and populations (Haider and Haider 2006; Narayanan 2015). The parameters for urban governance in South Asia thus spatially far exceeds the metropolitan and suburban bounds of cities, and typically also covers large conurbations of surrounding districts and regions.

The manner in which the nations of South Asia urbanise has sustainability implications worldwide. The much invoked Perlman Principles systematically link the achievement of global sustainability itself, to the eradication of urban poverty in the developing regions of the world (Perlman 2007). Janice Perlman emphasised the need for inclusivity in eliminating poverty – inclusivity of these regions in determining and implementing global urban sustainable development, but also, of the disenfranchised, minorities and others within developing cities who had thus far been excluded from political participation in the making of their cities. Perlman (2007) argued that in addition to ecological restoration, economic vitality and social justice (the three universally acknowledged pillars of sustainable development), a 'sustainable city' depends on the equitable political participation of its citizens, and cannot exist without this. The ultimate conclusion of the Perlman Principles is that 'There can be no sustainable city in the twenty-first century without social justice and political participation as well as economic vitality and ecological regeneration' (Perlman 2007: 173). In contrast, Indian cities continue to be 'developed' under a Master Plan, with no or minimal citizen participation (Downton 2000). Neither do the planning models for the cities of South Asia account for critical categories of identity – such as religion – which can emphatically impact inclusivity (Narayanan 2015).

Sustainable development is now a significant planning concept and strategy for South Asian cities. Almost all recent Master Plans in India for instance emphasise its importance as one of the foremost guiding principles. It is clear that sustainable development itself, with its broad applicability to ecological, economic and socially equitable development is desirable. The elements that define sustainable development in the clearest and most meaningful ways must however be drawn from insight and practices locally. Haas (2009: 7–8): 'To create sustainable living places, what we need from urbanism is a broad coalition of progressive ideas at a systems level, one which will offer a synthesis of skills, innovation, and knowledge . . . Sustainability is . . . a necessity'. In particular, Bolay (2011: 85) identifies four aspects of urbanism that must be considered in any strategy for sustainable urban development in the South:

1. 'a multidimensional perspective on new urban forms, in both diagnosing problems (inter-disciplinary vision) and devising proposals (holistic approach and inter-sectorial actions);

2. the participation of all stakeholders involved in designing and implementing the city's transformation;
3. the multiplicity of scales to take into consideration [from neighbourhoods to the city fringe to the regional outreach of urbanisation in developing countries];
4. [the different] social and urban processes' available that make place and space in cities.

However the focus of urban planning has generally always been the solution of 'immediate problems' related to housing, transportation and employment (Sanchez-Rodriguez 2008). What this has resulted in is a form of piecemeal spatial planning process with imbalanced access to infrastructure, leading to a sharp polarisation of assets and real income. Sanchez-Rodriguez (2008: 150) writes, 'This fragmented vision overlooks the wide range of multidimensional social, economic, political, cultural and biophysical interactions behind each urban problem'.

Considering the factors that determine identity politics is a critical step in identifying the ways in which they obstruct or enable a just society. Pacione (1999: 120) argued, 'In a just society a principal aim would be the amelioration of excessive inequalities, as manifested in spatial or opportunity terms, between persons, groups and communities'. As Pacione (1999: 120) further wrote, 'A religious perspective embedded in a particular spatial and temporal context merits as much consideration as a source of emancipatory and socially-progressive action as any other "meta-theory" – such as socialism, liberalism, feminism, humanism or postmodernism'. In multifaith, highly pluralistic South Asian cities, religion emerges strongly as one of the most critical categories that determines justice, and by extension, sustainability (Narayanan 2015: 26).

> Socio-spatial justice can best be enabled when dimensions that constitute context-specific development such as a range of anthropological, socio-cultural and political factors are considered by formal planning. In the context of Indian cities (and arguably elsewhere in the subcontinent), religion emerges as one critical analytical factor that determines socio-spatial justice, especially for the poor.

In order to develop planning protocols that reflect the social, cultural, political and environmental realities of cities as accurately as possible, a localised sense of place, place identity and placemaking have been identified as vital elements of sustainable cities (Sepe 2013), and which modernist planning in Indian cities has almost entirely neglected to consider. Religion is a vital category that demonstrably makes place in South Asian cities, in both positive and problematic ways (Gayer and Jaffrelot 2012). The older conceptual differentiations between 'space' and 'place' have specific resonances when religion is understood as a spatial category. Philosophers like Tilley (1994) tend to view space as the primary

10 Yamini Narayanan

motherhood notion from which 'place' is derived as opposed to geographers who argue for a primary focus on 'place' that may be directly experienced as opposed to space which is more abstract. Urban theorist H. S. Geyer uses Weber's (1929) model depicting different layers of human activities starting from agrarian/rural to increasingly industrialised/urban, to show how different human activities in distinct and real ways attach different 'place' qualities to urban space. Space becomes place when infused with identity (Hague and Jenkins 2005).

Religion is so fundamentally intrinsic to identity in India and its neighbours that anthropologist Gerald Larson (1995: 280) argues for an understanding of 'religion' as an essentially anthropological construct, comparable with other identity-forming concepts such as 'culture', 'language' and 'society'. By no means, clarifies Larson, does this mean that it is necessary to claim allegiance or sympathy to any religion; indeed, one may claim agnosticism or atheism. Larson here stresses that religion in India or elsewhere in South Asia may not be simplistically understood purely in terms of sacrality, but mundanity and secularity are shaped by religion, as they shape religion. Religion is life-encompassing in its ambit rather than only its sacred dimensions.

How may religion pragmatically be identified in its multifarious forms as an element that determines urbanism? The urban heritage discourse presents a functional possibility of considering religion in terms of its tangible and intangible heritage. As intangible heritage, Pacione's (1999: 118) deconstruction of religion in six ways further furnishes a useful frame of reference as 'doctrine, sacred narrative, ethics, ritual, experience and social institutions'.

In addition, religion can also be conceptualised in terms of space and built form. Framing religion as tangible or intangible heritage also offers the greater consideration of the range of informal development in cities which are often determined by religious structures, sites, identities and rituals (Davis 2006; Narayanan 2015). The UNESCO (2003) *Convention for the Safeguarding of Intangible Cultural Heritage* describes tangible heritage such as 'monuments, groups of buildings, sites and cultural landscapes' and intangible heritage as 'the practices, representations, expressions, knowledge, skills of communities and groups, and sometimes individuals, as well as the instruments, objects, artefacts and cultural spaces associated therewith' (Roders and van Oers 2011: 6). The Convention emphasises that intangible heritage was as important as tangible, material heritage to cultural diversity and sustainable development, and they both share a 'deep-seated interdependence' with natural heritage (UNESCO 2003). While some scholars question the classification of heritage as tangible or intangible, arguing that ultimately the experience of heritage makes all heritage intangible (Munjeri 2004; Smith 2006), this distinction is useful for the purposes of policymaking.

Urban histories and heritage: space, built form and living traditions

Urban history and heritage in their various tangible and intangible forms have strong resonances for contemporary urban sustainable development for South Asia (Narayanan 2015, Patel 2009). While city planning is certainly a 'prospective'

Sustainable cities in South Asia   11

project, planners are necessarily required to adopt a clear position in regards to history and the past, while orienting policy towards the future, 'whether they cling to legacies, memories and precedents or reject them' (Hebbert and Sonne 2006: 3). As Gottmann (1954: 2) wrote, 'the geographer must keep the past in mind if he wants to understand the "whys" behind the present problems and the present landscapes'.

The trajectories of urbanism in South Asia particularly make a historical analysis relevant and imperative to contemporary urban planning. Without critical inquiry into the history and heritage of cities, it would be difficult, if not impossible, to understand what constitutes the vital *genius loci* or 'spirit of place', and how current planning can take this account while planning sustainable cities. Precolonial urban heritage, tangible and intangible, continues to exert a palpable influence on the nature of the commonplace and everyday in many historic South Asian cities as well as the modern, postcolonial urban forms built over and around the old historic cores. Precolonial cities like Varanasi or Kathmandu, or modern postcolonial urban centres like Delhi, Colombo or Jaipur with an older, historic, 'native' core often had strong historical royal and religious patronage.

Further, the wide income gap in the Indian subcontinent, the history of privilege and power – or lack thereof – conferred by religion and caste, the fluidities of rural/ urban migrations, and the quickened pace of urbanisation since European colonisation mandate the questioning of the ways in which anthropological categories like religion continue to determine social and spatial hierarchies. Emphasising the links between urbanism and capitalism, Indian urban historian Sujata Patel (2009: 31) argues for the 'need to evolve an interdisciplinary historical perspective that can explore the uneven and transitional character of the urban process structured by colonial capitalism'. She notes that the analysis of five themes – all of which rely on a clear understanding and analysis of past and contemporary histories – can provide insights the real nature of urbanisation in the region, and further claims that these themes can also become the building blocks for fashioning a new urban sociology not only in India but the developing world in general:

> uneven capitalist development and its impact on urbanisation; the nature of urban inequalities; the influence of globalisation on city forms and structures; the intervention of state policies and the impact of collective action; and the various dimensions of urban cultures and modernities.
>
> (Patel 2009: 31)

However inserting religion as a category – or yet another theme, as it were – for an urban historical analysis deepens and illuminates even more clearly the enduring impact of the past on present and future processes of urban development in the region stretching further back in precolonial urban history and beyond. South Asia undoubtedly is one of the richest regions to uncover the extent to which tangible and intangible religious heritage has been influential in influencing its urbanscapes, and in turn being influenced by it. Cities like Varanasi, Taxila, Madurai, Kathmandu Valley, Delhi and even Visakhapatnam among others

12   *Yamini Narayanan*

are regarded as 'living cities' for the continuity of built form and living traditions over millennia, and were among the first to have a history of religion in their built and cultural environments. Buddhist and Jain monasteries dating back to 1st millennium BC existed in these sites, which later gave way to more temple-centric urban sites, as in Varanasi itself or Madurai (Hancock and Srinivas 2008). Indeed, whole cities actually evolved out of spaces that contained institutions of religious learning like Amritsar city, or the sacred site and later shrine of the great Sufi teacher Nizamuddin Auliya around which grew Shahjahanabad or Old Delhi (Hancock and Srinivas 2008).

Urban studies have been most preoccupied with the physical sites, architectures and the planning and design of cities, and this is also one of the vital running themes across most of the contributions of this book. Historians and anthropologists of South Asia have closely studied several key physical sites of cities in relation to religion – the gendered negotiations of space based on religious frameworks for feminine engagement, in high-rise apartments in Karachi (Ring 2006); tourism and heritage sites to pilgrimage sites like temples and natural heritage sites (Sachdev and Tillotson 2002; Tillotson 1987), urban design, layout and planning based on classical planning literacies inspired by religion (Sachdev 2001, 2005), and last but not the least, sacred spaces and sites like temples (Hancock 1999, 2002) and mosques (Asher 2000, 2001, 2012). In their utilisation of common spaces and celebrations around it, physical structures of religion, sacred and secular, often tend to have an overtly public engagement with the surrounding community. Hancock (1999: 178) writes in her study of the temple spaces in cities in Tamil Nadu, 'Temples, as loci for collective ritual activity and sumptuary display, are certainly public places insofar as they are open and accessible to large sections of the populace'.

The nodes and networks in turn influence the spatial dynamics of spatiality, mobility and access through the distinctive ways in which religion and heritage organises their everyday life. Religious heritage sites, observances, public celebrations and protocols, gendered participation and inhibition in the city, the organisation of trade and economics, political and cultural festivals in the city, and the ecology are all influenced by the different ways in which religion might engage with the modern city. The city has unique, detailed and complicated religious dimensions in material forms such as symbols which are significant in the experience and placemaking of the city, and cultivating identities. In his detailed study of the utilisation of Hindu symbols, rituals and histories in the making of the contemporary city of Bhaktapur in Nepal, anthropologist Robert Levy writes (1997: 52), 'In Bhaktapur sacralized symbols were extensively put to work to organize much of the time, space, status, economic and psychological life of the city, helping, in short, to shape it into a community'. Religion mediates the relationship between people and place, and as Bhaktapur demonstrates, can play even a central role in the creation of sites, structures, urban artefacts, and the utilisation of natural resources and space.

> The layering of religious meaning throughout the city – expressed in art and iconography, embodied in architecture and the exact citing of temples and

Sustainable cities in South Asia   13

shrines in city space, achieved in the representation of the city and its space in religious terms, constituted in action by way of rituals, processions and festivals – means that the city itself becomes a kind of sign of the sacred.

(Parish 1997: 453)

Religion does not refer only to sacrality, but it encompasses that the secular (Bailey 2001) and religious symbols and meaning-making devices deployed throughout the city are not necessarily distinct from secular ones at all. Space can be framed as an empirical reality, as well as a symbolic, theoretical site. Levy (1997: 56) for instance, understands Bhaktapur's urban space in two ways: sacralised space, and 'at the level of city-as-city'. He defines sacralised space thus:

> Sacralized space contrasts with mundane, ordinary space and is (in company with sacralized images, times, status divisions, and actions) clearly marked through various devices as being extraordinary, powerful, and participant in a transcendent world, a world elaborately defined by means of the extensive meaning-giving resources of Hinduism.

The non-sacred elements of the built environment develop and are utilised in similar ways to the sacred dimensions, and together, they form a coherent narrative of the heritage of the city. The symbols develop in

> responses to its topography, material witnesses to a variety of historical projects and happenings, responses to and indexes of the economic, utilitarian, and communicative needs of the city . . . Sometimes these other spaces are related to sacred ones, sometimes they are quite independent and secular.

(Parish 1997: 453)

However the rapid pace of growth of cities in South Asia, especially of the million-plus cities that are at risk of becoming megacities with large outlying conurbations make it very difficult to properly analyse urban history for the purposes of policymaking. Archaeological sites and structures are rapidly being destroyed or degraded to accommodate the escalating demand for growing cities. The change involves not merely a population spurt but associated changes and transformations caused by modernisation such as mechanisation, lifestyles, housing, leisure, gendered experiences and religio-cultural changes. Heitzman (2008: 36) writes:

> [T]here is the problem of conducting ethno-historical investigation within hundreds of sites where the population may be increasing so rapidly, and the conditions of existence altering so utterly, that the theorization and even the description of the contemporary middle city may remain undone or impossible.

In addition, other valuable heritage such as entire precolonial knowledge systems relating to building and design are being lost. South Asian urban historian

14   *Yamini Narayanan*

James Heitzman (2008) notes that the South Asian city is losing its identity, sense of place and history through

> source degradation through rapid construction or renovation of the built environment, resulting in the rapid erasure of older housing and business/ commercial districts and the replacement of older buildings (many, admittedly, of limited aesthetic appeal) by the blockular brick-and-concrete architecture of South Asian modernity.
>
> (Heitzman 2008: 36)

Sacred tangible and intangible heritage however are more likely of all other heritage to endure and be preserved in South Asia. The perception, utilisation and claims on all urban heritage intersect with the socio-economic-cultural complexities that constitute formal and informal urbanism, and the spatial fractures of 'gray spacing' between these constructs. The section below surveys religion's role in mediating such informal urbanism in South Asia.

Identities and informality: marginalisation and violence

The introduction of municipalities as nodes of authority for urban governance in the British colonies of South Asia (as elsewhere) privileged elite – the colonialists and then native Indian – participation and governance of the city (Beverley 2011). From the very beginning, only the small minority of the elite and powerful dictated the formal planning of the city, reinforcing existing social inequalities and introducing new ones. However there was also a constant – and an extremely large – 'counter-discourse' that sought to occupy and use spaces in ways not envisaged by the British colonists (Legg 2007). The everyday life and practices of the millions of citizens in South Asian cities, and their utilisation of and negotiations over the city's spaces, formed the infinitely larger scale of informal growth that came to characterise the split or even schizophrenic, uneven development in these cities.

These practices and spatial assertions have come to define the different types of informal development, understood as such essentially by the general incapacity of formal planning to control, manage or intervene in such development. Roy (2005: 147–148) refers to 'informality as a state of exception from the formal order of urbanization'. The informality in the city destabilises any perception of the city as 'a space of control' and instead allows the South Asian urban space to be one of 'autonomy and ambivalence' (Beverley 2011: 494). As informality is founded in the lived processes and structures of – generally poorer or more disenfranchised – citizens everyday rather than iconic milestones of planned development, it 'is fundamentally a process rather than a norm' (Dovey and King 2012: 276). Beverley (2011: 493–94) writes, 'focus on everyday practices reveals non-elite interventions in the late colonial city, parallel to the formal political domain of elites who entered into, and later inherited, the

Sustainable cities in South Asia   15

institutions of colonial urbanism'. The informal spaces show the 'complexity, ingenuity and creativity of everyday adaptations' (Dovey and King 2012: 276) as the non-elite/non-privileged conceptualise of innovative ways to claim and live in the city.

The social hierarchies in highly diverse South Asian cities are reflected spatially when the benefits of formal planning such as public transportation and other urban infrastructures are selectively available in some spaces, and not in the other parts of the city. Indeed, these wide differences in identities are one of the primary reasons for the large structures of informal spaces that exist in developing cities, and which generally fall outside of the formally 'plannable', rendering them 'unplannable' (Roy 2005: 147). Israeli urban planner Oren Yiftachel argues (2012: 150) that the 'new political geography, characterized by the proliferation of "gray spaces" of informalities . . . thrusts the politics of identity as a central foundation of urban regimes'. Yiftachel (2012: 153) defines gray spaces thus:

> (as) developments, enclaves, populations, and transactions positioned between the "lightness" of legality/approval/safety, and the "darkness" of eviction/destruction/death. Gray spaces are neither integrated nor eliminated, forming pseudo-permanent margins of today's urban regions, which exist partially outside the gaze of state authorities and city plans.

The intersections between religion and informality is one of the largest gaps of formal policymaking for South Asian cities. Religion is central to the making of the great social diversity of South Asian cities, and their highly variegated organisation and codified stratification. Geographers have generally shied away from exploring ethics and morality too deeply; however the pursuit of 'relevant' social policy for managing spaces requires an understanding and appreciation of the significance of these frameworks on the everyday life of citizens and communities (Pacione 1999).

How does religion contribute to the organisation of the city in terms of space, access to resources, rationale of religious priorities and opportunities for individual self-development? How do religious politics of urban space impact flow and fluidity of the interactions between people, and between people and place? What sorts of symbols and rituals are employed to assert rights to the city and its resources? Do questions of privilege and vulnerability apply only to human communities in the city? Where can we begin to see the development of a post-human, non-anthropocentric politics and worldview in relation to animal/nonhuman citizens of a city, and their utilisation as religious icons and/or urban resources?

Understanding the 'workings' of religion in identity and spatial politics is necessary in pluralistic cities to uncover the configurations of power that crosscut space and identity, and to plan for inclusive cities and empower communities. Patel (2009: 33) explicitly links space to identity formation itself, and she asks, 'How does space construct identities? What is the relationship between spatial segregation and identity formation?' Intersecting religion with identity exposes how spatial issues directly relate to equity such as ghettoisation (Rathore 2012), marginalisation, informal development and even gendered inequalities (Narayanan forthcoming; Hosagrahar 2005; Matin et al. 2002; Ranade 2007). Ahearne and Bennet (2011: 111) note that religions 'shed revealing light on underlying relations between the 'cultures' and 'policies' that maintain and divide human social groupings across time'.

The links between identity, privilege and powerlessness are enacted as well as reinforced through differential spatial rights and multiple options – or not – for mobilities. It is well established that mobilities enable economic empowerment, and inadequate capacity for mobility can intensify impoverishment (Uteng and Cresswell 2008). Dissimilar spatial rights further intensify privilege as well as vulnerabilities shaped by individual and communal identities and can actively contribute to the continued impoverishment and disempowerment of historically unprotected or weaker groups. A study in the city of Old Hyderabad in India shows that minority religious groups can experience a total inability to move at all outside of the bounded precincts of their ghettoes without fears for their safety, leading to a state of feeling 'landlocked' in the old walled city (Rao and Thaha 2012). Predictably, these limitations on spatial and mobility rights lead to increased impoverishment of minority religious groups in India (and other South Asian nations), destabilising caste as an indicator of poverty, and establishing religious identity instead as a more relevant marker in the current millennium (Gayer and Jaffrelot 2012; Sachar Commission Report 2006).

The identification and consideration of religious identities and politics thus become vital to address in development and planning protocols to reduce or eliminate any social and political vulnerabilities in different communities, which limit or control rights to urban spaces. All of these various aspects of the community contribute meaning and structure to the urban form, through space, symbols, rituals in public spaces, and other meaning-making devices that are used to lend hierarchy coherence and legitimacy. Parish (1997: 449) writes:

> Hierarchy is . . . meaningful [because] it acquires meaning, moral force, psychological significance, and political gravity because a variety of symbolic forms make it palpable and compelling and because people struggle against hierarchy, and for it, elaborating on it as they actively enact, defend, reject, and contest it. Boundaries and hierarchies are redundantly constructed, defended, breached and resisted.

The chapters in the book scrutinise the intersections of religion, and informality and informal development in two ways: one, in the commonly understood framework of the spread of slums and the unstable nature of livelihoods and security implied therein. Dovey and King (2012: 276) write, 'Informality emerged initially from critiques of the informal economy and now applies also to people (floating populations) and places (informal settlements). Informality is a framework for understanding the encroachment of informal activities and settlements within formally planned cities'. However there is need for an understanding of the informal beyond squatter settlements as 'informality is not a separate sector but rather a series of transactions that connect different economies and spaces to one another (Roy 2005: 148). The second focus for informality will examine the organisation of spaces, communities and economies around religious structures and rituals in public spaces as 'states of exceptions' to the order of formal planning. How can this state of exception 'be strategically used by planners to mitigate some of the vulnerabilities of the urban poor', as advised by Roy (2005: 148)?

Ten years ago, it was estimated that more than a billion people worldwide lived in slums (Bolay 2011); of these, the cities of South Asia accounted for some 24.13 per cent of this population (UN-Habitat 2009). The UNEP (2004: 12) report *Sustainable Development Priorities for South Asia* notes that at least half the area of almost all towns and cities in region have become shanties and slums due to migration and the excessive pressure on existing urban infrastructure. Likewise, almost half the land area is also environmentally degraded because of increased vulnerability to cyclones, earthquakes, tsunamis, droughts and floods, as well as over-exploitation of water and green resources (UNEP 2004).

Violence and insecurity have also become strongly associated with informality. UN-Habitat (2009: 38) notes that 'income inequality and spatial fragmentation are mutually reinforcing, leading to segregated and violent cities' Like many of the cities of north India, the large cities of Pakistan too, immediately upon freedom, had to deal with the one of the most destabilising and enduring impacts of the Partition, the great influx of arriving refugees. Karachi in particular faced – and in many respects, continues to experience – 'the refugee problem', creating almost 'intractable' tensions between the native residents or the 'sons of the soil' and the immigrants, who called themselves as *mujhahirs*, an almost provocative self-identification with the Prophet's own migration from Mecca to Medina (Daeschel 2013: 89). Daeschel notes (2013: 89) that 'the city of government was a city blighted like no other by uprooted and dislocated populations, leading to chronic housing shortages and burgeoning slum settlements close to the very hearts of power'.

The sacred and other religious structures and sites in the urban built environment also play a vital role in organising space, identities, and thereby privileging or compromising rights to the city. The assertion politics of religious minorities is usually strategised around meaningful religious structures, and can in fact be unstable spaces between informality and formality, as they struggle for recognition and resources from governance. The state typically deals with informal spaces either through continued tolerance by turning a blind eye, by legitimising the 'gray space' into white by formalising the informality of development, or by aggressively initiating slum demolition movements and definitively marking such areas as black (Yiftachel 2012).

18 *Yamini Narayanan*

It falls upon sensitive and attentive urban planning to address several issues related to spatial inequality such as 'urbanization of poverty and the prevalence of slums; income inequality and the resultant social exclusion; uncertain economic growth; and poor urban unemployment prospects' (UN-Habitat's 2009: 38). While urban governance cannot counter the forces of neoliberal growth, it can attempt to manage its impact on cities through inventive ways of achieving 'social integration and cohesion' (UN-Habitat 2009: 38). The intersections of religion and informality offer realistic lessons and opportunities in urban management. This book offers a modest starting point to the challenge of exploring radical new frameworks of sustainable cities for South Asia that recognise these realities and intersections.

Overview of chapters

This volume aims to reconceptualise the notion of sustainable cities in South Asia in two novel ways. One, it presents as a thematic study focussing closely on two ideas in particular: the relevance of an urban historical approach in studying sustainability in South Asian cities, religion as tangible and intangible heritage. The chapters also address the other great theme of informality, and the links between informality and religion, that is beyond the scope of formal planning. All chapters demonstrate the intricate ways in which heritage, religion, informality and sustainable development intersect. Two, the authors have utilised a case-study approach to explore the nexus between religion, urbanism and sustainable development in their selected cities. In this way, the book demonstrates how religion in fact centrally determines urban development by playing a role in some of the greatest challenges confronting South Asian cities. Yet when it comes to policymaking, there is a resounding silence on accommodating religion as an analytical category, leaving large gaps in the conceptualisation, planning and implementing of sustainable development. Discourses and policies that skirt around religion rather than engaging with religion cannot thus possibly address the gamut of issues relating to equity, ecological sustainability, violence and welfare in these cities.

Next, Anthony Ware locates religion's organising of identities and spaces in precolonial and colonial Burma, and the use of religious identities to assert space in the independent nation state of Myanmar. The site for ultra-nationalist politics is unsurprisingly the capital of Yangon (formerly Rangoon) and the deep historical analysis demonstrates that urban cosmopolitanism can be a narrative of privileged dominance. Inclusivity must necessarily be considered in terms of religious pluralism, which theme is further developed by Stephanie Matti in her exploration of the important concept of 'intangible values/goods' in Kabul which dialectically engage with material values and goods to form a deep and satisfying urban experience and identity.

Continuing on the theme of the critical importance of historical analyses for the contemporary development of South Asian cities, particularly cities with strong precolonial planning traditions, Shikha Jain emphasises the connection

Sustainable cities in South Asia   19

between cultural/religious patronage and urban planning for the city of Amritsar. PRASAD, an integrated type of planning based on pilgrimage and spiritual materialities that is explored here has implications for the countless pilgrimage cities of South Asia, and also other cities with a historic and/or religious core. Vera Lazzaretti neatly brings together the unstable binaries of religion and secularism to show the context of religious disputes within communal unrest and violence. Her analysis of the politicisation of a major intra-city pilgrimage route in Varanasi underpins the need for multi-vocal and inclusive concept of sustainability that uses traditional religious insights, allowing religion to be the way planning disputes are resolved.

Rohan Bastin uses the concept of the politics of recognition as a means of finding out how religious structures draw out specific spatial configurations of power, and explores how multifaith communities can co-exist in the city of Colombo. Using Karachi, one of the most violent cities in South Asia as an illustrative example, Claude Rakisits provides a historical overview that shows how violent origins begets future violence. The resolution of the gamut of issues confronting Karachi – violence, corruption, religious fundamentalism and nationalism, which are further reflected spatially through ghettoisation of ethnic communities – require among other things, a further conceptualisation of religion itself as progressive, liberal and post-secular construct.

The idea of informality is vastly expanded in Surjit Chakravarty's historical analysis and reading of the formal planning around mosques in Delhi, projecting informality as a strategic outcome of formality, rather as an absence of the commonly understood characteristics of formality. Informality is further extended as a post-humanist, non-anthropocentric worldview and reality in Yamini Narayanan's analysis of how the animal/nonhuman condition might complicate the notion of sustainable cities in South Asia where the varied animal population are highly visible. Using the example of male calf donations to Hindu temples in Vishakapatnam city, she critiques how iconic status of animals such as cattle in Hinduism determines how these animals are regarded as heritage as well as economic resource, and how neoliberal planning supports animal exploitation.

In the final analysis, renowned feminist urban planner Clara Greed analyses the long tradition of regarding town planning as a secular humanistic profession. She reminds us of two lessons in particular for planning in India and elsewhere in the South Asia – the consequences of ignoring religion as well as gender in framing sustainable cities. Greed proposes a useful model for mainstreaming gender as well as religion into planning policies in the Indian subcontinent.

Note

1 In 2002, a train filled with Hindu *kar sevaks* (workers of the nationalist RSS and BJP parties) returning from Ayodhya city was halted and burnt in Godhra city in Gujarat, presumably by Muslim fundamentalists. This led to a three-day pogrom of Muslims

20 Yamini Narayanan

across the state of Gujarat with Godhra and Ahmedabad cities reporting the highest casualties.

References

Agyeman, Julian, and Jesse McEntee. 2012. 'Reimagining Sustainable Urbanism'. In *Sustainable Urbanism and Beyond: Rethinking Cities for the Future* (pp. 208–211), ed. Tigran Haas. New York: Rizzoli.

Ahearne, Jeremy, and Oliver Bennett. 2011. Cultural policies and religion. *International Journal of Cultural Policy* 17 (2): 111–114.

Asher, Catherine, B. 2000. 'Mapping Hindu-Muslim identities through the architecture of Shahjahanabad and Jaipur'. In *Beyond Turk and Hindu: Rethinking Religious Identities in Islamicate South Asia* (pp. 121–148), eds. David Gilmartin and Bruce Lawrence, B. Gainesville, FL: University Press of Florida.

———. 2001. 'Amber and Jaipur: Temples in a changing state'. In *Stones in the Sand: The Architecture of Rajasthan* (pp. 68–77), ed. Giles Tillotson. Mumbai: Marg Publications.

———. 2012. 'The case of the Jaipur Jami Mosque: Prayer and politics disruptive'. In *Prayer in the City: The Making of Muslim Sacred Places and Urban Life* (pp. 113–136), eds. Patrick Desplat, A. and Dorothea Schulz, E. New Brunswick and London: Transaction Publishers.

Bailey, Edward I. 2001. *The Secular Faith Controversy: Religion in Three Dimensions*. London and New York: Continuum.

Bandyopadhyay, Ranjan, Duarte Morais, B. and Garry Chick. 2008. Religion and identity in India's heritage tourism. *Annals of Tourism Research* 35 (3): 790–808.

Beatley, T., and K. Manning. 1997. *The Ecology of Place: Planning for Environment, Economy and Community*. Washington: Island Press.

Beverley, Eric Lewis. 2011. Colonial urbanism and South Asian cities. *Social History* 36 (4): 482–497.

Bolay, Jean-Claude. 2011. What sustainable development for the cities of the South? Urban issues for a third millennium. *International Journal of Urban Sustainable Development* 4 (1): 76–93.

Brugmann, J. 1996. Planning for Sustainability at the Local Government Level. *Environmental Impact Assessment Review: Special Issue: Managing Urban Sustainability* 16 (4–6): 363–379.

Brundtland Commission. 1987. *Our Common Future: The World Commission on Environment and Development*. Melbourne: Oxford University Press.

Bulankulame, Indika. 2013. 'Convictions beyond the bomb: Interplays between violence, religion and development in Sri Lanka'. In *International Development Policy: Religion and Development* (pp.192–206), ed. Giles Carbonnier. New York: Palgrave Macmillan.

Daeschel, Michael. 2013. Misplaced ekistics: Islamabad and the politics of urban development in Pakistan. *Journal of South Asian History and Culture* 4 (1): 87–106.

Davis, Mike. 2006. *Planet of Slums*. London and New York: Verso.

Dovey, Kim, and Ross King. 2012. Informal urbanism and the taste for slums. *Tourism Geographies: An International Journal of Tourism Space, Place and Environment* 14 (2): 275–293.

Downton, P.F. 2000. 'Compact City Environment Strategies: Calcutta's Urban Ecosystem'. In *Compact Cities: Sustainable Urban Forms for Developing Countries* (pp. 311–320), eds. R. Burgess and M. Jenks. London: Spon Press.

Gandhi, Ajay. 2011. 'Crowds, congestion, conviviality: The enduring life of the old city'. In *A Companion to the Anthropology of India* (pp. 202–222), ed. Isabelle Clark-Deces: Wiley.

Gayer, Laurent, and Christophe Jaffrelot, eds. 2012. *Muslims in Indian Cities: Trajectories of Marginalisation*. New Delhi: HarperCollins.

Gottman, Jean. 1954. *A Geography of Europe*. London: Harper.

Haas, Tigran. 2009. The necessity of sustainability. *Journal of Urbanism: International Research on Placemaking and Urban Sustainability* 2 (1): 7–8.

Hague, C., and P. Jenkins, eds. 2005. *Place Identity, Participation and Planning*. Abingdon: Routledge.

Haider, Murtaza, and Irteza Haider. 2006. 'Pakistan'. In *Urbanization and Sustainability in Asia: Case Studies of Good Practice* (pp. 245–271), eds. Brian Roberts and Trevor Kanaley. Philippines: Asian Development Bank.

Hancock, Mary. 1999. *Woman in the Making: Domestic Ritual and Public Culture in Urban South India*. Colorado and Oxford: Westview Press.

———. 2002. Subjects of heritage in urban southern India. *Environment and Planning D: Society and Space* 20: 693–717.

Hancock, Mary, and Smriti Srinivas. 2008. Spaces of modernity: Religion and the urban in Asia and Africa. *International Journal of Urban & Regional Research* 32 (3): 617–630.

Harvey, David. 1994. 'Class relations, social justice and the politics of difference'. In *Place and the Politics of Identity* (pp. 41–68), eds. M. Keith and S. Pile. London: Routledge.

Hebbert, Michael, and Wolfgang Sonne. 2006. 'History builds the town: on the uses of history in twentieth-century city planning'. In *Culture, Urbanism and Planning*, (pp. 3–19), eds. Javier Monclus and Manuel Guardia. Aldershot: Ashgate.

Heitzman, James 2008. Middle towns to middle cities in South Asia, 1800–2000. *Journal of Urban History* 35 (1): 15–38.

Hopkins, Peter, Lily Kong, and Elizabeth Olson, eds. 2013. *Religion and Place: Landscapes, Politics, Piety*. London: Springer.

Hosagrahar, Jyoti. 2005. *Indigenous Modernities: Negotiating Architecture and Urbanism*. Oxford: Routledge.

Kauffman, Eric. 2010. *Shall the Religious Inherit the Earth? Demography and Politics in the Twenty-First Century*. London: Profile Books.

Larson, Gerald, J. 1995. *India's Agony Over Religion*. Albany: State University of New York Press.

Legg, Stephen. 2007. *Spaces of Colonialism: Delhi's Urban Governmentalities*. Malden, MA: Wiley-Blackwell.

Levy, Robert. 1997. The power of space in a traditional Hindu city. *International Journal of Hindu Studies* 1 (1): 55–71.

Martinez-Alier, Juan. 2002. *The Environmentalism of the Poor: A Study of Ecological Conflicts and Valuation*. Cheltenham: Edward Elgar.

Matin, Nilufar, Mahjabeen Mukib, Hasina Begum, and Delwara Khanam. 2002. 'Women's empowerment and physical mobility'. In *Balancing the Load: Women, Gender and Transport*, (pp. 128–150), eds. Priyanthi Fernando and Gina Porter. London: Zed Books.

McGranahan, G., P. Jacobi, J. Songsore, C. Surjadi, and M. Kjellen. 2001. *The Citizens at Risk: From Urban Sanitations to Sustainable Cities*. London: Earthscan.

McKinsey Global Institute. 2010. 'India's urban awakening: Building inclusive cities, sustaining economic growth'. www.mckinsey.com/insights/urbanization/urban_awakening_in_india (10th April 2014).

22 *Yamini Narayanan*

Munjeri, Dawson. 2004. Tangible and intangible heritage: from difference to convergence. *Museum International* 56 (1–2): 12–20.

Narayanan, Yamini. 2015. *Religion, Heritage and the Sustainable City: Hinduism and Urbanisation in Jaipur*. London: Routledge.

Neuwirth, Robert. 2011. *Stealth of Nations: The Global Rise of the Informal Economy*. New York: Pantheon Books.

Newman, P.W.G., and J. Kenworthy. 1999. *Sustainability and Cities: Overcoming Automobile Dependence*. Washington, D.C.: Island Press.

Pacione, Michael. 1999. The relevance of religion for a relevant human geography. *Scottish Geographical Journal* 115 (2): 117–131.

Parish, Steven, M. 1997. Goddesses dancing in the city: Hinduism in an urban incarnation: A review article. *International Journal of Hindu Studies* 1 (3): 441–484.

Patel, Sujata. 2009. Doing urban studies in India: The challenges. *South African Review of Sociology* 40 (1): 31–46.

Patra, Reena. 2009. Vaastu Shastra: Towards sustainable development. *Sustainable Development* 17: 244–256.

Perlman, Janice. 2007. 'Fighting poverty and environmental injustice in cities'. In *State of the World's Cities 2007: Our Urban Future* (pp. 172–239). WorldWatch Institute.

Ranade, S. 2007. The way she moves: mapping the everyday production of gender-space. *Economic and Political Weekly*: 1519–1526.

Rao, Neena Ambre, and Abdul Thaha, S. 2012. 'Muslims of Hyderabad: landlocked in the walled city'. In *Muslims in Indian Cities: Trajectories of Marginalisation*, (pp. 189–212), eds. Laurent Gayer and Christophe Jaffrelot. New Delhi: HarperCollins Publishers.

Rathore, Gayatri Jai Singh. 2012. 'Ramganj, Jaipur: From occupation-based to "communal' neighbourhood?". In *Muslims in Indian Cities: Trajectories of Marginalisation*, (pp. 81–104), eds. Laurent Gayer and Christophe Jaffrelot. New Delhi: HarperCollins.

Ring, Laura, A. 2006. *Zenana: Everyday Peace in a Karachi Apartment Building*. Bloomingtom and Indianapolis: Indiana University Press.

Roders, Ana Pereira, and Ron van Oers. 2011. Editorial: bridging cultural heritage and sustainable development. *Journal of Cultural Heritage Management and Sustainable Development* 1 (1): 5–14.

Roy, Ananya. 2005. Urban informality: Toward an epistemology of planning. *American Planning Association. Journal of the American Planning Association* 71 (2): 147–169.

Sachar Committee Report. 2006. *Social, Economic and Educational Status of the Muslim Community of India*. New Delhi: Prime Minister's High Level Committee Cabinet Secretariat, Government of India.

Sachdev, Vibhuti. 2001. 'Mandala by design: The courtyard of a Haveli Temple in Jaipur'. In *Stones in the Sand: The Architecture of Rajasthan* (pp. 28–41), ed. Giles Tillotson. Mumbai: Marg Publications.

———. 2005. A Vastu text in the modern age: Vishvakarma Darpan, 1969. *Journal of the Royal Asiatic Society, Series 3* 15 (2): 165–187.

Sachdev, Vibhuti, and Giles Tillotson. 2002. *Building Jaipur: The Making of an Indian City*. London: Reaktion Books Ltd.

Sanchez-Rodriguez, Roberto. 2008. 'Urban sustainability and global environmental change: reflections for an urban agenda'. In *The New Global Frontier: Urbanization, Poverty and Environment in the 21st Century* (pp. 149–163), eds. George Martine, Gordon McGranahan, Mark Montgomery and Rogelio Fernandez-Castilla. Oxon: Earthscan.

Sandercock, Leonie. 1998. *Towards Cosmopolis*. Chichester: John Wiley and Sons.

Sepe, Marichela. 2013. *Planning and Place in the City: Mapping Place Identity*. New York: Routledge.

Smith, Laurajane. 2006. *Uses of Heritage*. London: Routledge.

Stephens, C. 2000. Inequalities in Urban Environments, Health and Power: Reflections on Theory and Practice'. In *Sustainable Cities in Developing Countries*, ed. C. Pugh. London and Sterling: Earthscan.

Tillotson, Giles, H.R. 1987. 'Jaipur City and palace: The call to order'. In *The Rajpur Palaces: The Development of an Architectural Style, 1450–1750* (pp. 167–185), ed. Giles Tillotson, H.R. New Haven: Yale University Press.

Tilley, Christopher. 1994. *A Phenomenology of Landscape: Places, Paths and Monuments*. Oxford, Providence: Berg.

United Nations. 2014. 'World Urbanization Prospects'. http://esa.un.org/unpd/wup/High lights/WUP2014-Highlights.pdf (9th April 2015).

UNEP (United Nations Environment Programme). 2004. *Sustainable Development Priorities for South Asia*. Pathumthani, Thailand: UNEP.

UN-Habitat [United Nations Human Settlements Programme]. 2009. *Planning sustainable cities: global report on human settlements*. Sterling, VA: Earthscan.

UN-Habitat. 2012. 'State of the World's Cities 2012/2013: Prosperity of Cities'. www.unhabitat.org/pmss/listItemDetails.aspx?publicationID=3387 (20th March 2015).

UN-Habitat. 2014. 'Afghanistan's Urban Future'. http://unhabitat.org/afghanistans-urban-future/ (15th April 2015).

UN-Habitat Nepal. 2012. 'UN-Habitat in Nepal'. http://unhabitat.org.np/about/unhabitat-in-nepal/ (9th April 2015).

UNESCO. 2003. 'Convention for the Safeguarding of the Intangible Cultural Heritage 2003'. http://portal.unesco.org/en/ev.php-URL_ID=17716&URL_DO=DO_TOPIC&URL_SECTION=201.html (12th September 2013).

Uteng, Tanu Priya, and Tim Cresswell, eds. 2008. *Gendered Mobilities*. Aldershot: Ashgate.

Weber, A. 1929. *Theory of the location of industries* Edited by (translated by C.J. Friedrich). Chicago: University of Chicago Press.

Yanarella, E.J., and R.S. Levine. 1992. Does Sustainable Development Lead to Sustainability? *Futures* 24 (8): 759–774.

Yiftachel, Oren. 2012. 'Critical theory and "gray space": Mobilization of the colonized'. In *Cities for People, Not for Profit: Critical Urban Theory and The Right to the City*, eds. Neil Brenner, Peter Marcuse and Margit Mayer (pp. 150–170). Oxford and New York: Routledge.

Part I

Urban history, religion and heritage

2   Origins of Buddhist nationalism in Myanmar/Burma

An urban history of religious space, social integration and marginalisation in colonial Rangoon after 1852

Anthony Ware

> Yangon boasts one of the most spectacular and diverse urban landscapes: famous Buddhist buildings like the Shwedagon Pagoda, Anglican and Roman Catholic Cathedrals, Baptist and Methodist churches, over a dozen Sunni and Shia mosques, Hindu, Parsi and Sikh temples, and even a Jewish synagogue and an Armenian church. The city retains one of the most complete ensembles of colonial architecture in the world.
>
> ('History', Yangon Heritage Trust website, YHT 2014)

Britain captured Rangoon from the Burmese in April 1852, incorporating the new territory into an expanded British India. Most of the local Buddhist population fled, and during the conflict, all of the old port-city and a good deal of the new city inland around the Shwedagon Pagoda were destroyed, with the exception of a limited number of temples and pagodas. After the war, this desolate landscape provided the basis for the British to disregard all prior land title claims and set out to build a new, major colonial trading city *ab initio* – the first Indian city to be planned *from inception* along modern lines (Pearn 1939; Webb 1923).

One of the most striking features of the downtown urban grid today is the concentration and diversity of religious buildings, as noted in the opening quote from the Yangon Heritage Trust, implying close co-location of diverse religious communities in the new city built after the war. This chapter explores the narratives embodied in this spatial organisation of religious communities in Rangoon, through an examination of the urban history of its (re)construction after the 1852 war. In particular, it examines the politics of planning and of space embodied in developing the new urban grid area, particularly the allocation of religious space. In this sense, this chapter explores the religious, ethnic and political narratives reflected in the urban religious landscape and their impact on sustainable sociopolitical development. It draws on the themes of this volume by demonstrating ways in which the privileging of space is inherently political, and also often, as here, religious and ethnic.

28 *Anthony Ware*

This chapter argues that although the landscape of religious space created after 1852 reflects modernist colonial ideals, it more particularly reflects the colonial imperative to bulwark political power against excessive influence over their new domain by the Burmese king, the nominal head of the Buddhist faith, still ruling in Upper Burma. This recasting of the social position of Buddhism resulted, probably inadvertently, in an increasing marginalisation of the local Buddhist Burman people by a new, multi-religious migrant community, rebounding a generation later in strong Burmese nationalistic sentiment. It is argued that the colonial narratives about identity and power embedded in this use of urban space, displayed clearly through the religious spatial layout in colonial Rangoon, has fuelled Burmese–Buddhist nationalism since the early twentieth century, which in turn has driven ethnic and religious conflict since independence, including the recent re-emergence of anti-Muslim Buddhist ultra-nationalism.

The chapter is based on primary and secondary research, including some new interview and archival research. The remainder of the chapter is divided into four major sections. The first sets the scene by describing the spatial organisation of religious communities in downtown colonial Rangoon in greater detail. The second section documents the destruction of the old city and the planning processes which led to the layout of the urban grid, particularly noting the planning role in the development of religious spaces for new migrant communities in relation to local Buddhist sites. The third section discusses the meta-narratives this spatial organisation conveys about power, religion, ethnicity, identity and the state, before the final section offers some concluding thoughts about the relevance of this historical exploration to contemporary issues, particularly the underlying causes of ethnic and religious conflict in the country.

Downtown Yangon: religious diversity and juxtaposition

The spectacular golden spire of the Sule Pagoda sits in the heart of downtown Yangon, right at the centre of the urban grid (see Figures 2.1 and 2.2). With a major roundabout built around the ancient pagoda, this distinctive Buddhist landmark projects a proud image up and down the length of Sule Pagoda and Mahabandoola Roads in the main commercial district. One of the few remaining structures within the grid surviving from pre-colonial times, the pagoda sits in what, by the end of the colonial era, was a seemingly powerful position in the middle of town, at the southwest corner of City Hall (built in 1926) and just across Mahabandoola Garden (formerly Fytche Square) from the former Supreme Court (built in 1905–1911). While in the years immediately after the 1852 war the focus of the new city was around The Strand, along the river front, by the end of the colonial era this Buddhist icon was the single most visible downtown building, the most prominent religious edifice, prominently positioned in the heart of the city and next to the levers of power. Together with the glorious image of the even more spectacular Shwedagon Pagoda 3 kilometres to the north, the Sule makes a significant statement about the important place of Buddhism in Burmese society.

Origins of Buddhist nationalism 29

Figure 2.1 The Sule Pagoda in the heart of the central business district of Yangon. Adjacent buildings include (left to right): City Hall (white building with palm tree frontage), Immanuel Baptist church (twin white steeples), the former Supreme Court (red clock tower behind the trees) and the Bengali Sunni Jaime Mosque (right foreground).

Copyright: Rupert Mann 2014, used with permission

Or does it? Despite its prominence and despite the city grid having been planned around it, the Sule Pagoda does not project an uncontested message. Far from it! Barely 100m east of the Sule are the twin spires of Immanuel Baptist Church, whose first building on this site was constructed in 1885, and which now stands between the Supreme Court building and City Hall, directly across the front of City Hall from the Sule (see Figure 2.1). Its position is almost a counterweight to the statement otherwise made by the Sule. On the other side of the Sule, just 25m away, stands the Bengali Sunni Jaime Mosque, built in 1862 on land that had been attached to the Sule prior to the British conquest.

Indeed, the Sule is surrounded by numerous Christian, Muslim, Hindu, Jewish, Chinese, Sikh and even Parsi places of worship, all within just a kilometre of the famous pagoda (see Figure 2.2). As early as 1856, the Roman Catholics obtained land and built diagonally opposite Fytche Square (now Mahabandoola Garden) from the Sule, and the Baptists were granted a free allotment nearby. The Anglicans were as granted land in Barr St (now Mahabandoola Park Street) in 1855, land they later exchanged for the Holy Trinity site in 1865. The Armenian church, which had existed in the city before the war, was rebuilt on the corner of Merchant and Bo Aung Kyaw Road, the 'Soortees' Mosque was rebuilt in 1855 on Shwebontha Street near Mahabandoola Street, and the Hokkien Kheng

30 Anthony Ware

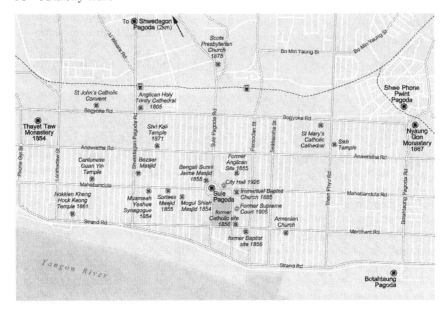

Figure 2.2 Map of the downtown urban grid area of contemporary Yangon, highlighting the juxtaposition of some of the key religious buildings (Buddhist places of worship shown in bold).

Hock Keong Chinese temple was built on Strand Road in 1861. In addition, an Anglican church was built on Strand Road, a Cantonese temple on Latha Street, a Hindu temple on Fraser Street (now Anawrahta Road), a Catholic convent on Montgomerie Street (now Bogyoke Road), and the Mogul Shiah Mosque plus a Jewish synagogue built on Dalhousie St (now Mahabandoola Road). As if to offer a final juxtaposition against the Sule Pagoda, Scots Presbyterian Church, built in 1875 with a significant contribution from the colonial administration, stands less than a kilometre north of the Sule, directly up Sule Pagoda Road on a rise at a bend in the road such that it has an elevated direct line of sight staring back down, as it were, on the Sule.

This spatial juxtaposition illustrates the fact that there are complex sociopolitical narratives embedded in the religious configuration of downtown Rangoon. In stark contrast to first impressions about the centrality of Buddhism through positioning of the Sule Pagoda, the dislocation of most other Buddhist spaces away from the downtown area becomes highly apparent. As Figure 3.2 shows, the only other Burmese Buddhist places of worship to remain from the pre-war era were all on the margins of the urban grid: pagodas in Pazundaung and Botahtaung townships (northeast and southeast sides of the urban grid) and monasteries in Lanmadaw and Pazundaung (west and east of the grid). This displacement of Buddhist religious spaces is a visible indicator of the displacement of the Burmese Buddhist population to the margins of the new colonial city, to make way for the new Christian, Muslim, Hindu, Sikh and even Jewish migrant bureaucrats, traders and labourers.

War and reconstruction: destruction of the Burmese and development of the colonial

A clean slate: destruction during the 1852 Anglo–Burmese war

Rangoon, meaning 'end of strife', was built as a trading port and fort city by King Alaungpaya in 1755, the founder of the Konbaung dynasty, as a strategic defence post after the defeat of a Mon uprising.[1] It was built on the river bank 3 kilometres south of the historic township of Dagon, home to the Shwedagon Pagoda, which has a long tradition in Burmese folklore and history. Dagon was clearly known to Burmese and Mon kings at least as early during the fourteenth and fifteenth centuries, many of whom visited the pagoda, and was probably known much earlier. By contrast, Alaungpaya's Rangoon was a riverside city with a port protected by a wooden-pile stockade. The port grew in significance with its export of teak and shipbuilding, until the British captured the city during the First Anglo–Burmese War (1824–1826). It was returned it to the Burmese as part of the Treaty of Yandabo after the war, but destroyed a few years later, in 1841, by a devastating fire. When King Tharrawaddy arrived and rebuilt the city, he relocated the fortifications back to Dagon, 3 kilometres inland around the Shwedagon Pagoda, using the pagoda hill to afford greater defence for a new walled city.

The Second Anglo–Burmese War broke out in 1852. In January a small fleet of British warships arrived in the Rangoon River, ostensibly to apply pressure for redress of fines against traders that the British considered spurious and obstructionist. Led by Commodore Lambert, who was later described by British observers as 'too hot-headed' for such 'delicate negotiations' (Pearn 1939, p. 168), tensions quickly escalated. A lack of cultural understanding and inept negotiations culminated in an acute sense of insult being felt by both the Commodore and the local governor. By April the Commodore had commandeered one of King Tharawaddy's ships and initiated a blockade of the River, which was followed by an ultimatum of war if a humbling abjection was not forthcoming.

As war became immanent, the distance between the port and the new city allowed the Burmese to adopt a radical defence strategy: the Burmese adopted a 'scorched-earth' tactic and burned everything from the port to the walls of the new city. They were likely attempting to recreate the conditions of their first war with the British, and building on their memory of the devastating 1841 fire. Despite an eventual victory, that earlier First Anglo–Burmese War has been labelled the 'worst-managed war in British military history', in which 45 per cent of the 40,000 British troops died when they were cut off from supplies (Hall, DGE 1956, pp. 103–105). The Burmese defence in the second war hoped to repeat that, by obliterating shelter and easy supplies for the British forces, as well as driving away locals living outside the city, preventing any chance of them aiding the British (Pearn 1939).

32 *Anthony Ware*

While providing some advantage to the Burmese, this almost total destruction of the port and land all the way to the new city wall only temporarily slowed the British. It did, however, have significant, unforeseen consequences for the reconstruction of Rangoon after the war. The British captured the city after an intense but short battle, but by then few buildings of substance remained. Most troops had to live under canvas, while most surviving Buddhist monasteries were appropriated as offices and quarters. Faced with such a desolate landscape, one of the first decisions of the Government of India after the annexation was to declare all land from the river to the Shwedagon Pagoda as belonging to the government. For both security and because of a lack of accommodation, civilians were banned from what remained of Tharrawaddy's new town near the Shwedagon Pagoda, which was annexed as the British military Cantonment. Meanwhile, accommodation also had to be found for the hundreds of Indian immigrants who had accompanied the expeditionary force, and the Europeans and traders who had remained. General Godwin allowed them to construct temporary huts on the burnt-out land between the river and the new town, now appropriated as government land.

Few Burmese remained in the region. Most of the population fled, many making their way to the relative safety of Upper Burma and the protection of the Burmese king (Furnivall 1957). Few returned before 1857, particularly given all land was appropriated by the colonial administration and military. With most monasteries damaged then arrogated for use by the military, large numbers of monks led the exodus to Upper Burma. Without monasteries to return to, and because the monarchy's patronage of Buddhism gave them greater freedom and security, most monks remained in Upper Burma until it, too, fell to the British in 1886.

Immediately after the conflict, General Godwin wrote that 'everything was burned', with 'bricks lying in heaps' and the old town 'utterly destroyed' (1852, quoted in Pearn 1939, p. 176). 'The old town, such as still existed, was razed to the ground. Thus the final destruction of Alaungpaya's Rangoon took place and nothing was now left of the town' (Pearn 1939, p. 169). An unnamed traveller visiting Rangoon in January 1854, less than 2 years after the war, described the scene by saying, 'Every vestige of the old city of Rangoon (except some portion of its brick pavements, some of its wells, a select few of its pagodas and shrines, and a small number of Kyoungs or Burmese monasteries), had been utterly destroyed' (Pearn 1939, p. 196). And it was, of course, almost completely devoid of locals claiming ownership.

Laying out a new urban grid

Faced with such a desolate landscape, the decision to appropriate all land from the river to the Shwedagon Pagoda paved the way to plan the redevelopment of the vacant land into a new city (Webb 1923). The expenses incurred in reclaiming swampland and constructing new roads and drainage could be subsidised by the proceeds of land sales. The colonial authorities decided that the area was a clean slate on which they could build a new city '*ab initio* (from inception)':

> The architects of modern Rangoon were fortunate in that they had a clean sheet on which to work: Alaungpaya's Rangoon had completely disappeared,

Origins of Buddhist nationalism 33

while Tharrawaddy's city had suffered much damage . . . [and] contained no secular buildings of any structural or architectural value. It was thus possible and necessary to design a completely new city on completely new lines; there was no obligation to adhere to the old plan in any respect, for no property in the land of Rangoon was admitted to any private person, all being regarded as Government land.

(Pearn 1939, p. 182)

The initial plans for the urban grid were laid out by Dr Montgomerie, a surgeon who had been secretary to the Singapore town committee during the period Raffles laid out that city, and who had come to Burma with the troops in 1852 (Pearn 1939). His September 1852 plan completely ignored the remains of all pre-existing buildings, including the Sule Pagoda. Lieutenant Fraser, the engineer tasked with the duty, submitted a more detailed proposal shortly thereafter, involving a similar grid system that likewise completely ignored the remains of all pre-existing buildings including the Sule. It was only when these plans were considered too small for the new city that Fraser modified and extended those plans into the current urban grid, utilising the Sule Pagoda as a centrepiece, plans that were confirmed in December 1852.

Thus the Sule Pagoda survived within the urban grid not so much out of deference to the position of Buddhism in the country, but because of its utilitarian position within the spatial layout of an expanded Rangoon city plan. It was, however, also the most revered of all the pagodas in the area and its destruction would have antagonised the local Burmese, so it served a dual purpose. Nonetheless, virtually all other sites within the grid zone were destroyed, including most Buddhist pagodas and monasteries; for example, dozens of monastery buildings were destroyed, as was the Kyaik Than Karo Pagoda in the current Theingyi Zay market area and another on Pongyi Street (originally known as Paya Mato Street, literally 'broken pagoda road') (Sayadaw U Pyin Nga Jaw Da 2014).

The decision that all land was the property of Government and might therefore be disposed of at the will of the Government was essential if the new town were to be laid out on the lines proposed, since the plan cut across the old roads and therefore all existing buildings would have to be destroyed. (Pearn 1939, p. 191)

Other than the Sule, the only other remaining structures in the urban grid area from before the 1852 war are a few small stupas, for example, the stupa on Anawrahta Road opposite 10th Street and the Botahtaung Pagoda on Strand Road. In 1852, the few monks remaining in 50 Buddhist monasteries which had been located within the urban grid area, all damaged or destroyed during the fire and war, were relocated to the Thayet Taw Monastery site in Lanmadaw.[2] This monastery on the Western edge of the grid area consisted of 16 acres of heavily vegetated land, and had not been damaged. Ownership of this land was granted to the monastery in 1854, but only after the other 50-odd former-monastic sites were irreversibly appropriated by the colonial authority for the urban redevelopment.

While there were numerous claims of compensation for loss during the war and 'reasonable claims were paid' to British subjects who suffered loss (Pearn 1939, p. 180), no claims were paid for the loss of buildings nor for land, as it

34 Anthony Ware

was deemed that the Burmese had never given land to foreigners anyway and rarely allowed permanent buildings to be erected (for examples of decisions, see National Archives 1854c, 1855a). No restitution was paid for the loss of Buddhist temple lands.

Town planning and the new urban grid

It is interesting to 'compare the town planning around religious space in pre-colonial Burma and post-1852 Rangoon. Pre-colonial Burma had significantly advanced town planning practices, with large regularly planned cities (U Kan Hla 1978) and detailed *yazadaing* (sumptuary) rules governing things like materials, height, size, etc. in the planning and construction of residential and sacred buildings (Lim 2006). Pyu cities, for example, dating to the first century AD, and the construction of the Burman capitals at Pagan during the ninth to thirteenth centuries, demonstrated advanced regular planning (U Kan Hla 1977, 1978).

Commenting on the sixteenth century Mon city of Bago as it existed during one of their periods of autonomy from the Burman empire, U Kan Hla notes that,

> Instead of narrow, curved, dirty, semidark, treeless streets, typical of European, Persian, and Indian medieval cities, the European visitor was presented with straight, wide avenues, palm trees to both sides, leading to the refined gilded turrets over the town gates. Similar avenues would not appear in Paris or Petersburg for another 150 years.
>
> (U Kan Hla 1978, p. 97)

In Pyu, Mon and Burman cities, clear architectural distinctions were made between residential and sacred buildings, and both civil and religious spaces were well-provided. Interestingly, prior to the 1841 fire Alaungpaya's river-front Rangoon contained no Buddhist temples within the city walls; an old map of Rangoon, drawn from memory after the war to show the city landscape between 1836–1849, shows no temples within the old city but the city surrounded by a large number of Buddhist monasteries on ground later occupied by the urban grid (see also U Kan Hla 1978; Webb 1923). However, this was clearly not a reflection of a widespread pre-colonial planning scheme, as King Tharrawaddy's 1841 reconstruction of Rangoon and the imperial cities of Pagan and Ava both contained Buddhist temples (U Kan Hla 1977). Rather, it related to the needs of Rangoon as a small fort and seaport rather than a royal city. Also interestingly, the same old map shows three mosques and two churches had been permitted inside the stockade walls, with several more nearby, highlighting the accommodation of the governor in allowing the religious expression of foreign traders in the city, building a sense of inclusion and facilitating intercultural social integration and trade. Pearn (1939) identifies five churches in Rangoon and its suburb prior to the first war (1824–1826): Armenian (built 1766), Portuguese Catholic (built 1760), two Italian Catholic (1782–1808), and English Baptist, later taken over by American Baptists (built 1807). This appears to mirror many pre-colonial Indian medieval cities that were not explicitly pilgrimage cities, in which the rulers actively sought religious diversity as a driver of economic growth and trade.

Urban planning in the (re)construction of Rangoon after the 1852 war was minimal, consistent with the laissez-faire British administrative practices of the day. Webb (1923) argues this was the first time an Indian city was planned out and built as a modern city by the British – but these planning activities were limited to the colonial authority's claims of ownership of all land in the development zone, laying out the grid system of roads and drains and allocating lots based on sales and occasional gifts. Modern town planning, based on structure plans, zoning and building permits developed in response to the social and economic issues caused by industrialisation and rapid urban growth. In Britain, the origins of these modern practices can be traced to the Municipal Corporations Act (1835), Royal Commission on the State of Large Towns (1844–1845) and the Public Health Act of 1848, although British local authorities only began to adopt by-laws regulating construction from the 1870s onwards (Hall and Tewdwr-Jones 2011). In Rangoon then, while modern town planning practices were being developed during this (re-)construction period, the extent of that planning was minimal until the municipal authority was formed in 1872, and by then, almost all valuable land in the urban grid had been sold.

In the years immediately following the war, all applications for free allotments, compensation or financial assistance were decided from Calcutta, not Rangoon. Applications made to the Chief Commissioner in Rangoon were sent to the Foreign Department of the Government of India, with recommendations by the Commissioner based in Rangoon (for example, National Archives 1854a; National Archives 1854b, 1855a, 1855c, 1855d, 1856, 1857, 1859). The Governor General, based in Calcutta, did at times ignore the recommendations of the Commissioner (for example, National Archives 1854a), and the Rangoon administration's lack of decision-making authority is highlighted by the fact that matters, including terms of sale of lots, boundaries and prices; whether a rent-to-buy could be allowed for the poor; land allocation for a police station, the magistrate and public officials; arrangements for the construction of roads and the wharf – even the salary for the chief engineer and the appraisal and sale of valuables found in damaged Pagodas – were all decisions taken in Calcutta, not Rangoon (for example, National Archives 1854c, 1855b). The first clear example of town planning decisions being made by the Chief Commissioner in Rangoon without reference to Calcutta were in 1867 (National Archives 1867a, 1867b). This underscores the limited control the local colonial authorities based in Rangoon had over the urban landscape, and the manner in which decisions were made at distance with minimal reference to local factors or knowledge. The first record of building plans being required to be submitted to the authorities for approval is dated 1867, and was in the context of a mosque to which a free grant of land had been provided (National Archives 1867a).

36 Anthony Ware

Town planning and religious space

Primarily, therefore, the impact of the colonial administration on planning or regulating religious space was felt through decisions about which religious groups they would facilitate through free grants of land, or occasionally cash grants, and whether religious sites would be allowed to persist from pre-war Rangoon or be destroyed. These decisions were largely made on the basis of readiness to construct and need, as demonstrated by numbers of worshippers and organised leadership. In other words, the religious spaces almost invariably followed groups of residents settling in the various geographical quarters of the new city, then seeking a local place of worship. Yet, despite this relatively minimal role in planning or regulating religious space by modern standards, the impact of the colonial administration through these means is still significant.

The evidence of records in the national archives shows that numerous grants were made in response to written applications, and that parties appear to have requested particular allotments chosen by themselves. Thus the juxtaposition of religious space in the downtown grid reflects the dispersal of ethnic and religious groups in the new city, as permitted or encouraged by the colonial authorities. There is no evidence of the sort of modern structure planning that would allocate a site for a religious building, then seek an organisation to either buy or receive the site, or of the colonial authorities making planned decisions about the location of religious facilities. Rather, religious spaces in the new city seem to have been selected, designed and constructed by self-forming local migrant communities with shared ethnic and religious ties, resulting in what Appadurai (1995) calls the 'religious production of locality'.

Nonetheless, this apparently laissez-faire and community-led development of religious space still embodied a 'politics of place-making' (Burchardt and Becci 2013), shaped, for example, through selectivity as to whether pre-existing religious communities would be granted free allotments by the colonial administration allowing them to return to their land, or be pushed aside by the urban redevelopment. By the end of 1853, at least nine free allotments had been granted to immigrant communities: two churches, one convent, two mosques, one Hindu temple, one synagogue and two Chinese temples (Pearn 1939, p. 195), all in very close proximity to one another. This juxtaposition could only be described as an ideological belief that a multi-religious modernist or cosmopolitan mix of ethnicities was advantageous to stability and economic productivity. While a few of these were effectively replacing property destroyed in the war, of significance is that, apart from allowing the Sule Pagoda to continue as a place of worship (but stripped of the land previously dedicated to an on-site monastery), only one such land grant was given to local Burmese Buddhists in the decade after the war, being for the reconstruction of the Theingyi (ordination hall) on Dalhousie Street (now Mahabandoola Road) (Pearn 1939, p. 195). Even more significantly, that grant was made only after the damaged Kyaik Than Karo Pagoda attached to it had been destroyed and its land given for the construction of a mosque, popularly known today as the Bazaar Masjid (Sayadaw U Pyin Nga Jaw Da 2014),

Origins of Buddhist nationalism   37

and only the ordination hall was re-constructed, not the attached monastery. The only other grant of redeveloped land to Burmese Buddhists noted in the national archives was in 1867, for the Nyaung Gon monastery in Pazundaung on the Eastern edge of the grid area (National Archives 1867b). This reduction in the number of monasteries and relocation to the periphery is illustrative of, if not a driver of, the marginalisation of the local Burman-Buddhist population in the face of a fast-growing migrant workforce being imported into the new colonial Rangoon from elsewhere in British India.

Further grants for religious purposes were made over the subsequent years, and this does not count churches in the Cantonment to which the authorities made cash contributions, nor religious groups who purchased their own land such as the Catholic Cathedral completed in 1859 and the Anglican church originally planned for Barr St, built in 1865 at the Holy Trinity site. (Both of these churches requested government contributions to their construction costs – see National Archives 1856, 1859).

The historical legacy of this urban planning lives on in the architecture and public space land use in the downtown urban grid. The displacement of local Buddhists also explains much of the subsequent Burman nationalism and the pro-jection of dominance by the Burmans over other ethnic minorities, particularly those who embraced or shared the Christianity or Islamic faiths connected with the coloniser. This intense nationalism is one key factor underlying the ethnic conflict plaguing the country since independence, and indeed, one reason behind the 'need' to establish a new in capital city on a greenfield site at Naypyitaw in 2005, away from the colonial politics embedded into the very spacial layout of Rangoon. The need was felt to disconnect the country's future from the colonial and distinctly non-Buddhist heritage of that city, together with the difficulty of defending the administrative functions from the restive civilian population, the large non-Burman community and perceived international threats.

Meta-narratives about identity, integration and power

Urban planning and sustainable urban development

As Worpole & Greenhalgh (1999, p. 4) say, 'urban planning is, by definition, a form of cultural planning' in that the urban form mediates social interaction and social change, and either facilitates or inhibits the communication of certain values. Thus, while the development of Rangoon was not controlled in the mod-ernist sense, the colonial administration's decisions to discontinue some religious land use and facilitate, if not promote, the development of other religious spaces, allowing a particular diversity and juxtaposition, does constitute a form of political cultural planning. Even at the most basic level, the relationship between religious and secular spaces in Rangoon was changed markedly with the British abolition of the traditional Burmese *yazadaing* (sumptuary) rules, something which had a great impact on the daily religious experience of the Burmese. The question could even be posed as to whether the granting of land appropriated from the Sule

38 *Anthony Ware*

Pagoda to the Bengali Mosque, and land appropriated from the Kyaik Than Karo Pagoda at the Theingyi ordination hall to the Bazaar Mosque, represents a deliberate agenda pursued by some of the largely Muslim immigrant administrators in the Indian Civil Service bureaucracy, or was purely coincidental.

While the sustainable urban development literature focuses primarily on 'macro scale processes, issues of governance, institutional capacity and the political economy of urban environmental sustainability . . . ordinary spaces, places, and the form, design, use and activity patterns of localities and neighbourhoods' are also a of significant interest' (Zetter and Watson 2006, p. 4). Likewise, sustainable urban development wants to not only explore the environmental impact of development, but also the political economy and make explicit the social, ethical and economic issues undermining sustainability (Pugh 2000a, 2000b). UN-Habitat (2009), for example, suggest that a central element of sustainability is design of physical space that encourages positive interaction and reduces socio-spatial inequalities.

The meanings associated with place, what might be termed 'place-identity', contribute significantly to the construction of personal and social identities. Watson (2013) argues that the degree to which any religious or ethnic 'imagined community' (as per Anderson 2006) experience inclusion and social integration depends, in large part, on the extent to which they experience empowerment and ownership within the process of constructing 'place-identity' and meaning. As Burchardt and Becci (2013) argue, the spatial organisation of religious communities contributes powerfully to this construction of meaning. 'Place-identity', they argue, impacts on collective and individual identity formation, as well as the construction and maintenance of power relations and cultural hierarchies, while the spatial organisation that shapes it is itself highly dependent on patterns of migration and engagement with globalisation. The already-noted displacement of Buddhist sites, together with the indigenous Buddhist population, to the peripheries of the new city conveyed a powerful message about the marginalised identity of these people, and the Buddhist religion, in the colonial hierarchy.

Identity, integration and power meta-narratives in Rangoon post-1852

Moore and Osiri (2014) offer a very useful comparison between Bangkok and Rangoon in the nineteenth and early twentieth centuries, in terms of the role of visual and spatial urban form (both religious and civic) in the legitimisation of political authority and the regulation of social integration. They argue that changes in urban space were central to the social and political reforms of the Siamese Kings Mongkut (r. 1851–1868) and Chulalongkorn (r. 1868–1910), with things like the opening of temples once reserved for the monarchy as cultural spaces for festivals and events resulting in strong national identity-building and social integration. The removal of elite privilege and the royal sponsorship of events in civil and religious spaces promoted much wider social interaction than had previously been the case, and an inclusive reimagining of the monarchy. This

Origins of Buddhist nationalism 39

was part of a strategic program of modernisation to avoid colonisation, by presenting Siam as equal to the imperial powers. By contrast, they argue, a high degree of segregation between European, Indian-Chinese and Burmese populations in Rangoon during the same era exacerbated social differences. Some commentators see a deliberate manipulation of cultural, ethnic and religious differences for the political benefit of the colonisers, with impacts that have echoed to this day.

Moore and Osiri argue that in the planning and development of Rangoon

> The bulk of the population, Indian and Chinese, lived in the closely laid web of the 'work premises' areas near the river, with other areas allocated for residential and 'open spaces' to the north . . . Although spatially integrated with existing urban precents, the new civic spaces gave little impetus for any integration of local and colonial cultural life in Rangoon.
>
> (Moore and Osiri 2014, p. 159)

Early maps indicate that the downtown grid was conceived of by the British as a close network of 'work premises' (Pearn 1939, Map 7) around the port and administrative centres, with imported labourers living on site in clusters around similar work areas. This patterning is still evident in the urban grid area, with streets dedicated to printing, stationary supplies, art and other single industry clusters. Moore an Osiri (2014) argue that

> The British brought little of London's civic space to colonial Rangoon, concentrating instead on the construction of a profitable port city spatially segregated in three main areas: the congested multiethnic 'downtown' street grid, the residential areas of Europeans and a few Burmese and Chinese elite surrounded by open spaces, and, at the center of the city, the Shwedagon pagoda surrounded by large tracts of British cantonment and garden lands.
>
> (Moore and Osiri 2014, p. 167)

Notably absent from Moore and Osiri's 'three main areas' are the marginalised Burmese population, who, as previously noted, by the 1872 census numbered over 60,000 and constituted 70 per cent of the population, yet are barely regarded in any analysis of the socio-spatial landscape. The absence of the local Burmese during the crucial first years of the (re)development of the city entrenched their marginalised position in Rangoon, and hence in British India, as well as the marginalised position of Buddhism. For example, all blocks between Strand and Merchant roads were allocated as early as 1853 (Pearn 1939, p. 191). By the time large numbers of Burmese returned, Indians and Chinese already dominated the downtown area and almost all downtown land had been sold without compensation to the traditional owners. The first British census, taken in 1872, found that 70 per cent of the population of the city were Burmese, but that they were marginalised into outer wards, such as to the west of the Thayet Taw monastery in Lanmadaw, or in Botahtaung and Pazundaung near the rebuilt Nyaung Gon monastery, or further from the downtown area on either side of the Cantonment.

40 Anthony Ware

Most of the European-Armenian-Anglo Indian population lived in the Cantonment with its spacious parkland and facilities. The Burmese had only a marginal presence in the city until some Western-educated Burmese were able to join the lower and middle echelons of the colonial administration and commercial enterprises in later years of the colonial period.

Rangoon, as constructed after 1852, was therefore, as Charney (2009, p. 2) so eloquently expresses it, 'a colonial possession within a colonial possession', a colony of British India, as it were, more than of Britain. The colonial administration promoted Indian migration, even subsidising travel costs, until Rangoon had the world's highest rate of migration (Taylor 2009, Charney 2009). The reliance on Indians for the administration, defence and development of the colony led to the alienation and disenfranchisement of the marginalised Burmese, which grew throughout the colonial era into a staunch Burman-Buddhist nationalism. The Burmese found themselves 'not only under the British, but also at the bottom of a social hierarchy headed by Europeans and a range of Asian immigrant minorities' (Charney 2009, p. 2). Comparison of the 1872 and 1881 census data shows the Indian population of the city grew by over 50,000 in just 9 years, to be 47 per cent of the population just 30 years after the war, equal to the Burmese population (in Pearn 1939, p. 234). Rangoon was, in most regards, 'a foreign city erected on Burmese soil' and '[t]he Burmese who attempted to make a life for themselves in Rangoon were the outsiders in a very real sense' (Charney 2009, pp. 18, 24).

Rangoon was British, Indian and colonial, lacking a 'Burmese' sense of place. Later analysis suggests that the great weakness of the colonial state in Burma was 'its inability to sustain support from the indigenous population' (Lim 2006, p. 43), unsurprising given these dynamics. While the diverse religious juxtaposition in the downtown urban grid contributed a degree of social integration between the Indian and Chinese immigrant groups, the majority Burman population – and Buddhism – were marginalised, resulting over time in mounting nationalistic fervour and tensions between the Burmese, Indian and other minorities, tensions which in many ways continue today.

Burman-Buddhist nationalism

The final, explicitly Buddhist, dimension of this marginalisation is worth mentioning. The Buddhist patronage of the monarchy still enthroned in Upper Burma, the formal defender of the Buddhist faith in Burma, was a matter of some concern to the colonial administration. Not only were large numbers of Buddhist monks remaining in Upper Burma for the security and freedom the monarch provided, but the danger existed that the local Buddhist population would look to the monarchy for spiritual, if not political, leadership, and that unrest might ensue. For a transplanted colonial administration lacking local legitimacy, the legitimacy of the monarch derived from Buddhist patronage was considerable – and was threatening.

For example, in 1871 King Mindon donated a new *hti* ('umbrella' or gilded crown encrusted with precious stones) to the Shwedagon Pagoda, a common enough demonstration of royal Buddhist patronage, but the potential prospect of a royal visit to colonial-controlled Rangoon provoked serious concerns. The link between Buddhism and the monarchy, and the inclination of the Burmese to look to the monarchy for Buddhist patronage, presented a direct threat to the legitimacy of the colonial authorities, requiring deliberate repositioning of the sociopolitical position of Buddhism in the colonial domain. It is possible (although conjecture) that some the marginalisation of Buddhism, not just local Burmese, was in some ways deliberate, as a necessary and inevitable repositioning of Buddhism in the social order as a bulwark for colonial rule. If not deliberate, this appears to have been at least a subconscious dynamic or fortuitous political outcome (for the British).

As the marginalisation of the Burmese was not only ethnic and political, but also religious, it should not be surprising that the nationalist Burman response has had a strong Buddhist aspect from the early twentieth century until the present day. The nationalist response to their marginalisation is a subject which really requires another whole chapter, but has included not only strong anti-Indian (and anti-Chinese) sentiment, but equally strong anti-Muslim (and sometimes anti-Christian) sentiment. It is not without relevance that the earliest nationalist movement towards independence grew out of the Young Men's Buddhist Association, and then that the nationalist Burma Independence Army recruited during World War II was almost totally Burman and Buddhist. Many (although by no means all) of the longest running ethnic separatist struggles in the country have been by largely Christian minorities, concerned as much as anything else at what they saw as a nationalist 'Burmanisation' and 'Buddhafication' agenda post-Independence, and the most fiercely contested separatist conflict was the one led by Muslims on the Western frontier. The religious dimension has not been dominant in the armed ethnic conflict ongoing since Independence, but neither has it been absent. Forwarding to the present day, the ability of nationalist Buddhist monks, such as U Wirathu and the 969 movement, to preach vitriolic rhetoric inciting violence against Muslims and instilling fear of their supposed designs to control the country is wrapped up in the strong urge to not only reassert Burmese identity, but also Buddhist identity. The impact of colonial marginalisation of Buddhism, not just the Burmese people, is still being felt today.

Conclusion

This chapter has presented an urban history exploring the politics of place-making inherent in the spatial organisation of religious communities within the downtown urban centre of Rangoon, as it was planned and (re)developed as a colonial city after the 1852 war. The charred and burnt-out landscape at the end of the war, and absence of most of the local population, facilitated the construction of a new downtown urban grid without regard to pre-existing structures and land titles. What resulted was a modern, cosmopolitan colonial city that appeared multi-religious and multi-ethnic, but which under the surface involved

42 Anthony Ware

marginalisation of both the local ethnic Burman population and, to a large extent, Buddhism as a religion.

While the urban planning of downtown Yangon during the first decades after the war remained relatively laissez-faire, it still constituted cultural planning and was still highly political and religious, perpetrated through decisions such as the appropriation of previously Buddhist land for redevelopment into the urban centre, control over the location of ongoing Buddhist worship and the concomitant granting of free land or offers of other support for the development of other, non-Buddhist places of worship in the city centre.

'Place-identity' contributes significantly to the construction of personal and social identities, and the extent to which any community experience inclusion and social integration depends, in large part, on the extent to which they experience empowerment in the process of constructing this place-identity. The politics of place-making, whether the result of the colonial authorities as a whole or individual bureaucrats, while potentially not conscious, resulted in a configuration of religious space that helped scaffold the colonial narrative of British India and bulwark colonial rule against undue influence by the Burmese king in Upper Burma, marginalising both the Burmese and Buddhism. It is argued that while planning for religious space *appeared* to follow the settlement of new (largely migrant) communities into the emerging city, clustered around work premises and function, the relegation of the previous privileged position of Buddhist space was more than just a result of accidental marginalisation of a Burmese population who returned too slowly after the war, and who lacked understanding of and willingness to fit into the colonial social and economic order. Consciously or otherwise, the relegation of Buddhism to being one religion among many, and one largely located at the margins of the new society, served a political and religious purpose, making a clear statement about colonial sociopolitical domination of the defeated local population, and the subjugated power of the Burmese king, the principal patron and defender of the Buddhist faith.

This marginalisation of the Burmese and the recasting of the social position of Buddhism in colonial Rangoon, this chapter argues, has been a contributing factor fuelling Burmese nationalism, as well as making this nationalism as much Buddhist as ethnic. This reactive Buddhist-plus-ethnic nationalism has contributed negatively, it is argued, to everything from the long-standing ethnic conflict in the country to the ability of nationalist Buddhist monks, such as U Wirathu and the 969 movement, to preach vitriolic rhetoric and incite violence against Muslims.

Notes

1 The Mon had a thriving Buddhist kingdom, with a capital at the port city of Bago, 125 kilometres northwest of Yangon, prior to the rise of the first Burmese empire. The Mon were first defeated in 1057 by King Anawrahta, but rebelled repeatedly over subsequent centuries and enjoyed several periods of autonomy. Many of the battles between Mon and Burmese were quite ferocious. Today, a majority of Mon have been assimilated into Burman ethnicity, while a minority maintain a separate identity as an ethnic minority in the country.

2 Inscriptions were erected in 1998 at each gateway into the Thayet Taw monastery complex, in both English and Burmese. These were headed "A Brief History of Thayettaw Kyaungtaik", and they began with the following text (sic):

This auspicious and legendary Thayettaw Kyaungtaik which is made up of sixty-six monasteries at present was once a mango garden. During King Thayawadi konbaung (1837–1846) Yangon Mayor U Shangalay and the Royal messenger and port-officer Maung Tu build a monastery on it and donated it to ven. Sayadaw U Mani of Ava of Upper Burma. In 1985 when British occupied the whole of Lower Burma, fifty monasteries scattered around downtown area of Yangon, such as Theingyi bazaar, Bogyoke market, Mogul street and Sule pagoda etc, were displaced and concentrated by Sir Arthur Phayre – the first commissioner of Yangon of British Burma in the mango-garden in the name of Thayettaw Kyaungtaik. The population of Yangon at that time was about 40000. On March 11, 1854, Queen Victoria issued a royal decree conferring the Kyuaungtaik into a religious freehold piece of land . . .

References

Anderson, B. (2006), *Imagined Communities*, revised edn., London and New York: Verso.

Appadurai, A. (1995), 'The Production of Locality', in Fardon, R. (ed.), *Counterworks: Managing the Diversity of Knowledge*, London: Routledge.

Burchardt, M. and Becci, I. (2013), 'Religion Takes Place: Producing urban locality', in Becci, I., et al. (eds), *Topographies of Faith: Religion in urban spaces*, Leiden and London: BRILL.

Charney, M. W. (2009), *A History of Modern Burma*, Cambridge: Cambridge University Press.

Furnivall, J. S. (1957), *Colonial Policy and Practice: A comparative study of Burma and Netherlands India*, London: Cambridge University Press.

Hall, D. G. E. (1956), *Burma*, 2nd edn., London: Hutchinson's University Library.

Hall, P. and Tewdwr-Jones, M. (2011), *Urban and Regional Planning*, 5th edn., London: Routledge.

Lim, R. M. (2006), 'Cultural Sustainability and Development: Drukpa and Burman vernacular architecture', in Zetter, R. and Watson, G. B. (eds.), *Designing Sustainable Cities in the Developing World* (pp. 21–49), Aldershot: Ashgate.

Moore, E. H. and Osiri, N. (2014), 'Urban Forms and Civic Space in Nineteenth- to Early Twentieth-Century Bangkok and Rangoon', *Journal of Urban History*, Vol. 40, No. 1, pp. 157–177.

National Archives (1854a), 'Application for Grant of Land for the Masonic Lodge "Star of Burma"', Yangon: National Archive of Myanmar, Ministry of National Planning and Economic Development, Ac. No. 1AO-00093, Series 1/1(A), No. 93, File 36, Box 1854(3).

National Archives (1854b), 'Grant of Land to American Baptist Mission in Rangoon', Yangon: National Archive of Myanmar, Ministry of National Planning and Economic Development, Ac. No. 1AO-00082, Series 1/1(A), No. 82, File 24, Box 1854(2).

National Archives (1854c), 'Rangoon Town Land, Laying Out of the Town of Rangoon', Yangon: National Archive of Myanmar, Ministry of National Planning and Economic Development, Ac. No. 1AO-00141, Series 1/1(A), No. 77, File 19, Box 1854(2).

National Archives (1855a), 'Claims by Messers Cohen and Zacchariah for Compensation for Losses Sustained by Them During War of 1852', Yangon: National Archive of Myanmar, Ministry of National Planning and Economic Development, Ac. No. 1AO-00165, Series 1/1(A), No. 165, File 53, Box 1855(2).

44 *Anthony Ware*

National Archives (1855b), 'Disposal of Articles of Value Found on the Demolition of a Pagoda in the Cantonment of Rangoon', Yangon: National Archive of Myanmar, Ministry of National Planning and Economic Development, Ac. No. 1AO-00165, Series 1/1(A), No. 177, File 65, Box 1855(2).

National Archives (1855c), 'Proposed Erection of Church at Each of the Military Stations of Rangoon, Thayetmyo and Taungoo', Yangon: National Archive of Myanmar, Ministry of National Planning and Economic Development, Ac. No. 1AO-00165, Series 1/1(A), No. 170, File 58, Box 1855(2).

National Archives (1855d), 'Rangoon General Hospital & Rangoon Lunatic Asylum', Yangon: National Archive of Myanmar, Ministry of National Planning and Economic Development, Ac. No. 1AO-00141, Series 1/1(A), No. 141, File 25, Box 1855(1).

National Archives (1856), 'Erection of a Roman Catholic Church in the Cantonment at Rangoon', Yangon: National Archive of Myanmar, Ministry of National Planning and Economic Development, Ac. No. 1AO-00165, Series 1/1(A), No. 194, File 12, Box 1856(1).

National Archives (1857), 'Memorial from Dr Dawson on Behalf of the American Baptist Mission for the Exemption of the Land and Houses Occupied by Them from the Usual Taxes in Rangoon', Yangon: National Archive of Myanmar, Ministry of National Planning and Economic Development, Ac. No. 1AO-00322, Series 1/1(A), No. 322, File 51, Box 1857(3).

National Archives (1859), 'Application for a Grant of Money from Government Towards the Erection of a Second Church in the Town of Rangoon', Yangon: National Archive of Myanmar, Ministry of National Planning and Economic Development, Ac. No. 1AO-00412, Series 1/1(A), No. 412, File 8, Box 1859(1).

National Archives (1867a), 'Petition from a Number of Mahomedan Residents for Rangoon for a Small Grant of Land for a Mosque', Yangon: National Archive of Myanmar, Ministry of National Planning and Economic Development, Ac. No. 1AO-00903, Series 1/1(A), No. 903, File 241, Box 1867(5).

National Archives (1867b), 'To Mg Pan Yah and Ma Kya Ngone: Free Grant of Land at Pazundaung to Erect a Kyaung on It', Yangon: National Archive of Myanmar, Ministry of National Planning and Economic Development, Ac. No. 1AO-00982, Series 1/1(A), No. 982, File 373, Box 1867(8).

Pearn, B.R. (1939), *A History of Rangoon*, Rangoon: American Baptist Mission Press.

Pugh, C. (2000a), 'Introduction', in Pugh, C. (ed.), *Sustainable Cities in Developing Countries* (pp. 35–71), London and Sterling, VA: Earthscan.

Pugh, C. (2000b), 'Sustainable Urban Development: Some millennial reflections on theory and application', in Pugh, C. (ed.), *Sustainable Cities in Developing Countries* (pp. 73–173), London and Sterling, VA: Earthscan.

Sayadaw U Pyin Nga Jaw Da (2014). Interview by Rupert Mann, Yangon Heritage Trust, at Mhan Kyaung Monastery, Thayet Taw Complex, Bogyoke Aung San Road, 9:10AM 22 May 2014.

Taylor, R.H. (2009), *The State in Myanmar*, London: Hurst & Company.

U Kan Hla (1977), 'Pagan: Development and Town Planning', *Journal of the Society of Architectural Historians*, Vol. 36, No. 1, pp. 15–29.

U Kan Hla (1978), 'Traditional Town Planning in Burma', *Journal of the Society of Architectural Historians*, Vol. 37, No. 2, pp. 92–104.

UN-Habitat (2009), *Planning Sustainable Cities*, Global Report on Human Settlements 2009, London and Sterling, VA: United Nations Human Settlements Programme (UN-Habitat) and Earthscan.

Watson, G. B. (2013), 'The Art of Place-Making', in Krause, L. (ed.), *Sustaining Cities: Urban Policies, Practices, and Perceptions*, New Brunswick, NJ Rutgers University Press.

Webb, M. (1923), 'The Development of Rangoon', *The Town Planning Review*, Vol. 10, No. 1, pp. 37–42.

Worpole, K. and Greenhalgh, P. (1999), *The Richness of Cities: Urban Policy in a New Landscape*, London: Comedia/Demos.

YHT (2014), 'History (website)', Yangon: Yangon Heritage Trust. Available: http://yangonheritagetrust.org/history, accessed 11 June 2014.

Zetter, R. and Watson, G. B. (2006), 'Desiging Sustainable Cities', in Zetter, R. and Watson, G. B. (eds.), *Designing Sustainable Cities in the Developing World* (pp. 3–18), Aldershot: Ashgate.

3 Religious heritage in the old city of Kabul

Stephanie Matti

Introduction

Tall blank walls with high small windows and winding pedestrian-orientated alleys dominate the urban landscape of the Murad Khani district in the old city of Kabul. The upper storeys of houses jut out over the streets; on some of the narrower streets, they cover the street entirely. Behind heavy-set carved wooden doors, gardens flourish in private courtyards. The stout blue and turquoise minaret of the Abu'l Fazl shrine stands at the centre of the bazaar street, surrounded by jewellery shops, fortune-tellers and beggars. With its traditional earth architecture, historic bazaar, and labyrinth of alleys and places of worship, the urban fabric of Murad Khani is laden with meaning infused with different dimensions of religiosity.

Since it was first settled in the 18th century, Murad Khani has been inhabited by the Qizilbash – an ethnic minority who are Shi'a Muslims in predominantly Sunni Afghanistan. The district houses several places of religious significance including *Takiya Khanas* and the Abu'l Fazl shrine, one of the most important Shi'a sites in Afghanistan. However, the influence of religion on the urban fabric of Murad Khani is not just limited to sacred sites: it can be seen in the layout of the streets, the structure of the houses, the laws governing property ownership and the way people relate to space.

This chapter explores the tangible and intangible dimensions of the urban history of Murad Khani, drawing attention to the various influences of religion – specifically Shi'a Islam – on the planning of sacred and secular spaces. What emerges is the story of Murad Khani as home to a historically persecuted religious minority whose identity and sense of belonging draw heavily on sacred sites in the local area. This chapter argues that the mutually constructed tangible and intangible components of religious heritage constitute a key resource in enhancing the liveability of Murad Khani and sustaining social cohesion. As such, they must be taken into account when framing strategies for sustainable urban development in the city.

Murad Khani is situated at the centre of one of the fastest growing cities in the world (Setchell and Luther 2009: 1). Kabul is a city beset by problems of insecurity, underdevelopment and weak governance. In the past decade, there has been significant growth in the body of literature on urban planning in Kabul. Much of this pertains to the rapid expansion of informal and unplanned settlements in the city since 2001. These studies tend to focus on the housing crisis, property rights and the newer, modern growth of Kabul. While there are passing references to religious spaces, a study on the influence of the nexus between religion, sense of place and urban planning in Kabul represents an important gap in the literature. As one of the best restored historic urban areas in the country, Murad Khani is a particularly useful site for studying the relevance of religion and sense of place to urban development. The study of Murad Khani is also particularly important as it helps document a living historic city centre, in addition to shedding light on the particular heritage and experience of a religious and ethnic minority.

The chapter draws on a review of the relevant literature and a range of primary sources including: an in-depth socio-economic survey of the area; interviews I conducted with national and international staff of Turquoise Mountain; and an oral history project of residents in the local area conducted by Turquoise Mountain staff in 2008. While this material has informed Turquoise Mountain planning and project implementation, it has not been published before. In writing the chapter, I also drew heavily on my own experiences having worked at Turquoise Mountain from March 2013 till July 2014.

This chapter is structured as follows. The first section introduces the urban heritage discourse and oral histories that form the foundation for the rest of the chapter. The second section provides a brief introduction to the geography,

Figure 3.1 The historic district of Murad Khani is situated at the centre of rapidly expanding Kabul.[1]

48   *Stephanie Matti*

people and history of the district. The third identifies and analyses how religion has influenced the urban landscape of Murad Khani focusing on the district as home to a religious and ethnic minority. The forth traces the different approaches to urban planning that have been applied to Murad Khani, as well as exploring other threats to the urban heritage of the area. The final section examines what this means in terms of sustainable development and concludes the chapter.

Mapping urban heritage in Murad Khani

In recent decades, there has been a shift in the urban heritage conservation discourse from a focus on specific architectural monuments to a broader recognition of the built environment including the social, economic, cultural and spiritual context as well as cultural diversity and identity (UNESCO 2011: 10; ICOMOS 2008: 1; UNESCO 2009: 6). In addition to the conservation of tangible heritage such as the physical, built and natural, this approach draws attention to the conservation of 'intangible values (memory, beliefs, traditional knowledge, attachment to place) and the local communities that are the custodians of these values in the management' (ICOMOS 2008: 1). The 2008 ICOMOS Quebec Declaration states that it is in fact 'the interaction and mutual construction between the tangible and the intangible elements that give meaning, value, emotion and mystery to place' (2008: 2). To access these intangible dimensions in a particular context requires examining and listening to the local communities.

In 2006, British non-government organisation, Turquoise Mountain, began working in Murad Khani with the aim of regenerating the historic area. Substantial work was done by Turquoise Mountain, especially in the first years of operation, not only to map the physical structures in the area, but also to undertake what Young (2006: 50) terms a 'cultural mapping' of the area. This involved mapping the interplay between the tangible and intangible aspects of the urban environment through extensive documentary and oral history research, as well as a detailed charting of physical structures in the area.

The Turquoise Mountain Oral History Project, undertaken by anthropologist Noah Coburn, with interviews conducted by Seddiq Seddiqi in 2008, set out to answer a number of questions including 'what did residents remember of the past?' and 'what could they tell us about the place of Murad Khani in Kabul's urban fabric?' In doing so, the project aimed to develop an understanding of Murad Khani both historically and sociologically based on the memories, attitudes, values and personal histories of its residents. Coburn argued that the findings of the project 'allow outsiders an insight into how Murad Khani residents talk about themselves and their history' (2008).

Oral histories are especially important in places such as Kabul where there are few written sources especially on topics such as culture, belonging and how residents interact with their built environment. The historical record in Afghanistan from the past three hundred years focuses on the main power dynamics between the Kabul-based ruler and tribal power brokers with little attention paid to what was happening within Afghan cities (Coburn 2008). Even less is said about the role of minority groups such as the Qizilbash in Kabul (Legendy 2007). Oral histories represent a crucial way to fill some of these gaps by giving 'voice to cultures and communities that would otherwise be unnoticed, neglected, or suffering marginalisation within a wider metropolitan stage, or urban research and policy context' (Young 2006, 50). These oral histories provide an invaluable insight into the Murad Khani community and are drawn on extensively in the present chapter.

History of Murad Khani

Murad Khani is a district in the old city of Kabul; located north of the Kabul River; it covers an area of approximately 3.5 hectares. Community elders claim that Murad Khani was once considerably larger and more difficult to define than at present (Coburn 2008: 5). The Head Engineer at Turquoise Mountain estimates that at its peak there were between 700 and 1,000 houses in the area. However, by the late 1970s, much of the residential housing had been destroyed to make room for a new business district and government buildings. Today, there are approximately 200 buildings in Murad Khani (Ahmadzia 2014).

The elders of Murad Khani tell various stories about how the area was first settled (Legendy 2007). The most credible story, which has wide support among the community, is that settlement of the area dates back to 1776 when Timur Shah transferred the capital of the Durrani Empire from Kandahar to Kabul (Sharifi

Figure 3.2 The traditional-style buildings of Murad Khani at sunrise. Unplanned and poorly regulated settlements are visible on the hills in the background.

50 Stephanie Matti

2007). Distrustful of the Afghan tribes that brought his father to power, Timur Shah had formed an elite bodyguard of Qizilbash troops – a people of Turkic descent who had previously provided military support to the Safavids in their rise to power in Iran (Huart 1934: 1053; Kakar 1979: 138). After successfully moving the capital to Kabul, the captain of Timur Shah's Qizilbash bodyguard was awarded the land that was to become Murad Khani in return for his support (Legendy 2007).[2] The population of Murad Khani grew as Qizilbash from other areas of the old city as well as new migrants from Iran began to move to the area. By the 19th century, Murad Khani had become one of the most densely populated areas of the city (Legendy 2007).

While the ethnic composition of the area has undergone significant changes in the past decade, for most of its history the residents of Murad Khani have come from the Shi'a Qizilbash minority. Afghanistan is a multi-ethnic society with a large number of minority groups; Orywal (1986) identifies 55 different ethnic groups in the country. Religious affiliation tends to be split along ethnic lines with each group identifying with one of the two main denominations of Islam: Sunni or Shi'a. The Hazara are the largest minority that adheres to Shi'a Islam and the third largest ethnic group in the country representing approximately 19 per cent of the population (Library of Congress 1997). The Qizilbash meanwhile represent approximately 1 per cent of the Afghan population (Library of Congress 1997). Murad Khani, historically home to an ethnic and religious minority, therefore, is not unique in the Afghan context. Understanding how urban planning influences the sense of belonging of the Qizilbash Shi'a minority in Murad Khani provides some insight into the situation faced by religious and ethnic minorities across the country.

Historically, the Qizilbash have occupied a unique position within Afghan society. Writing in the 19th century, Vigne (1840: 168) notes that at the time there were between 18,000 and 20,000 Qizilbash in Kabul. He adds that their leaders were 'by far the most wealthy, the most intelligent, and the most influential men at Kabul'. In addition to occupying important positions in the military, they were also among the elite at the royal court filling positions as scribes, courtiers and administrators. The wealth they acquired allowed them to build grand houses adorned with intricate carvings and lavish courtyards (Legendy 2007).

However, as a wealthy well-educated non-native Shi'a group living in predominantly Sunni Afghanistan, the Qizilbash occupied a vulnerable position in society. In various periods of the 19th century, the Qizilbash were victims of vicious oppression and religious pogroms. This reached a peak in the 1880s and 1890s when Shi'a Islam was banned by the regime and Shi'a Muslims were actively persecuted (Coburn 2008: 6). With a change in regime in 1901, the Qizilbash were returned to their former positions of power. Persecution flared again in 1929 under the brief reign of Bacha Saqâo, during which the royal family commissioned a *fatwa* calling on residents of the city to rob and murder any Shi'a Muslim in Kabul (Legendy 2007). Oral histories from Murad Khani residents indicate that while the rhetoric of this oppression and persecution has historically been anti-Shi'a, the motives were often political in nature (Coburn 2008: 6).

The past 20 years have seen a rapid change in the demographic composition of Murad Khani. While the Qizilbash were the main ethnic group in the district as late as the early 1990s, by 2013 they only constituted 22 per cent of the population (Matti 2013). Most of the previous inhabitants fled the area during the civil war in the early 1990s, with many remaining abroad afterwards. Most residents in Murad Khani are now Sunni Tajiks but many properties are still owned by the previous Qizilbash inhabitants (Matti 2013). While little information is available on the distribution of ethnic Qizilbash in present-day Kabul, the spatial demarcation of the city tends to run along religious and ethnic lines with Shi'a Muslims predominantly living in Dasht-e-Barchi and Kart-e-Seh districts.

Sense of place and religious heritage in Murad Khani

Beatley and Manning (1997) identify 'sense of place as an important dimension of sustainable places, strengthening local identity, contributing to investment, and retaining communities'. This section maps how the tangible and intangible aspects of religious heritage contribute to the sense of place of Murad Khani residents. There is a high concentration of spaces devoted to Shi'a worship in Murad Khani including two major shrines (Abu'l Fazl and Panjtan), two minor shrines (Zain al-Abedin and Yahya), two mosques (Murad Khan and Bibi Zeinab) and several *Takiya Khanas* or places of Shi'a worship used during Ashura on the tenth day of Muharram. This section provides an overview of these religious sites and the broader influence of religion on the urban design of the area, as well as examining how the residents of the area engage with these tangible aspects of the urban environment. It argues that the sense of place and identity of Murad Khani residents are deeply rooted in the religious heritage of the area. This section also argues that the unique position of the Shi'a Qizilbash in Afghan society – shifting between privilege and persecution – has impacted the urban design of Murad Khani.

The most well-known religious site in Murad Khani is undoubtedly the Abu'l Fazl Shrine, one of the most important places of Shi'a worship in Afghanistan. The shrine is named after Abbas (also known as Abu'l Fazl), son of Ali and the fourth Caliph of Islam, and is considered to be the most sacred Shi'a site in Kabul (Sharifi 2007). Throughout the year, large numbers of men and women regularly visit the shrine to pray and to listen to Qur'an recitals. However, the shrine rises to prominence during the annual festival of Ashura when Shi'a Muslims hold processions in and around the shrine, singing religious songs while some worshippers flagellate themselves (BBC 2011).

In terms of land-ownership, the Abu'l Fazl shrine is designated as waqf: common land used for religious purposes. Waqf is legal category of ownership in many societies with a historic presence of Islam; such property cannot be sold, rented, inherited, mortgaged or gifted (Baird-Zars et al. 2014: 2). In Afghanistan, by law all waqf assets should be registered with the Afghan Ministry of Hajj and Endowments. However, despite large waqf holdings, as of 2014 no properties had been registered (Baird-Zars et al. 2014: 6). While traditionally administered by religious authorities, waqf lands across Afghanistan have either been merged into the broader category of public land, are now controlled by local leaders or are managed privately. In the case of the Abu'l Fazl shrine, a community-based shrine shura (shrine council or board of trustees) manages the site. It is unclear the amount of control, if any, the central government has over the shrine, and what this means in the context of urban planning.

The shrine plays an important role in building attachment and belonging for Murad Khani residents. Some see their residence in the area as being intrinsically linked to the shrine. One resident sums this view in the statement that residents 'live here from the blessing of this shrine's power.'[3] Other oral histories link the power of the shrine to important planning decisions. During the reign of King Zahir Shah (1933–1973), for example, the government planned to build a paved road through the district that would destroy the shrine. According to community elders, a holy man came to Zahir Shah in his dreams and told him not to destroy the shrine. The story goes that the next morning the King visited the municipality and ordered the workers not to harm the shrine (Sharifi 2006: 10). These oral histories point to the central role that the Abu'l Fazl Shrine plays in the identity formation of its predominantly Shi'a residents and how they interact with their urban environment. The mutual construction of the tangible shrine and the intangible – how the local community interacts with the shrine – and the importance given to both by residents in telling their stories, points to the centrality of religion in the daily lives of members of the local community.

Takiya Khanas, sites where Shi'a Muslims worship during Ashura, represent another site where the nexus between religion and urban planning comes to the fore. Known by various names such as *Ashurakhana*, *Hussainiya* and *Imambargah* across the Shi'a Muslim world, *Takiya Khanas* are gathering places that play a particularly important role for Shi'a Muslims. For much of the 20th century, Shi'a Muslims in Kabul were banned from praying or performing religious ceremonies in public; instead these practices around the day of Ashura were carried out in secret in *Takiya Khanas* (Sharifi 2006). There are currently seven *Takiya Khanas* in Murad Khani; they are generally situated on the second floor of private houses, surrounded by high blank walls to hide their location (Wide 2014). These *Takiya Khanas* acted as spaces for the empowerment and communal resistance by Shi'a minorities living in a hostile environment.

With the fall of the Taliban in 2001, restrictions on the practice of Shi'a Islam were lifted. As a result, *Takiya Khanas* began became increasingly public and open. Interviews with community elders indicate that while in the past many houses were used as *Takiya Khanas*,[4] now only seven remain. Since Turquoise Mountain began working in the area in 2006, there has been no evidence of any new *Takiya Khanas* being developed or revived (Ahmadzia 2014). The existing *Takiya Khanas* are mainly visited during the month of Muharram; at other times of the year they are used as community spaces where people gather to pray and talk with each other.

There are several other Shi'a shrines and mosques in the Murad Khani area. The Panjtan shrine, located nearby the Abu'l Fazl shrine, is less important in religious terms, however pilgrims often visit both in the same trip (Wide 2014). The Zain al-Abedin shrine is located in a section of Murad Khani that was largely knocked down and replaced by the Ministry of Finance. The shrine still stands in the courtyard of the Ministry of Finance though public access is limited (Sharifi 2006). In addition to those listed at the beginning of this section, other religious sites in Murad Khani were destroyed or fell into disuse during the civil war. For example, one elderly resident remembers a mosque that was destroyed during the war and later replaced with a café (Coburn 2008). It is difficult to determine the effect of such changes on the sense of belonging of the residents especially given the scale of displacement and destruction at the time.

Aside from sites of Shi'a worship, the layout and architecture of the area were also influenced by the defense needs of its Shi'a Qizilbash inhabitants. The tall blank walls with small high windows and the labyrinth of narrow alleys that dominate the urban landscape of Murad Khani point to the defensive needs of its population. Furthermore, until recent decades, the quarter was walled and could only be accessed through thick wooden gates that were closed at night (Legendy 2007). Elders in Murad Khani explain that low underpasses were designed to prevent mounted horsemen from entering the district (Martin 1907: 44). Wide notes that the Qizilbash residents of Murad Khani were 'an embattled minority whose architecture reflects their defensiveness'. He adds that while this defensiveness was not only due to the resident's status as a religious minority, this was an important component (Wide 2014).

Figure 3.3 The private courtyard and inward-facing windows of Great Serai (recently restored by Turquoise Mountain) is typical of traditional buildings in Murad Khani.

54 Stephanie Matti

Religion has also affected the urban design of Murad Khani indirectly including through the economic structure of the community. Over time, a religion-based economy has developed around the Abu'l Fazl shrine. The emergence of bazaars close to places of religious worship is common across the Islamic (and Christian) world (Wide 2014). While some merchants sell goods that have religious or spiritual value, others take advantage of the increased pedestrian traffic (due to pilgrims visiting the shrine) to sell a wide variety of goods. In the absence of a strict urban plan when the area was first settled, it is unsurprising that the shrines – acting as a central hub of the community – had such a powerful influence on the location of the adjacent central market street and the broader development of the district.

As Hebbert and Sonne (2006: 11) argue, 'town planning may draw on universal types but it is also an encounter with specific place and people'. This is the case for Murad Khani where the practice of Shi'a Islam is interwoven into the fabric of Murad Khani and how the inhabitants engage with their urban environment. The sacred and secular elements of the environment identified above have empowered the Qizilbash minority at the local level in the face of historic persecution by providing a sense of belonging, hidden spaces where they were able to practice their faith, and common identification with a shared belief system and the rituals that come with it.

However, while there are many positive aspects of having a sense of place that is deeply rooted in the local urban fabric of a society, it can also have adverse

Figure 3.4 The Abu'l Fazl Shrine (pictured on the right) is at the centre of a large bazaar and economic hub.

effects on 'cognition of self and cognition of place of the inhabitants, and accordingly impact their status and roles in society' (Narayanan 2015: 3). Throughout much of history, Murad Khani has been a Qizilbash-dominated community with all known religious sites devoted to the worship of Shi'a Islam. While on the one hand helping to protect the Qizilbash and create spaces of empowerment, this also reinforced the segregation of the Qizilbash from majority Sunni Kabul. As Murad Khani has become increasingly diversified in recent years it is unclear how this Qizilbash and Shi'a-centric sense of place in Murad Khani has affected the sense of place of more recent non-Qizilbash arrivals to the community. It is also unclear whether they are excluded from some aspects of community life or whether the urban heritage of the area is expanding to include this increased diversification. It is important to remember that urban heritage and sense of place are not static; rather they are constantly being further enriched through interaction with people and ideas.

The various elements of religious heritage outlined in this section give Murad Khani a unique and culturally rich sense of place that stands out against the relatively homogenous uncontrolled urban sprawl of Kabul. The area, is a human and social asset that has developed through the layering of cultural values and the accumulation of traditions over successive generations. If urban planning is to be sustainable and build on, rather than erode this urban heritage, it needs to take into account the role of religion and religious spaces in the community.

Urban planning and other threats to urban heritage

Writing in 1904, Patrick Geddes likened the phases of a city to 'the layers of a coral reef in which each generation constructs its characteristic stony skeleton as a contribution to the growing yet dying and wearying whole' (Geddes 1904). The past century has seen regimes come and go in Afghanistan as different foreign powers and domestic groups vie for power. With these regimes come different approaches to urban planning that have been influenced by various approaches to, and interpretations of, Islam. Urban planning in Kabul, and Murad Khani, has come under the sway of a highly diverse set of influences: from the organic development of Murad Khani along traditional Islamic lines, the secular modernist urban design of the first half of the 20th century, and atheistic Soviet redevelopment to the anti-planning of the Taliban and Western-driven urban regeneration.

As you move around Kabul, the imprint of different approaches to urban planning is clearly visible: from the old city's complex of narrow streets and hidden courtyards, to the wide boulevards and spacious villas Shahr-e-Nau, and from the high-rise Soviet apartments of Microrayon to the unplanned settlements extending up the hillsides. Having explored some of the influences of religion on sense of place and urban structures in Murad Khani, this section now examines how this has developed and been threatened by different influences including various approaches to urban planning. This section also examines some of the threats to

56   *Stephanie Matti*

the historic city's physical, visual and social fabric including plans for redevelopment, infrastructure projects and market liberalisation.

When it was first settled in the 18th and 19th centuries, Murad Khani did not develop according to a planned, geometric blueprint. Rather, it developed organically responding to the different requirements of its residents including defence and the religious and cultural traditions outlined in the previous section (Arez and Dittmann 2005: 34). In the absence of a clear urban plan, the layout and structure of the area was deeply rooted in the values – including religious values – of the society.

Towards the end of the 19th century, and gathering pace in the early 20th century, the royal family started planning new urban spaces in Kabul as part of their modernisation push. The Shahr-e-Nau (New City) district, for example, was planned according to a 'gridiron layout, typical of new western cities but not previously seen in Kabul' (Kazimee 1997: 5). The construction of these new 'modern' districts changed the demographic structure of the city with divisions between neighbourhoods increasingly based on socio-economic status rather than ethnicity or religion (Breshna 2004: 36). This stymies the development of a sense of place and empowerment based on shared ethnicity or religion; this is particularly significant in the case of persecuted minority groups.

Changes in the perception of threat – linked to increased tensions between Sunni and Shi'a Muslims – also influenced the growth and development of the city. The Sunni ruling elite began to view the residents of Kabul (including Shi'a Muslims living in Kabul) as a greater threat with the dense defensive network of alleyways in the old city considered as an ideal place for unrest to ferment. In response, the gates of the old city were torn down and wide streets intersecting the old city were constructed (Kazimee 1977, 5). Some attempts were made to construct similar streets through Murad Khani with the government going so far as 'hang red flags on all the houses chosen to be demolished' (Coburn 2008, 8). However, these plans for Murad Khani did not materialise.

With the planned modernist districts came a new division between private and public spaces and the increasing detachment of religion from the urban fabric of Kabul. The individual plots and detached houses of the new neighbourhoods contrasted with the dense array of attached houses in the old city. In the open social climate of the time, public spaces such as parks and gardens grew in importance. Nabizada argues that the existence of such public spaces together with a lack of outdoor semi-communal private spaces in Kabul led to changes in the way women access the city including greater use of public spaces (Nabizada 2012: 79). However this modernising vision of urban life, in which women enjoyed more legal equality and freedoms and much greater access to the city (Breshna 2004: 36) was at odds with traditional religious and cultural preferences of much of the population. Esser (2012: 306) argues that this disconnect acted as a catalyst for 'rising political tensions within the capital city'.

In the early 1960s, the Soviet Union started assisting Soviet and Soviet-allied countries to design and implement large-scale construction developments based on strict urban plans. In Kabul, this assistance took the form of a series of urban development plans finalised in 1964, 1970 and 1978. The plans, developed by Afghan government officials with technical assistance from the Soviet planning experts, were based on a top-down model for modernist urbanisation. The first plan for Kabul, finalised in 1964, was a comprehensive plan for a city of 800,000 people (Nabizada 2012: 32). This was revised in 1970 due to a projected increase in population to 1.4 million people over 25 years, and again in 1978 for a population of 2 million by 2003 (Calogero 2011: 72; Nabizada 2012: 33). The plans closely resemble urban plans for European cities developed the 1960s. With extensive parks in the centre, independent districts and formal zones dividing industrial and residential areas, the plans for Kabul bear strong similarities to the 1965 Master Plan of Geneva, Switzerland (Viaro 2004).

The implementation of all three Master Plans was beset by problems. The authorities struggled to keep pace with the rapidly growing population and were unable to effectively enforce the plan (Nabizada 2012: 32). As a result, informal and unplanned settlements flourished. Moreover, the plans were overly proscriptive and did not resonate with the cultural and religious values of many Kabul residents (Habib 2011: 368). Consistent with Soviet ideology, religious buildings were neglected in favour of secular recreational institutions. Meanwhile, some public facilities incorporated into the plans such as open-air swimming pools ran directly counter to the traditional religious values of modesty and gender-segregation (Habib 2011: 368). By the late 1970s, the regime came under strong pressure from traditionalists and religious authorities partially as a backlash against this approach to urban planning (Esser 2012: 307). With the communist revolution of 1978 and the invasion by the Soviet Army in 1979, urban planning became even more dominated by communist ideology and further removed from the traditional values of Afghan society (Habib 2011: 368). As the country descended into war between the Mujahedeen and the Soviet-backed regime, the government was not able to implement any significant plans for urban development. The combination of these issues meant that by 2002, only about 20 per cent of the 1978 Master Plan had been implemented (Viaro 2004).

Under the Master Plans for Kabul, Murad Khani was earmarked for redevelopment with the historic district to be almost entirely razed and replaced by a commercial and residential neighbourhood based on typical Soviet high-rise apartment buildings and public recreational facilities. Under the plan for Murad Khani finalised in 1971 and incorporated into the 1978 plan for Kabul, all buildings, including the *Takiya Khanas*, were earmarked for demolition and redevelopment. The only structure remaining in its original form in the district was the Abu'l Fazl shrine, which is labelled on the official plan simply as an 'existing building'. This removal of any reference the religious nature of the structure may have been done to comply with the secular Soviet ideology (Wide 2014). Such redevelopment would have almost entirely destroyed the sense of place and the religious heritage of the area. While the plans for Murad Khani were ultimately never carried out, the district became increasingly neglected throughout this period. Earmarked for destruction, once grand homes fell into ruin while rubbish started to build up in the courtyards and streets (Radio Free Europe 2010).

58   *Stephanie Matti*

The civil war from 1992 to 1995, following years of Mujahedeen insurgency, left the physical, social and economic fabric of Kabul in ruins. An estimated 60 per cent of the infrastructure in Kabul and approximately 63,000 houses were destroyed between 1993 and 1994 alone with entire neighbourhoods reduced to rubble (Nabizada 2012: 40; Warah 2002: 63). Located in the heart of the city and besieged by warring factions, Murad Khani was hit particularly hard with an estimated 80 per cent of the structural fabric of the old city destroyed in this period (Breshna 2004: 25). Many mosques and religious sites were also destroyed. The conflict was also massively destabilising for the inhabitants of Kabul; by 1994, half the city's population, approximately one million people, had been displaced by the conflict (Nabizada 2012: 40).

Following the civil war, Kabul came under the rule of the Taliban (1996–2001) who applied an approach of 'anti-planning' towards the city (Esser 2012, 308). The Taliban, with their conservative rural ideology, believed that Kabul was the centre of anti-religious modernisation and was, therefore, in need of moral purification (Esser 2012, 308). Esser (2012, 308) argues that the 'neglect of urban recovery or any significant development measures under the Taliban should therefore be understood, not as a measure of their ignorance, but as their determined expression of revenge upon the city'. The Shi'a religious sites in Murad Khani do not seem to have been specifically targeted by the Sunni Taliban in this period as the Abu'l Fazl shrine and several other structures remain intact.

The Taliban also targeted the intangible elements of urban heritage, destroying the urban cosmopolitanism of the city through a range of prohibitions. The Taliban enforced strict gender segregation and placed heavy restrictions on the presence of women in public. One current resident stated that during the Taliban time, no woman 'dared to come out of her house' (Coburn 2008). Finally, the massive displacement of people from Kabul and the accompanying rupture in social fabric of the area was hugely damaging for identity and other intangible dimensions of urban heritage that were fundamentally linked to Murad Khani as a place.

In addition to the destruction of the physical and social fabric of the city, Kabul was further set back by the exodus of the educated elite, including urban planners, in the preceding decades (Viaro 2004). During 23 years of conflict, the country had also been cut off from developments in urban planning that were happening around the world. In the 1980s and early 1990s, there had been a dramatic shift away from the de-cultured modernist planning of the 20th century, to a more culture-led approach to urban planning (Frestone and Gibson 2006: 25). As part of this, there was a shift from top-down planning to greater community participation. This shift is visible in changes to the theory of urban heritage, which has developed a stronger focus on intangible aspects of heritage and the important role of local communities. After the US-led invasion in 2001, Afghanistan re-engaged with an international system that had undergone huge changes in terms of politics and economics, but also, in approaches to urban planning and heritage conservation.

Urban planning in Kabul in the post-2001 period has been dominated by the massive expansion of the population of the city from one million to five million

Figure 3.5 Decades of civil war and neglect left the physical structures of Murad Khani in ruins with much of the area buried under several metres of accumulated garbage. The area was named on the World Monuments Fund Watch List of the world's most endangered sites (Turquoise Mountain Website, 2014). Turquoise Mountain has since cleared over 33,000 m^3 of built-up garbage.

in 10 years (van der Tas 2004: 67). Much has been written about the rampant expansion of unplanned settlements that have grown as the population tries to compensate for insufficient housing (Habib 2011: 369; Miszak and Monsutti 2014: 184; van der Tas 2004: 67). With no comprehensive plan to take its place, the 1978 Plan is still used by the Municipality when making decisions about planning and building permissions despite the fact that a Presidential Decree was passed suspending the plan in 2005 (Calogero 2011: 74). In Murad Khani, there has been much uncertainty over plans for the district with many pushing for the area to be demolished and redeveloped into a modern city centre; the liberalisation of the market makes this a real possibility, while poorly regulated and enforced property rights heighten this uncertainty.

In 2006, Turquoise Mountain, a British NGO under the patronage of HRH the Prince of Wales and President Karzai, began working in Murad Khani with the aim of regenerating the historic area focusing on both the tangible and intangible dimensions. In terms of tangible assets, by 2014 the organisation had 'cleared over 33,000 m^3 of built-up rubbish from the streets, restored over 112 historic buildings, established a clinic and primary school, and installed utilities throughout the community' (Turquoise Mountain website 2014). Turquoise Mountain has restored a number of the *Takiya Khanas* and some of the smaller shrines, but no work has been done directly on the Abu'l Fazl shrine. Meanwhile, regular community events including Qu'ran recitals and celebrations have been held by Turquoise Mountain in an attempt to encourage the development of community

Figure 3.6 Together with the community, Turquoise Mountain has restored over 112 historic structures in the area (Turquoise Mountain Website, 2014).

spirit and connection to the area. This work has been carried out in close collaboration with the community through various forums including the Shrine *Shura* (elected trustees of the shrine), as well in dialogue with local business owners, elders, women, property owners and other sections of the community. In in the process, Turquoise Mountain has drawn attention to the uniqueness of the inherited architectural form, and its role in the formation of the identity and character of Murad Khani.

Turquoise Mountain emphasises the role of the community in the project and the sustainable development of the area, arguing that the 'rich cultural heritage of Murad Khani provides the basis for its regeneration and for the community's long-term social and economic wellbeing' (Turquoise Mountain website 2014). The approach taken by the Turquoise Mountain has been deeply influenced by postmodern social and cultural theory that emphasises the importance of the values, diversity and history of an area and its inhabitants as well as the urban heritage discourse. Restoring the historic buildings, including those with religious significance, of the area is viewed by the organisation's founder and staff members as central to creating a greater sense of pride in the past and community feeling in the present. Turquoise Mountain has implemented an approach that is deeply rooted in the mutual construction of tangible and intangible dimensions of urban heritage. Understanding how the local community relates to religious structures and the role they play in the identity and sense of place of Murad Khani residents has been a core component of the Turquoise Mountain approach.

Figure 3.7 A large mosque is being constructed alongside the Abu'l Fazl Shrine.

62   *Stephanie Matti*

Despite various attempts by Turquoise Mountain to protect the area from redevelopment,[5] the conservation of the area and important religious sites within it is by no means certain. In 2010, the Mayor of Kabul developed a plan to significantly widen one of the roads bordering Murad Khani, a plan that would have involved the destruction of half of the Abu'l Fazl shrine. Turquoise Mountain and the Murad Khani community campaigned against the plan, which was subsequently dropped. More recently, in early 2014, a long-standing plan to build a new Shi'a mosque alongside the Abu'l Fazl shrine was put into action by the Shrine Council together with the predominantly Shi'a Ministry of Urban Development Affairs (Wide 2014). Without prior warning, a large hole (approximately 20m wide, 20m long and 3m deep) was dug next to the shrine, knocking down several shops in the historic bazaar, cutting off the water supply to the district and threatening the structural integrity of the shrine. Turquoise Mountain has been working together with the *Wakil Gozar* – or community leader – of Murad Khani, and government bodies to ensure that the mosque is built in the historical style and the bazaar shops are reconstructed (Clark Stewart 2014). It is clear that urban planning and the effect of religion on it in the context of Murad Khani continues to be fluid and changing with variety of different policies and actions continuing to threaten the urban and religious heritage of the area.

Conclusion

The district of Murad Khani in the old city of Kabul is an area rich in history and steeped in different dimensions of religiosity. From the Abu'l Fazl shrine and hidden *Takiya Khanas* to the layout of the streets and the sense of place of its residents, religion has had a powerful influence on the development of the area over successive generations. The result is a district endowed with a unique and rich sense of place that stands out against the relatively homogenous and uncontrolled urban sprawl of Kabul.

This chapter has drawn heavily on the oral history research carried out by Turquoise Mountain to develop an understanding of how the tangible and intangible dimensions of religious heritage are mutually constructed in the context of Murad Khani. The picture that emerges is of an historic area in which religion and religious sites form an important element of the sense of place, heritage and identity of the local community. The importance of religion is particularly pronounced due to the religious persecution that has been directed towards the Qizilbash residents of the area.

The urban heritage that has developed is a human and social asset built through the accumulation of traditions and values over centuries and that continues to sustain and reinvigorate the people who live in the area (Schneekloth and Shibley 1995). This heritage and sense of place is particularly important in the context of Afghanistan where the fabric of society has been eroded by decades of conflict, displacement and extremist Taliban rule.

This chapter has also drawn attention to a several threats to the cultural and religious heritage of the Murad Khani. These have included rapid urban growth,

Figure 3.8 Members of the Murad Khani community come together to celebrate *Nawruz* (New Year).

modernist urban planning, infrastructure projects, economic pressures and the destruction of the physical and social structures during the civil war and Taliban periods. These developments have threatened to transform Murad Khani in ways that would have detrimental and potentially irreversible effects on both the physical and visual integrity of the historic urban centre as well as on the social values and interactions of the local community. By researching the tangible and intangible heritage of the area, renovating historic structures and promoting the cultural development of the community in addition to protecting the area against the threat of redevelopment, Turquoise Mountain has worked to mitigate these threats, and revive the unique cultural heritage of the area.

As Kabul and other cities in Afghanistan expand rapidly, the decline of historic centres due to development, neglect and the other threats mentioned above requires urgent and ongoing policy attention. The important role of religion in the formation of sense of place and the close participation of the communities concerned should be at the centre of any policies for urban planning. It is only through contemporary interventions that respect the cultural and religious heritage of Murad Khani that this powerful asset will be maintained for future generations.

Notes

1 All photos in this chapter were taken by Homayun Baig for Turquoise Mountain between 2006 and 2015.

64 *Stephanie Matti*

2 A second story tells that Murad Khan was a General under King Ahmad Shah Durani (1747–1773) who awarded him the lands in the north of the Kabul River which later became Murad Khani.
3 Interview with Khala Mahgul, 15 July 2008. Khala Mahgul, 90 years old, Murad Khani resident.
4 Interview with Khala Mahgul, 15 July 2008. Khala Mahgul, 90 years old, Murad Khani resident. Interview Zarghuna 5–12–07.
5 Legal instruments protecting the area include: two presidential decrees protecting the historic district of Murad Khani (2006 and 2008); the registration of Murad Khani as a historic area with the Ministry of Culture; the registration of every historic building in the area with the Ministry of Culture; the passing of a law by Afghan Parliament protecting Murad Khani as a heritage zone; and the development of an urban regeneration plan for the area together with the Ministry of Urban Development Affairs to replace the 1978 Master Plan. In addition to this, the area was placed on the 2008 World Monuments Fund watchlist of most endangered sites in the world. Turquoise Mountain has also received a UNESCO prize for its conservation work on specific sites within Murad Khani. Finally, the organisation has 'worked to make the area it as beautiful and as living as we can to make people want to protect it' (Clark Stewart 2014).

Bibliography

Ahmadzia, H, 2014, interviewed by S. Matti Kabul (13 April 2014).

Arez, G. and Dittmann, A. 2005, *Kabul – Aspects of Urban Geography*, Peshawar.

Baird-Zars, B. et al. 2014, 'Unlocking Islamic endowments of land (waqf) for poverty alleviation: findings from a multi-country survey of contemporary waqf administration and management', draft available at www.conftool.com/landandpoverty2014/index.php/ [4 January 2015].

BBC 6 December 2011, *Abu Fazal: Shrine of Kabul Shias*, available at www.bbc.co.uk/news/world-asia-16045206 [1 March 2014].

Beatley, T. and Manning, K. 1997, *The Ecology of Place: Planning for Environment, Economy and Community*. Washington: Island Press.

Breshna, Z. 2004, 'A program for the rehabilitation and development of Kabul's historic centre', in *Development of Kabul Reconstruction and Planning Issues: 10th Architecture & Behaviour Colloquium*, eds. B. Mumtaz and K. Noschis, Ascona, 4 to 7 April 2004.

Calogero, P. 2011, 'Kabul cosmopolitan: geopolitical empire from the planner's viewpoint', *Planning Theory*, vol. 10, no. 66, pp. 66–78.

Clark Stewart, S. 2014, interviewed by S Matti, Kabul (11 March 2014).

Coburn, N. 2008, 'Oral history from Murad Khani (interviews by Seddiq Seddiqi)', *Turquoise Mountain Archives*, Kabul.

Esser, D. 2012, 'Kabul: urban politics since Zaher Shah', *Encyclopedia Iranica*, vol. 15, no. 3, pp. 306–310.

Frestone, R. and Gibson, C. 2006, 'The cultural Dimension of Urban Planning Strategies: An Historical Perspective' in *Culture, Urbanism and Planning*, eds. J. Monclús and M. Guàrdia, Ashgate, Hampshire.

Geddes, P. 1904, 'Civics: as applied sociology', presented at *Sociological Society*, University of London, London, on 18 July 1904.

Glatzer, B. 1998, 'Is Afghanistan on the brink of ethnic and tribal disintegration?' in *Fundamentalist Reborn? Afghanistan and the Taliban*, ed. W. Maley, Hurst & Co., London.

Religious heritage in Kabul 65

Habib, J. 2011, 'Urban cohesiveness in Kabul city: challenges and threats', *International Journal of Environmental Studies*, vol. 68, no. 3, pp. 363–371.

Hebbert, M. and Sonne, W. 2006, 'History builds the town: on the uses of history in twentieth-century city planning' in *Culture, Urbanism and Planning*, eds. J. Monclús and M. Guàrdia, Ashgate, Hampshire.

Huart, C. 1934, '*Kizil-B"sh*', *The Encyclopaedia of Islam: A Dictionary of the Geography, Ethnography and Biography of the Muhammadan Peoples*. Brill, London.

ICOMOS 2008, *Quebec Declaration on the Preservation of the Spirit of Place*, 4 October 2008, available at www.international.icomos.org/quebec2008/quebec_declaration/pdf/GA16_Quebec_Declaration_Final_en.pdf [3 January 2015].

Kakar, M. 1979, 'Government and society in Afghanistan: the reign of Amir 'Abd al-Rahman Khan', *Modern Middle East Series*, no. 5.

Kazimee, B. 1977, 'Urban/Rural Dwelling Environments: Kabul, Afghanistan', Master's thesis.

Legendy, C. 2007, 'Understanding Murad Khani', *Turquoise Mountain Urban Regeneration Project*, Kabul.

Library of Congress 1997, 'Ethnic groups in Afghanistan', *Library of Congress Country Studies*, Washington, DC.

Martin, F. 1907, *Under the Absolute Amir*. London and New York: Harper and Brothers.

Matti, S. 2013, 'Socio-economic survey of Murad Khani, Kabul 2013', *Turquoise Mountain Archives*, Kabul.

Miszak, N. and Monsutti, A. 2014, 'Landscapes of power: local struggles and national stakes at the rural-urban fringe of Kabul, Afghanistan', *The Journal of Peasant Studies*, vol. 2, pp. 183–198.

Nabizada, T. 2012, A study on the Spatial Structure of Houses and Open Spaces by the Analysis of Physical Improvements and Daily Activities in the Typical Residential Areas in Kabul City, Osaka University Knowledge Archive, Osaka.

Narayanan, Y. 2015, *Religion Heritage and the Sustainable City*, London: Taylor and Francis.

Orywal, E. 1986. Die ethnischen Gruppen Afghanistans: Fallstudien zu Gruppenidentität und Intergruppenbeziehungen, Wiesbaden.

Radio Free Europe 2010, 'Kabul's old city gets a face-lift and an injection of cash', Radio Free Europe Documents and Publications, 11 October 2010.

Schneekloth, L. and Shibley, R. 1995, *Placemaking: The Art and Practice of Building Communities*, John Wiley and Sons, Inc., New York.

Setchell, C. and Luther, C. 2009, 'Kabul, Afghanistan: a case study in responding to urban displacement', *Humanitarian Exchange Magazine*, vol. 45.

Sharifi, O. 2007, 'Historic background of Murad Khani', Revised by Javid R., *Turquoise Mountain Archives*, Kabul.

Turquoise Mountain, *Turquoise Mountain Website*, available at www.turquoisemountain. org [accessed: 1 November 2014]

UNESCO 2009, 'Preliminary study on technical and legal aspects relating to the desirability of a standard-setting instrument on the conservation of the historic urban landscape', *Executive Board Session 181*, 20 March 2009, available at http://unesdoc.unesco. org/images/0018/001811/181132e.pdf [3 January 2015].

UNESCO 2011, 'A new international instrument: the proposed UNESCO recommendation on the historic urban landscape (HUL)', *Report to the Intergovernmental Committee of Experts*, 25–27 May 2011.

Van der Tas, J. 2004, 'Social services, access to land and transportation as core sectors for the future economic growth of Kabul', in *Development of Kabul Reconstruction and Planning Issues: 10th Architecture & Behaviour Colloquium*, eds. B. Mumtaz and K. Noschis, Ascona, 4 to 7 April 2004.

Viaro, A. 2004, 'What is the use of a Master Plan for Kabul?' in *Development of Kabul Reconstruction and Planning Issues: 10th Architecture & Behaviour Colloquium*, eds. B. Mumtaz and K. Noschis, Ascona, 4 to 7 April 2004.

Vigne, G. 1840, A Personal Narrative of a Visit to Ghuzni, Kabul, and Afghanistan, and of a Residence at the Court of Dost Mohamed, London.

Warah, R. 2002, 'Re-emerging Kabul', *UN Chronicle*, vol. 39, no. 2, p. 63.

Wide, T. 2014, interviewed by S. Matti, Kabul (11 April 2014).

Young, G. 2006, 'Speak, culture! – culture in planning's past, present and future' in *Culture, Urbanism and Planning*, eds. J. Monclús and M. Guàrdia, Ashgate, Hampshire.

4 Revisiting planning for Indian cities
The pilgrim city of Amritsar

Shikha Jain

Introduction

In a country where national highways often transform into pilgrim routes, urban streets and squares corroborate as ritual spaces, stones on pavements evolve into living temples and city adaptations to accommodate mega-scale *Kumbh melas* become accepted role models,[1] clearly the significance of religion in urban planning cannot be undermined.

The use of the term 'sustainability' for cities remains in vogue in global conventions and charters since the last two decades, though it is well researched and established that historic cities across the world were envisioned, conceived and functioned on sound sustainability models for centuries by interpreting and translating natural resources into associative religious values that were subsequently safeguarded by the ruler and the citizens through their strong commitment to religion.

Historic urban settlements in India show a planning order that distinctly marks a religious centre as the genius loci of any urban pattern, be it the temple towns of southern India or medieval princely cities where the ruler's abode was first marked with the temple of the presiding deity before the city was built around it. In that sense, traditional Indian urban planning was invariably centric in nature with the primary centre (topographical in case of a hilly terrain and geometrical in case of a levelled terrain) marked by the presiding or ruling deity of the town or the city. The daily life of the citizens as well as the ruler was governed primarily with the aim of serving the presiding deity who was the prime custodian as well as the raison d'être for the existence and prosperity of the city.

'Administratively and politically, the structure of human settlement has frequently engaged total landscapes. The agricultural and pastoral uses of towns have always been important, especially in pre-industrial cities. The issue of topography is indeed central – not only in the primary sense that hills and valley determine the configuration of settlements – but also, that pre extant rural order inevitably affects the developing city form'.[2] Extending this further to the case of Indian cities, the rural interpretations of faith and divinity of natural forms such as water, rocks, mountains are often found crystallised in urban settlement patterns and city design. Similar pattern of organization is observed at the cluster level too

68   *Shikha Jain*

where the subcentres are marked by the presence of a temple, well or shrine with some religious associations. It is the repetitive rituals that renew and demarcate the city centre and subcentres in a typical Indian settlement and ensure the sustenance of the city for the residents.

Though it is easy to write off this theory as a pre-industrial or rural syndrome, yet even the 21st century planned urban settlements in India exhibit such spontaneous features till date. For example, during a survey of the lake city of Udaipur in 2005, I observed that a group of women had formed an enclosure on the dry lakebed, and a municipal water tanker was parked close to this group supplying water. After inquiring from the locals, I gathered that it is a usual phenomenon since as part of their religious traditions, the women have to take bath in the lake after any death ceremony in the family. Even though they have bathrooms with tap water in their houses now, it is only the venerated spot of the lake that needs to be used for this ceremony so the women gather on the lakebed, and since it was dry that year due to drought, they ordered a municipal tanker. It clearly shows that often new technology is adapted by Indian citizens to cater to old religious rituals rather than shedding off the ritual. In another incident in 2010, I was informed by a resident of the newly planned New Friends Colony in the capital city of New Delhi as to how a small rock under a tree outside their pavement became a full-fledged shrine with a Friday bazaar in a few months as locals started venerating the rocky outcrop on road pavement as a shrine. Such phenomena are frequently found in most Indian settlements today and one thus finds religious associations and markers often overlaying the newly planned and defined urban layouts in most cases. One of the latest Bollywood movies, *Peekay*, released in India conveys this aspect of blind faith in religious associations of Indian citizens very well. However, while such religious associations may get misused into conning the general public, one needs to understand these inherent religious associations that govern the functioning of an average Indian mind and realise the potential of religion in guiding urban planning for Indian cities in future to provide long-term sustenance.

In India, we find several pockets of living historic cities even in this day and age that continue to function with inherent traditional knowledge systems ensuring sustenance of socio-economic and environmental aspects often grounded in religious beliefs of the locals. India has one of the longest histories of urbanisation spanning over the past 5,000 years. Today, Indian cities display the greatest capacity to react, withstand, adopt, accommodate, include, use and benefit from contemporary challenges while continuing to retain an indigenous mechanism for these adaptations.

The Indian cities present dual development strategies clearly marked between post-independence archaic colonial planning norms vis-à-vis local cultural aspirations that determine the design of improvised urban spaces. It is evident that history, culture, religion and faith play a more proactive role in urban planning at an informal level in India and there is a need to understand and integrate this aspect more formally in policy making and planning frameworks in future.

The city of Amritsar which has functioned as the seat of Sikhism for centuries with the Golden Temple as the genius loci is an ideal example to understand the role of religion in guiding urban form. The case study of pilgrim city of Amritsar presents an interesting example of living heritage where religion has predominantly determined the city form, functioning and economy through various centuries till today. This 16th century pilgrim city has now grown into an urban settlement with a population of 11 million with an additional 1 million pilgrims visiting every day. It is also one of the 12 cities identified under the national HRIDAY (Heritage Rejuvenation Development and Augmentation Yojana) scheme of the Ministry of Urban Development to be taken up for rejuvenation, so an understanding of the religious association with city development in this case may provide an approach for similar cases across India.

Sikhism and genesis of Amritsar: Sri Harmander Sahib

The tenets of Sikhism by Guru Nanak and later gurus outline secularism, equitability and service to mankind as key features that are essentials for sustainable communities. The city of Amritsar, was created as the centre for Sikhism and continues to flourish as such.

Guru Amar Das (1479–1579 AD), the third Guru of the Sikhs decided to establish a new place of pilgrimage for the Sikhs in late 16th century as the previous location of Goindwal seemed unsuitable for future expansion of Sikhism. The site of the pond identified for the holy shrine was located between the villages of Sultanwind, Tung, Gumtala and Gilwali. Amrit-Sar (Pool of Nectar) was this water body identified for building the holy shrine of the Sikhs in the 16th century. The city thus had a modest beginning around a low-lying area with a small pond with the famous tree, Dukh Bhanjani Beri that stands in the same location within the complex of the Holy Shrine of the Golden Temple (Sri Harmander Sahib) till today. The location of this site en route of caravans moving between India and Afghanistan on the historic trade route known as the Baadshahi Marg provided further impetus to its growth as a commercial centre.

The foundations of the city of Amritsar were laid by the next Guru Ramdas in 1577 AD around the holy shrine of Sri Harmandar Sahib, continued by Guru Arjun Dev in 1589 AD and the temple complex was finally completed by Guru Hargobind Singh in 1604 AD. The holy shrine itself predates the concept of a Gurudwara (the threshold or doorway of the guru) which was put forward few decades later by Guru Hargobind. With the compilation of the Guru Granth Sahib and its installation within Sri Harmandar Sahib in 1604, the Sikh faith was fundamentally redefined, the concept of a Gurudwara became synonymous with the structure and a new identity for sacred Sikh Architecture was born. All future Gurudwaras were thus based on this typology for Sri Harmandar Sahib. In 1606, Guru Hargobind Singh also laid the foundation of Akal Takht or the Eternal Throne facing the main shrine. This structure continues to serve as the centre of the temporal authority of the Sikhs since then.

The architectural style adopted by the Sikhs derives from an existing amalgamation of Mughal and Rajput architectural traditions which had reached their pinnacles between the 15th and 17th centuries. The diversity of the architectural

70 *Shikha Jain*

styles which had spread across northern and western India was aptly suited to the new typologies that Sikhism sought after, in the form of the Gurudwara and allied spaces. Thus, even though the origins of the architectural style used in Sri Harmander Sahib may be seen in pre-existing architectural vocabularies, the evolution of these styles marks the beginning of an entirely unique expression of Sikh beliefs and aesthetics that subsequently reflects in the urban fabric of Amritsar.

With the temple, as the genius loci, plans were made to develop and expand the existing settlements into a new town. The location of the new town and the emerging religion of Sikhism was a great threat for both the Mughals and the Afghans who plundered and demolished the temple and the city as many as seven times between 1739 and 1764 AD. With constant attacks from the Mughal and Afghan rulers, the temple complex and city faced a difficult time, but they were soon rebuilt, and the city expanded with a new vigour through the commitment of the Sikhs.

Rebuilding faith and the city

Surrounding the tank at Sri Harmander Sahib, the leading members of the Sikh *misls* (confederacies) first established their residences and palaces and *bungas* (rest places) at Amritsar in the late 18th century. There were over 84 bungas around this sacred pool and temple during this period. One of the more prominent bungas that still stands within the complex is the Ramgharia Bunga while others were removed post-independence. The bungas also served as important educational and training centre for the Sikhs until the colonial period. Further developments include construction of Lohagarh, a small fortress in the west of the city and cremation space for the young son of Guru Hargobind on the site that currently houses the structure of Baba Atal. The limits of city which was called Ramdaspura during this time expanded from the Shivala built by one of the nobles Jassa Singh Ahluwalia in the east along with extension to Katra Ahluwalia to the Darshini Deodhi providing a direct view of Sri Harmander Sahib on the southern side.

During this Misl period (1764–1802), the function of the city predominantly remained as a religious and pilgrimage centre. The trade was limited to meet the local needs, and each *Katra* (neighbourhood/residential cluster) functioned independently as a principality with its own policing under the Misl sardar. The development during this period includes Katras, forts, havelis, bungas gardens, tanks, etc. The various Misl Sardars who contributed to the development of city are: Sardar Jassa Singh Ramgarhia who converted fort of Ram Rauni to fort Ramgarh and built Katra Ramgarhia and Bunga Ramgarhia for defence of Sri Harmander Sahib; Bhangian who built Qila Bhangian, Katra Hari Singh, Katra Desa Singh, Katra Bhag Singh, Katra Dulo, Katra Chatar Singh, Tunda Talab area; Kanhaiya Sardar Jai Singh who built Katra Baggian, Katra Jaimal Singh and Karmo Deodhi; Sardar Jassa Singh Ahluwalia who constructed Qila Ahluwalia and Katra Ahluwalia and Faizal Puria Nawab Kapoor Singh who built Faizal Puria Katra now known as Bazaar Kaserian.[3] This period led to strengthening of the defence system for Sri Harmander Sahib as well as for the city. Further, many activity areas in the form of bazaars and katras were developed as subsidiaries to the main function of the city as a pilgrim place.

The golden period of Sikhism

Amritsar rose to the heights of its glory under the patronage and governance provided by Maharaja Ranjit Singh when he extended his custodianship to the city of Amritsar as his Summer Capital in 1805. He regained control of Sikh territory after conquering Amritsar, visited the temple and offered his homage at the Akal Takht and Sri Harmander Sahib in the form of large cash offerings. It was under Maharaja Ranjit Singh that the structures of Sri Harmander Sahib and holy tank were reconstructed and the main shrine attained an unmatched formal glory. Sri Harmander Sahib flourished and united the Sikhs like never before. Along with temple renovations such as addition of marble inlay cladding, wall paintings and gold gilding work in the main shrine (giving it the name of the Golden Temple), the complex was further expanded along with the surrounding city. New city walls were constructed with a surrounding moat and gates, Gobindgarh Fort was constructed using foundations of the initial mud fort structure of the Bhangis into a contemporary military defence structure inspired from French military fortress plans and the grand palatial structure of the Ram Bagh Palace Gardens introduced a new idiom of planning and architecture in the city of Amritsar. Its location on trade route from Afghanistan again helped Amritsar to come up as a flourishing trade centre which was at its peak in the early 19th century with trading of textiles and other goods traded by Hindu Khatris, Banias, Muslim Khojas, Kashmiri Muslims and Afghans.

The city developed a new legible urban form during this period including architectural typologies of forts, gates, gardens, havelis, akharas etc. Among the fourteen city gates built during this period, only Ram Bagh Gate remains in its original form today while all other gates were demolished and rebuilt by the British during 1866–1868. Besides the Ram Bagh Garden which was modelled on Shalimar Bagh of Lahore and housed the Maharaja's summer palace, there were several other gardens and open spaces in the city such as Bagh Akalian, Bagh Santokhsar, Ralia Ram and Bagh Ramanand. The Maharaja encouraged his noble sardars to expand the city by constructing their havelis and small gardens around which katras (mixed landuse clusters) developed. These were Katra Karam Singh, Katra Hakima, Katra Khazana, Katra Dal Singh, Katra Mit Singh, Katra Garba Singh, Katra Zamindar Khushal Singh and Katra Sher Singh.

This was truly the golden period of the city when it was at its peak of development as the Maharaja also invited Marwari merchants to the city and trade flourished. Besides salt market, grain market and timber market, a wholesale trade and yarn centre was established at Katra Ahluwalia. Others included Bazaar Patragan, Guru Bazaar (with jewellery), Misri Bazar, Bazaar Bansanwala, Bazaar Subunian (silk market), Karmo Deori, Bazaar Mumiaran, Bazaar Kathian, Mughal Darwaza, Bazaar Kaserian and Bazaar Mai Sewan as important markets of Amritsar at that time with trade connections within India and outside.

Institutionalisation of Sikhism

Sikh religion faced a serious setback after the death of Maharaja Ranjit Singh. With loss of one of the strongest political patronage of Sikhs and control of the British, other religions such as Hinduism and Christianity started influencing this sect within its seat at Amritsar. It is recorded that several Hindu idols were placed by the Hindu Brahmins in the Darbar Sahib (Sri Harmander Sahib) and misguided Sikhs paid their homage.[4] Moreover, the British strategically started controlling several Gurudwaras in Panjab State including Sri Harmander Sahib despite the Waqf Act of 1861 as per which the management of the holy places should be under the control of the local communities. During this period, aspects such as religion, the official language, the celebration of festivals: all these became open to contestation that was arbitrated upon by the officials of the British Raj.[5] As a response to this, the Singh Sabha Movement was born in 1873 in the name of Sri Guru Singh Sabha Amritsar duly registered through the Government Act XXI of 1860. In 1879, the priests of the Akal Takht and Sri Harmander Sahib issued a joint Hukumnama welcoming the Singh Sabha Movement as the restorer of the original form of Sikhism and calling upon the Sikhs to join the movement.[6] All matters related to modernisation and management of the religious premises were made through democratic decisions made at annual sessions.

One of the major contributions of Amritsar Singh Sabha to the city was the establishment of the Khalsa College at Amritsar in 1897 that gave an impetus to education of the Sikhs. The next few years saw further turmoil with the formation of the Lahore Singh Sabha as a counterpart and several smaller Singh Sabhas in various Gurudwaras across Panjab. Conflicts such as decisions regarding electrification of the Golden Temple and similar matters are well recorded in Sikh documents of this period. The electrification of the temple was a highly controversial matter and after a period of debate between the Amritsar Singh Sabha and the Lahore Singh Sabha, at the 1896 session, a Lighting Committee was set up under the presidency of Sardar Arjun Singh and funds were raised through devotees and from a generous donation by Maharaja Bikram Singh of Faridkot. He also donated money for installing permanent electricity and for raising a new *Langar* (kitchen) building.

In order to integrate all sabhas, it was decided to form a Khalsa Diwan Amritsar which soon led to a parallel formation of Khalsa Diwan at Lahore diluting the strength of sabhas under the Khalsa Diwan Amritsar. These internal issues were finally resolved with the formation of the Chief Khalsa Diwan at Amritsar in 1902.

This management and governance framework of the Sikhs was again disturbed after the historical Jallian Wala Bagh massacre of 1919 in Amritsar. The Gurudwara Reform Movement was taken up after the 1920 General assembly of the Sikhs held in the vicinity of the Akal Takht. The Sikhs took back control of several Sikh shrines including the Golden Temple and a mother body emerged with 175 members that took its final shape after some years as the Shiromani Gurdwara Prabandhak Committee (SGPC). The first memorable task undertaken by the SGPC was the first formal Kar Sewa (service for voluntary labour) in desilting and cleansing of the Amrit Sarovar at the Golden Temple in 1923. De-siltation, repairs to the substructure were carried out and tiles were laid which was completed over a period of 22 days (June 17th–July 8th) by a massive gathering of devotees from all over the world. Finally, after the Gurudwara Act came into force on November 1, 1925, SGPC officially took over the management and maintenance of the Golden Temple and its environs which continues till date.

The temple complex itself evolved and rapidly grew around Sri Harmandar Sahib during the mid-19th century, and many new structures were added, beginning with the widening of the outer 'parikrama' in 1928–1929. Other additions in the surroundings included the Guru Ram Das Sarai, Akal Rest House, Nanak Nivas, Teja Singh Samundri Hall, Manji Sahib and Diwan Halls. In 1949, Sikh Reference library formed and the Central Sikh museum was created in 1958. After the 1973, *kar sewa*, a firm tradition of maintenance, cleansing and governance by the devotees and their representatives, was established under SGPC.

The Indian Army invaded Sri Harmandar Sahib under orders from Prime Minister Indira Gandhi, between 3th and 8th June 1984 under the 'Operation Bluestar' with the intent to remove Jarnail Singh Bhindranwale and his armed followers from the premises. This event claimed thousands of innocent lives and resulted in extensive damage to the built fabric of Sri Harmandar Sahib. The Akal Takht building was completely destroyed and had to be extensively rebuilt. In 1988, several shops and houses were removed to make a corridor around the Sri Harmandar Sahib. This added lot of space for movement and significantly added to the visual impact and overall aesthetics of the Golden Temple complex. In 2004, Sri Harmander Sahib observed the first Kar Sewa of the 21st century for the purpose of installing water treatment plants. This year also observed the largest ever recorded strength of devotees visiting the Golden Temple, on the eve of 400 years centennial Installation celebrations of the Sikh Scripture in September 2004. And in 2014, after constant efforts of the Sikh community, the Government of India finally officiated compensation for innocent Sikh families of Amritsar who suffered during the 1984 riots.

Global and national agenda, local planning and religion

Today, the Sikh organisation SGPC is in complete charge of management and development of Sri Harmander Sahib in Amritsar and its surroundings. It owns several structures in the vicinity of the temple and is further involved in building new infrastructure for the visitors, *Serai* (hotel accommodation) etc. as per requirements of the increasing visitors to the Golden Temple. While SGPC is not directly involved in the city management which comes under the jurisdiction of the Municipal body of Amritsar, there is no doubt that SGPC and the rules outlined by this body as per *maryada* for Sikhs play an important role in contributing to the surrounding development of the city. The Golden Temple is one of the most visited sites in India recording close to 60,000 people every day, almost doubling at the weekends and reaching up to half a million during festivals.

74   *Shikha Jain*

Sri Harmander Sahib is an internationally renowned pilgrim site which is on the Tentative List of India to be proposed for nomination under the World Heritage UNESCO (United Nations Educational, Scientific, and Cultural Organization) listing. However, this process of nomination though initiated in 2004–2006 was stalled as SGPC withdrew the nomination dossier from the World Heritage Centre. One of the reasons to withdraw this nomination was that SGPC is not prepared to accept any involvement of an external agency or body whether national or international in the management of Sri Harmander Sahib. Clearly, Sikhism and its *maryada* (code of conduct) are the paramount features governing any decision for the Golden Temple and subsequently impact the city development in the vicinity. Even if a visitor mistakenly lights a cigarette outside the boundary of the Golden Temple, locals immediately ask him to stop. There are clear rules of behaviour that are followed beyond the premise of the main shrine even in the surrounding market areas.

The population of Amritsar today has a composition of Hindus that constitute 50.23 per cent of total population of Amritsar city, while 47.92 per cent are Sikhs and 1.85 per cent are Christians, and rest of the population belongs to other religions including Muslims, Jains and Buddhist, as per 2001 census. Yet, the Golden Temple is indisputably revered by all communities in the city besides the peaceful co-existence of Hindu temples, Muslim mosques and Churches for other communities as per secular tenets of Sikhism.

The city has expanded since 20th century, though the historic walled area around Sri Harmander Sahib is still legible, but it is under great pressure due to high density of population and increasing demands for accommodation from the pilgrim tourists. Besides the historic bazaars in the walled city, a number of informal markets are located around the major traffic nodes including railway station, bus stand and places of tourist interest and Golden Temple, Jallianwala Bagh, Durgiana Mandir, Baba Atal, etc., to supplement the commercial requirements of people living within the walled city and visitors to the city. The Master Plan of Amritsar identifies these informal markets located on road berms, vacant land/open spaces, parking lots etc. creating numerous problems in the efficient functioning of the city including traffic and transportation.[7] The Master Plan outlines that in order to rationalize the growth and development of the city, informal sector needs to be made integral part of the city planning and development process. Options for creating more affordable commercial areas in terms of day markets needs to be explored in order to enable the informal sector contribute to the economic growth of the city.

Some of the ongoing proposals for urban renewal of Amritsar include a heritage walk funded under the Asian Development Bank project in the walled city, sewerage and water supply within the walled city and decongestion of bazaars, the Galliara project around the Golden Temple, but there are several challenges in effective implementation of these projects due to the complexity of socio-economic and functional layers, as well as multiplicity of government organisations that need to be addressed during implementation of new schemes such as HRIDAY Scheme under the Ministry of Urban Development.

One of the significant aspect to be comprehended in Indian cities is the dynamics of their living heritage and perpetually flourishing religious urban nodes that often generate as part of ongoing cultural practices and defy planned development. For India's historic cities to retain their prime principles of sustainability, the Government of India has introduced a positive, heritage and resource-based approach to urban development through National Programmes such as HRIDAY and PRASAD (Pilgrimage Rejuvenation and Spiritual Augmentation Drive). The focus of revitalisation and rehabilitation of historic centres of India will be on whole areas, not just individual buildings, and on social communities, not just the physical environment. Future planning of Indian cities will be driven by environmental and social and not economic and political concerns alone with more attention to 'inclusive' planning rather than exclusive classes. It is commendable that these recent national schemes of HRIDAY and PRASAD launched by the Government of India in 2014–2015 have a special focus on these challenges of the urban cultural heritage of India. While HRIDAY Scheme is being implemented by the Ministry of Urban Development, the PRASAD Scheme focusing on Pilgrim cities is being implemented by the Ministry of Tourism. For cities like Amritsar, which fall under both schemes it needs to be ensured that the projects under HRIDAY and PRASAD are complimentary and address concerns related to pilgrim tourism as well as sustained urban development of the historic city.

At the global level, the recent adoption of a new policy instrument by UNESCO, the 2011 Recommendation on the Historic Urban Landscape, is a significant set of general principles in support of sustainable urban heritage management. Processes of renewal, regeneration, enhancement and management of historic cities require a medium-and long term vision that is both achievable and sustainable, embodying the concept of custodianship for future generations. In that sense, these guidelines are not much different from the principles of sustainability adapted and practiced in historic Indian cities for centuries until the advent of colonial rule and post-colonial development.

Despite more than two hundred World Heritage Cities inscribed on the UNESCO World Heritage List, the external auditor's report on World Heritage observes the need for more Asian and specifically Indian cities that need to be placed on the List.[8] At the same time, it points to the lack of legislation in Indian cities as a major challenge in achieving World Heritage Status for Indian cities. Recognition of urban heritage and aspirations for its significance at a global level is a fairly recent phenomenon in India evident in the listing of historic cores of Chandigarh Ahmadabad, Delhi, Mumbai and Jaipur on India's Tentative List for UNESCO World Heritage in last few years. While few Indian cities are striving hard to ensure sustainable management of their historic cities as per current Operational Guidelines of UNESCO, the dilemma remains in responding to universal norms that may not be locally applicable or effective in long term.

An integrated approach that reviews various tools for urban conservation in use at the local, regional, national and international level is essential for Indian cities. Mapping, protecting and planning for urban heritage landscapes through a reflection on national agendas as well as international applicability of UNESCO's

76 Shikha Jain

Historic Urban Landscape needs to be reviewed alongside matching local aspirations in customized contexts. UNESCO based programme of Indian Heritage Cities Network (now a Foundation) and parallel activities by other NGOs such as INTACH have helped in raising awareness on urban heritage in India and substantiating changes such as inclusion of a City Level Heritage Management Plan as part of the Master Planning exercise.

Few sectors of historic Indian cities have exemplary examples of urban renewal projects such as the Aga Khan – ASI urban renewal initiative in Nizammudin area of New Delhi though its replicability and sustainability across India is limited. Historic cores in cities of Mumbai, Delhi, Varanasi, Hyderabad, Madurai, Mysore, Jaipur, Udaipur, Ahmedabad and many more have taken initiatives in framing heritage management plans and heritage committees for conservation and development of historic areas. However, the challenge of understanding the localised cultural practices, religion, faith and their impact on city development is an area that still remains largely unaddressed. In fact, it is time that urban heritage solutions for Indian cities are derived through an empathy for such religious processes and practices to feed back into UNESCO documents on regional contexts.

Generic documents such as the UNESCO/UN-HABITAT Toolkit on 'Historic Districts for All – India: A Social and Human Approach for Sustainable Revitalisation' comprising of a manual for city professionals do not find much application. Similar exercises are being undertaken at the national level by the Ministry of Urban Development in working out recently announced schemes for urban renewal in pilgrim and heritage cities. However, unless the issue of sustainability and future urban planning in Amritsar and other pilgrim cities is addressed at the ground level through customised solutions adapted to synergise the activities between 'the City and the Shrine' along with reinforcement of religious patronage at city level, it will be difficult to achieve the desired status.

Conclusion

As a city inspired to be the seat of Sikhism, Amritsar presents an excellent case study to understand that religion is one of the key determinants in city building as opposed to conventional planning norms and global urban agendas. It is observed that during the Misl period and the reign of Maharaja Ranjit Singh, there was a synergy between patronage for religious activity and urban development. This connect was strong because the patronage for city development resided with the Sikh ruling elites with the paramount focus of defending Sri Harmander Sahib and developing Amritsar as the seat of Sikhism.

The colonial period under the British Raj saw the beginnings of disconnect between the state as a 'non-patron' and the community of Sikhs. The two parties were working to achieve different ends. During the British Rule, there was a deliberate disconnect between the religious centre and political/governance centre recorded in various incidents including the 1877 inscription in the Golden Temple that refers to intentions of the British to auction the Golden Temple which was finally saved by a miracle enumerated in the inscription.[9] The British monitored the activities of Sri Harmander Sahib and tried to dilute its influence in order to avoid any possibilities of a national espionage in its premise. This was also evident in the construction of the highly criticised incongruous Gothic Clock Tower built during the British period and removed later.

Unfortunately this disconnect in development of the Golden Temple area and urban projects in the surrounding city continues in the post-colonial period since the Indian state keeps working through an archaic and often condescending governance and legal mechanism laid down since colonial period.

The Golden Temple complex, its inception, practice and institution have been integral to the development of Amritsar and indeed the entire Sikh community worldwide. Every aspect of Sikh culture and society have been born out of the practices developed here, starting with the establishment of the Akal Takht or the Eternal Throne. The Golden Temple and its religious affiliations are evidently the most important determinants while planning for urban renewal of the historic city of Amritsar, and they also hold significance for assessing further city expansion to a large extent. It has been observed that a number of planned proposals and schemes for urban renewal are not being successfully implemented, while there are informal developments that are mushrooming with the increasing visitation and religious affiliations to the Golden Temple. Hence, it is essential to address the role of the Golden Temple, its visitors and management framework in an integrated manner with the Municipal planning for the surrounding areas as was the case historically through centuries.

An understanding of the religious core of Amritsar and its functioning will add significantly to the thought process and action plans for sustainability of the walled city. Such data and applications at city level may further provide exemplary cases to be used in policy making, while devising national schemes for Indian cities such as the recently launched National Mission on PRASAD and HRIDAY identified for Amritsar.

Sikh institutions like SGPC have adapted well by adding modern entities such as a library as well as a museum to the religious complex. The city of Amritsar like any other contemporary Indian city also reflects aspirational pressures of global urbanism such as malls, fancy restaurants, etc. Thus the actors in the city i.e. the State, citizens and the Sikh religious institutions are dynamic entities contributing to urban growth of Amritsar. But in order to allow a more coherent growth of this city, it is essential to reinforce the connection between cultural/religious patronage and urban planning. This is the biggest challenge for India in its secular state structure.

The historic Indian urban landscapes such as Amritsar are born out of the deeply rooted cultural and spiritual traditions and have evolved into spaces of timeless appeal over the centuries. These historic areas have undergone numerous physical, social and cultural transformations, yet they manage to conjure up the inherent values of the place often through a cultural continuity grounded in religious centres and associated faith. Despite the fact that physical planning around the Golden Temple shrine and surrounding urban area is now under different

78 *Shikha Jain*

stakeholders, the underlying rules of Sikhism does define the code of conduct for both areas to a large extent. Clearly faith and practices can have a greater impact than physical planning systems. Hence, urban solutions and national agendas need to be framed and implemented through such belief systems for example the practice of Kar Sewa (free service for maintenance and cleaning) of the Sikhs can easily be encouraged to extend beyond the Golden Temple to the surrounding city thus ensuring city maintenance. In fact the recent report prepared by ICLEI (International Council for Local Environmental Initiatives) South Asia in 2014 for the World Bank corroborates such examples for Amritsar city which show local babas (associated with the Golden Temple) who are providing voluntary service for solid waste management by organising collections at their level. Such community level innovative solutions grounded in religious commitment will go a long way to ensure sustainable measures for the city. These will further the cause of national agendas such as the 'Swach Bharat' (Clean India) campaign, and HRIDAY and PRASAD, which otherwise will be difficult to implement purely as central-level recommendations to the States and the city.

Notes

1 'At the Kumbh Mela, instant urbanization – a transformation in weeks from an underwater flood plain to a city of tens of millions unfolding in a thoughtful and planned way – can potentially be a model for the kinds of things [that should be] considered in the development of hundreds of other new, permanent cities', Prof. John Macomber, Harvard Business School in www.ibtimes.com/kumbh-mela-case-study-chaos-attracts-harvard-business-school-1076944
2 Spiro Kostof (1989), *Dwellings, Settlements and Tradition*, edited by Jean-Paul Bourdier and Nezar Alsayyad, University Press of America, p. 109.
3 District Gazetteer, Amritsar, Amritsar: A study in urban history (1840–1947), The city of Amritsar, An Introduction by Fauja Singh.
4 Madanjit Kaur (1983), *The Golden Temple: past and present*, Amritsar, Guru Nanak Dev University Press, p. 95.
5 Banerjee, Ashis, Book Review: Punjab, A History from Aurangzeb to Mountbatten, IIC Quarterly, Summer 2014.
6 Madanjit Kaur (1983), p. 99
7 Master Plan of Amritsar.
8 Article 103, WHC-11/35.COM/INF.8: 'Final report of the Audit of the Global Strategy and the PACT Initiative', p 26. http://whc.unesco.org/archive/2011/whc11-18ga-INF.8-en.pdf.
9 Narration by John Campbell Oman (2011) in *The Golden Temple of Amritsar, Reflections of the Past (1808–1959)* by Amandeep Singh Madra and Parmjit Singh, Kashi House.

Bibliography

Aggarwal, J.C. (1992), Modern History of Punjab: A Look Back Into Ancient Peaceful Punjab Focusing Confrontation and Failures Leading to Present Punjab Problem, and a Peep Ahead: Relevant Select Documents. Vol. 37. www.conceptpub.com.
Arshi, P.S. (1989), *The Golden Temple: history, art and architecture* (pp. 13–14), New Delhi, Harman Publishing House.

Dilgeer, H.S., (2001) Shiromani Gurdwara Parbandhak Committee Kiven Bani (Punjabi), Amritsar, S.G.P.C.

Dilgeer, H.S., (2000), *Shiromani Akali Dal (1920–2000),* Belgium, Sikh University Press.

Environmental Action Plan for Urban Transformation in Service Delivery for Amritsar and Ludhiana. Final Report on Amritsar prepared by ICLEI (2015) with support of the World Bank, UK Aid and Australian Aid (Unpublished).

Kang, K.S. (1977), *Art and Architecture of the Golden Temple,* Ed. Anand, Mulk Raj. Vol. 30, no. 3, Marg Publications.

Kaur, Madanjit, (1983), *The Golden Temple: past and present,* Amritsar, Guru Nanak Dev University Press.

Sai Consultants, Master Plan of Amritsar (Unpublished) prepared for Amritsar Development Authority, 2014.

Sandhu, Kiran and Gurpreet Singh Gill, 'Impact of Neo-Urban Paraphernalia on Amritsar City: of Transformations and Transgressions', in Department of Estate Management Valuation (p.1–17). University of Sri Jayewardenepura, *Sri Lankan Journal of Real Estate.*

Singh, Fauja, ed. (1978), *The City of Amritsar,* New Delhi: Oriental Publishers & Distributors.

Singh, Khushwant (2011), *A History of the Sikhs* (Volume 1 and Volume 2), New Delhi, Oxford University Press.

Singh Madra, Amandeep and Parmjit Singh (2011), *The Golden Temple of Amritsar, Reflections of the Past (1808–1959),* Kashi House.

5 Tradition versus urban public bureaucracy? Reshaping pilgrimage routes and religious heritage around contested space

Vera Lazzaretti

Setting the scene

This chapter deals with different visions of religious and spatial heritage in Varanasi (Banaras, as it is called by its inhabitants, Uttar Pradesh, India). By analyzing the changes to local urban processions as performed today by one of the city's main pilgrimage associations, the *Kashi Pradakshina Darshan Yatra Samiti* (KPDYS, a private and self-funded organization), I will highlight the current management of sacred space by urban authorities, and its effects in terms of access, community relationships and re-positioning of 'traditional' actors and practices. Furthermore, I will suggest that the practice of local pilgrimages constructively mediates between contrasting visions of religious heritage, as well as developing a particular way of experiencing place, and engaging with others.

Local processions and the production of locality developed through them will emerge as ways of constantly re-defining sense of place and belonging. As I will outline, sense of place and belonging, together with heritage, have been identified as crucial in renewing the discourse on urban development (for example, Beatley and Manning 1997, CABE and DETR 2000, Sepe 2013). Re-conceptualizing sustainable cities thus requires addressing local dynamics of dwelling in and being attached to places. Moreover, local pilgrimages will be seen as both tangible and intangible heritage; in fact, pilgrimage pertains to actual shrines, routes and resting places for pilgrims, as well as having ritual, symbolic and individual significance. My analysis also reflects on potentials and risks in the uses of religious heritage; these are linked to questions of privilege, access to space and the power to shape the urban fabric and its meanings for social actors. Such themes are clearly fundamental in rethinking urban sustainability.

I focus on a specific space where changes to local processions are especially evident: this is the Vyas Pith[1] and the nearby Jnanavapi, the Well of Knowledge, where pilgrims are supposed to pronounce their vows and perform starting rituals. This area is today at the core of multiple disputes. The Pith and the Well are situated between the famous Kashi Vishvanath temple and the Gyan Vapi mosque, named after the Well. The whole compound is considered a highly security-sensitive zone, especially after the demolition of the Babri *masjid* in Ayodhya in 1992 by

Hindu 'rightist' mobs, at which time Vishvanath was identified by Hindutva leaders as the next place to be 'freed' from the Muslim presence. These claims were based on the area's controversial past. Even though historical evidence is lacking, in fact, a popular narrative about the shrine and its several destructions has been promoted since the British period, through the interaction of colonial reports and local contributions (Desai 2007). Until recently, however, this area was a shared civic space for local inhabitants of both religious communities.

Moreover, the area between the two main shrines where the Vyas Pith dwells is at the centre of a local dispute between different conceptions and managements of sacred space. The rituals, offerings and pilgrims inflow of the Well area are, in fact, still run privately by the Vyas[2] family, while the surrounding Kashi Vishvanath temple and its compound have, since 1983, been controlled by a government trust, the Kashi Vishvanath Trust (KVT), in which urban authorities constitute the majority of the board of trustees and executive committee.[3]

I will argue that the current management of religious heritage in this space compromises an inclusive sense of place and is unsustainable for the city, in the sense that it alienates both people and space. As I will outline, it produces a filtered and to some extent manufactured heritage, rather than endorsing actual local traditions and performers. On the other hand, the practice of local urban processions will be seen to be historically adaptable to the changing urban territory and it emerges today as inclusive of various social actors. The KPDYS will be shown as capable of engaging in dialogue with both main opposing conceptions of religious heritage, the one represented by secular urban authorities and that of 'traditional' sacred specialists. I will suggest that cautious observation of such local practices can inform the discourse on sustainable cities for South Asia as one that has to enhance locality in its full complexity; therefore, looking at the multiple religious heritage of single places emerges as an important clue for such locally sensitive future planning.

The next section introduces some theoretical remarks: the anthropological perspective on place as a multivocal construction, which I adopt in the present analysis, will be linked to critical approaches to sustainability and heritage. The third section then deals with pilgrimage as a form of religious heritage and explores different layers, meanings, potentials and risks of such a practice in urban contexts, while also introducing the KPDYS and the performance of local urban processions in Banaras. Following that, the next section briefly outlines the origins of such practice and later focuses on the Vyas Pith. The dispute about its management in terms of access to space, security and community relationships will be outlined. In the fifth section, I will describe some of the consequences of the current management by highlighting changes to urban processions and bureaucratic procedures faced by the KPDYS. The final section presents concluding remarks and develops the critique of the current official management of religious heritage, while proposing the KPDYS activities as an alternative way that can contribute to re-thinking sustainability as a locally sensitive and inclusive concept, necessarily attached to and enhancing actual heritage bearers, their specific senses of place and their needs.

82 Vera Lazzaretti

Sustainability and heritage: an anthropological perspective

After having been for long treated as a simple inert scene for human actions, place has definitely emerged in the last few decades as a valid and complex anthropological subject (Appadurai 1988; Feld and Basso 1996: 4–5; Gupta and Ferguson 1992; Hirsch and O'Hanlon 1995; Rodman 1992). The phenomenological approach to the spatial dimension privileges experienced places over the abstract dimension of space, as it is in specific localities that people start to construct their ideas and concepts about space (Casey 1996). Therefore, the anthropological perspective on place has been thought of as the intent of collecting and transmitting 'local theories of dwelling' (Feld and Basso 1996: 8), that could enrich one's own understanding of the space dimension and inform future discourses and actions for and in places. The inner multivocality (Appadurai 1988) of places has been pointed out as the main quality to be considered in the study of spatial entities. Locality is not a given fact, but something constantly re-thought and reproduced (Appadurai 2001: 232–233), and place is the result of multiple social constructions. The multilocal perspective on place also conveys the idea that 'a single place may be experienced quite differently' and pursues constantly looking at places from the viewpoints of others (Rodman 1992). Such anthropological reflections on place are fundamental to the discourse on sustainable cities.

In cultural geography the notion of 'sense of place' defines attachment, belonging and dwelling (Tuan 1977). Anthropologists describe sense of place as something that is constantly negotiated by different voices, such as those of the variety of local inhabitants, those of the authorities, those coming from distant imageries of immigrants and even those of ethnographers, who have the power to re-construct others' places in their works. Understanding senses of place means identifying 'some of the ways in which people encounter places, perceive them and invest them with significance . . . and ways in which places naturalize different worlds of sense' (Feld and Basso 1996: 8). Addressing sense of place and local ways of place-making have been linked fruitfully to the discourse on sustainable cities (Beatley and Manning 1997, CABE and DETR 2000). Sustainability, in fact, has been re-thought as a vital concept that has to deal with local communities and their needs, and not as an imported label applied uncritically to development discourses for non-western realities (Mahadevia 2001, Patra 2009). Attention to elements that make place, and sense of place, for local actors has been pointed out as the clue to re-conceptualizing any sensible and sustainable planning for cities (Narayanan 2015, Sepe 2013). The focus on such concepts is even more meaningful in the delocalized world, and especially for Indian cities where the historical coexistence of diverse communities makes it even more necessary for urban planning to understand places in a multivocal and multilocal way.

Understanding local senses of place, forms of belonging and links between urban built environment and people, in order to rethink sustainable, and thus locally sensitive cities, means engaging with the history of places, their inhabitants and the products, tangible and intangible, of people-place interactions. In essence, sense of place is inextricably linked to heritage; and the latter has been defined as a present mode of cultural production that has recourse to the past (Kirschenblatt-Gimblett 2004).

Discourses on safeguarding heritage have become influential in international, national and local urban cultural policy, especially after the 2003 UNESCO (United Nations Educational, Scientific, and Cultural Organization) Convention on Intangible Cultural Heritage (ICH), which officially sanctioned the liveliness and pervasiveness of place-based forms of knowledge, such as masterpieces, rituals, performances, and indeed even practitioners, as intangible heritage. However, understanding heritage as a past resource that is being reshaped in the present (and for the future) means being aware of selective dynamics of power related to the process of making heritage. While even a tangible or natural heritage site is not universally identifiable, the criteria for selection are much more subtle in the case of intangible heritage. The creation and promotion of intangible heritage, indeed, requires access and, in essence, power, which sometimes are only in the hands of official authorities and not of the actual bearers of heritage themselves (Beardslee 2014).

Research on cultural heritage has, indeed, pointed out the strong discrepancies between professional heritage enterprises and the actual knowledge, practices and persons to be safeguarded (Kirschenblatt-Gimblett 2004, Marquart 2014, Santos 2014). Moreover, the possibly detrimental uses of the intangible heritage label and discourses can even be a means of disempowerment of local creativity (Hafstein 2007). This happens when the actions of official enterprises, such as UNESCO and its national branches, do not mirror local priorities but promote the superimposition of 'new' traditions, spaces and practitioners labeled as official intangible heritages to the detriment of actual living practices and performers (Beardslee 2014), and moreover to minority communities. The present case, for example, illustrates ways in which urban authorities are in a position of power to project a certain religious heritage and to deal as they see fit with actual traditional sacred specialists. Moreover, this manufactured religious heritage could also progressively result in the rejection of the Muslim community; however, a full discussion about details and consequences on the minority community are beyond the scope of the present chapter.

Addressing heritage, then, is a clue to rethinking sustainable places. Heritage, as is well known, is not a mere collections of monuments and artefacts, but is the multi-faceted expression of the history of communities and their places. It has immaterial aspects which allow people to identify, recognize and discover themselves, and thus has been identified as the womb of any discourse on future development (Carta 1999). Both the tangible fabric of the city and its intangible ways of life constitute its living heritage, that has been rethought as a necessary and evolving concept for urban development (Menon 2005). Heritage is, in fact, the mutable result of local action and thinking, both of which have to be considered in order to respect local sense of place. Highlighting the potentials of heritage for urban development means, in essence, being concerned with the 'connections between people and places, movement and urban form, nature and

84   *Vera Lazzaretti*

the built fabric, and the processes for ensuring successful villages, towns and cities' (CABE and DETR 2000).

However, the risks of particular uses of heritage should be carefully taken into consideration in discourses on sustainable cities. In fact, heritage, and especially religious heritage in the Indian context, is amenable to being rewritten differently according to various voices, forces and needs. This adaptability of Indian religious heritage has for long been a strength, as it has been reshaped and rethought over time, instead of being put aside. Today, however, the same quality also carries risks of excluding minorities and any discourse on sustainable planning for Indian cities needs to take this into account.

Pilgrimage as a multi-faceted heritage

Pilgrimage, together with other ritual practices, texts and oral transmissions, as well as shrines, institutions and sacred specialists, is part of both the tangible and intangible religious heritage of India. Its role within discourses on sustainable places is based on the fact that it is a highly diffused practice that influences the construction of local senses of place and contributes to settlement, maintenance and change in social roles. Sacred centres and pilgrimage destinations have, moreover, been crucial locations for social activities and economic exchange, and to define power relationships, since ancient times (Bakker 1992, Sax 2000).

Religious practices, then, have been highlighted as powerful means of shaping community belonging and settling the public sphere, and are as well easily amenable to abuse by political forces in modern and contemporary cities (AlSayyad and Massoumi 2011, Freitag 2008). In Indian cities, the rhetorical language of leading Hindutva movements is being propagated at various layers of society, so that religious performances can easily become symbols and flags of communal claims on urban spaces, where minority communities are marginalized (Gayer and Jaffrelot 2012). Pilgrimages especially have been re-invented and widely used at a pan-Indian level as means of political assertion and propaganda by 'rightist' associations, and as a popular way to mimic and pursue the (re)appropriation of contested space (Assayag 1997, Brosius 2005). Religious symbols and language, when presented as part of presumably secular actions and propositions especially in urban contexts (Prakash 2007), are a powerful means of subtly diffusing ideas about purity and authenticity of Hinduness within common people.

The potential politicization of pilgrimage should on the one hand be taken seriously into consideration by urban policy makers; on the other hand, however, the possible exploitation of religious heritage by Hindutva associations and forces cannot deny the inherent quality of pilgrimage as a powerful practice to develop sense of place and belonging, as well as comprehension of multiplicity of landscapes and their interconnections. Rituals have indeed been rethought as 'propositions for alternatives and as symbolic actions, thus as highly productive elements for social interaction and the creation of meaning' (Michaels and Mishra 2010: v–vi). Such meanings relate to actual places and make sense to the city's inhabitants by defining their ways of belonging to the urban territory.

The practice of trans-regional pilgrimage has contributed immensely to the development of a specific sense of place through the creation of an 'imagined landscape' (Eck 1988), where gods and heroes' adventures and marks are found in the various geographical, and human shaped locations. This landscape developed over time from the interaction between the Brahman *élite*, in the form of text compilers, and vivid popular and local practices. It is by no means understandable through the language of uniqueness and exclusivity; in such landscape, in fact, places are linked to each other, duplicated in various and far away locations, grouped in clusters and thus inherently plural. It was, in particular, the practice of listing deities, which is as well at the base of local processions in Banaras, that helped the compilers to project links between specific and scattered sites and to settle a systematic pan-Indian sacred landscape, where any local form could find a counterpart elsewhere (Eck 1988 and Gutschow 2006: 340–346 and 367).

A place, then, is not an isolated location but, on the contrary, has links to a variety of other sites, as well as bearing mythological, historical and symbolic meanings for its various actors. Moreover, pilgrimage, even if only temporarily, makes it possible to share a community experience; in fact, the journey not only creates connection between distant places, but it enables the encounter of different people in a time–space dimension where cultural diversity become less significant (Bhardwaj 1973, Varma 1990).

The layer of pilgrimage I address, however, is that of local urban processions, which are mostly unappreciated and excluded from the diffused and general understanding of pilgrimage as a journey to a final unique destination. These processions are very common in Banaras, and likely also in other cities, and are locally defined both as *yatras* and *parikramas*. The circuits strictly pertain to the city's places and forms of worship and convey the conception of urban territory as a net of pilgrims' trajectories with a series of divine destinations, each with a specific role, domain of action and meaning for the city's inhabitants.

Local urban pilgrimage is here approached as an inherently mutable religious form; in fact, as highlighted by recent reflections on ritual dynamics, changes within rituals and because of rituals have been shown as observable, not only in the light of the contrast between ancient and new, or tradition and modernity, but rather as implied by the existence of rites (Michaels and Mishra 2010, Husken 2007). Even deviations, mistakes and transformations of religious actions have been suggested to be meaningful and powerful means of re-settling power and social roles (Hüsken 2007).

Religious practices, however, hardly figure in city planning in Indian cities (Narayanan 2015). Even in a city like Banaras, where the industry and business of the sacred are surely crucial elements for its ongoing development, contemporary urban authorities seem to have adopted uncritically the language of eulogy and myth in city planning[4] and to address tourists and pan-Indian pilgrims, rather than taking account of the richness of the actual local practices. Although proposals have been made in the past few decades to promote, for example, the development of the most notable pilgrimage circuit in the city, through the institution of the 'Reformation Committee for a Development Plan for the Pancakroshi Yatra

86   *Vera Lazzaretti*

Circuit' in 1986, all Master Plans of the Varanasi Development Authority have up to now failed in implementation, and even in taking such proposals into serious consideration (Singh 2002: 178–180).

On the contrary, as I will show in the following section, the current management of the city's central compound which, as mentioned, is a crucial site for the performance of pilgrimage, is far from enhancing the actual religious heritage. 'Traditional' sacred specialists and local families previously in charge of the main temple, for instance, have been left aside and local processions are obstructed by rigid security procedures. A critical understanding of the bureaucracy of security (and fear) adopted by urban authorities to deal with urban contested places is necessary in order to define what kind of spatial and religious heritage is being promoted officially, who is being addressed by this sanctioned heritage and who, as a consequence, is being excluded.

Different visions of space: whose well of knowledge?

The origins of lists of deities, which are supposed to be the basis of urban processions in Banaras, and their evolution through the centuries, are far from clear. Early sources, such as glorifications and medieval digests, show a lack of uniformity in the enumeration system of deities and testify to a surprising diversification of lists and ways of enumeration (Gengnagel 2011: 43). Divine clusters are often seen as anticipating connected circuits; however, the relationship between textual lists, ways of composing them and the equivalent geographical practice are far from having been extensively examined. The *Kashikandha*, which is the most authoritative glorification text on Banaras (dated around 13th–14th century)[5] describes only 13 pilgrimages by explicitly calling them *yatras* (KKh 100), while modern pilgrims' guides list more than 50 urban processions (Vyas 1987). A structuring tendency, in fact, emerged only in secondary literature, beginning in the 19th century.

An intense period of construction and reconstruction of the city's sacred landscape took place on the wave of the revitalizing atmosphere of the 18th century. The city that we can observe today emerged as the result of the interaction between various factors and patrons: regional sovereigns sponsored the construction of shrines and palaces on the riverfront to highlight their power in such a notable and growing urban location,[6] and new social forces such as merchants and bankers emerged from the 18th century onwards and actively influenced Banaras' religious life, helping to produce the city's image as a Hindu center (Bayly 1999: 216–220, Cohn 1987: 341–342, Motichandra 1985: 313–330). These social groups, together with the Brahman *élite*, became the privileged interlocutors of the new colonial administration, whose role in filtering the local glorification tradition through the Orientalist imagination (Said 1978) and the colonial historical paradigm has been extensively documented. Urban projects and technologies of the colonial administration helped in (re)discovering presumably pre-existing and ancient sacred sites (described in Sherring 1868: 105–106), and consequently in enhancing the 'Hinduness' of Banaras in its physical sacred geography.

After major construction activities stopped around 1850 (Gutschow 2006: 36), printed pilgrims' maps realized by local sacred specialists became available in the city and elsewhere and helped in collecting and promoting the results of the newly projected urban geography. In the same period, modern pilgrims' guides reshaped previous textual materials by fixing more structured lists of deities, whose corresponding addresses in the urban space were now given.

In the 20th century, singular personalities and notable compilers of pilgrims' guides, such as Kubernath Sukul and Kedarnath Vyas, acted as pilgrimage promoters and specialists. An increasing number of religious associations was as well involved in the promotion of the performance of local pilgrimages and participated in the diffusion and multiplication of lists of divine clusters (Singh 2002: 176–177).

The emergence of the current activities of the KPDYS is part of this sketched panorama of last century Banaras. According to Uma Shankar Gupta ji, who is the main organizer of the group, the Association has been active since 1979 and was registered in 1999.[7]

Its religious leader is considered to be Dandi Svami Shivananda Sarasvati, disciple of the famous Svami Karpatri ji (1907–1982),[8] and today, the Association organizes about 20 processions to clusters of deities in the city's territory every year. Its activities are claimed as maintaining continuity with the local tradition settled by past pilgrimage promoters and specialists. However, the current performance of processions is both a resettlement of previous traditions and a multiply contested and opposed practice, which has the Vyas Pith and Jnanavapi as focus.

The centrality of the Jnanavapi area and, especially, of the Vyas Pith for pilgrimage was apparently settled in the last two centuries. This is attested by the statements of Kedarnath Vyas ji, current incumbent of the Vyas Pith and author of one of the more notable contemporary pilgrimage guide (Vyas 1987), and by the recognition granted to the Vyas family by the KPDYS and other personalities related to the practice of pilgrimage. A member of the family was, as Kedarnath Vyas ji *is* today, in charge of guiding pilgrims through the introductory rituals and, at the end of the circuit, sanctioning the accomplishment of their vow. The scheme of performance of initial and final rituals at Jnanavapi is described for the Pancakroshiyatra in the 17th century's *Kashirahasya* (KR 10.10–19)[9] and seems to have been later employed for the performance of other minor and less diffused pilgrimages, such as those performed today by the KPDYS.

As a marker of the place, a majestic seat for the sacred specialist in charge of the pilgrimage rituals was placed in the Well pavilion, most likely in the 19th century. The Pith is held as a hereditary right by the Vyas family, which still lives just in front of the Well of Knowledge and has charge of the offerings and inflow of devotees in this area. As witnessed by Vyas ji, the tradition of starting and concluding processions at the Vyas Pith was well established and validated by local political authorities, especially the Kashi Naresh of Ramnagar.[10] Members of the local royal family still come once a year to perform the Pancakroshiyatra with the service of the Vyas family.[11]

The Vyas Pith used to be the place where multitudes of pilgrims were supposed to perform the *sankalpa* (Michaels 2005: 45–63), through which they invoke the gods and pronounce their vows at the commencement of their paths. Today, however, the area is being projected and controlled by the security authorities as a transit zone, where pilgrims and devotees are required to follow a fixed path.

88   Vera Lazzaretti

As part of the security plan, which was implemented after the demolition of the Babri *masjid*, the Gyan Vapi *masjid* was caged to prevent it being the next flashpoint. Many neighbouring lanes, squares and narrow passages have been cordoned off and ultimately taken away from the city's inhabitants, apparently to protect them. As well, a layered and complex security hierarchy regularly controls the access of devotees to the four gates of the secluded compound and the rest of the surrounding space. The entire system is divided into three sectors controlled by different level of security forces (national, regional and local)[12].

A large number of Hindu devotees queues every day to enter the compound for *darshan*, the sacred visual contact with the deity. Those entering from the mosque side pass by the Well of Knowledge on the way to Vishvanath; others, however, who enter from the remaining gates, find it difficult to reach the Well at all, because of the security restrictions, especially during crowded festival days. As well, religious activities and visits to the mosque are frequently discouraged by the security authorities. Access for Muslims tends to be limited to prayer times (*namaz parhna*), and sometimes is completely denied, especially to worshippers from outside the local area, for apparently arbitrary security reasons.[13] Spontaneous worship at the Well and the surrounding minor shrines is discouraged by the security authorities, who invite devotees to keep walking in an ordered line on the way to Vishvanath. The temple is being projected as the unique acceptable destination within the entire compound.

Moreover, the Kashi Vishvanath Trust, which in 1983 took over from the local family which previously managed the temple, appears to be planning to gain control of the whole area. Their project is that of a large and unique compound, where for example they can build a 'traditional' school (*pathshala*) for the study of Sanskrit and a rest house for pilgrims (*dharmashala*),[14] and from which the Gyan Vapi mosque and the minority community could easily be isolated, or even entirely rejected. Furthermore, sacred specialists such as the local Brahmin family which was relieved of charge of the temple, and nowadays the Vyas family as well, are being distanced from their domain, and their knowledge left aside or at least not enhanced. For instance, the Vyas family is now being cordially invited by the Trust to sell its properties next to the Well of Knowledge in order to facilitate the above-mentioned project.

The pursuit of an allegedly *secular, neutral* and *secure* management policy seems to be instead allowing, if not promoting openly, the filtering and confining of part of the space's elements and actors. Borders, not to be crossed, have been defined and pertain to both architectural and human bodies. What was formerly a lively religious space is now kept as an orderly no man's land.

Tradition and bureaucracy: negotiating religious practices

That the urban civic arena in Banaras was in the past a shared one is testified by records of multi-religious participation in common religious feasts (Freitag 1989: 206) and by the memories of actors involved in the life of the area around Vishvanath.[15] As described above, however, a policy of seclusion of space, segregation of communities and alienation of both social actors and shrines seems to be promoted currently by authorities. It is, indeed, easy to imagine that such a developing process would lead to a more serious negation of the sites' inherent multiplicity, to the detriment of the Muslim community. Already, however, it is possible to describe the ongoing effects on the so-considered major religious tradition, which can already be seen in changes to the practice of local pilgrimage and to the relationship between previous pilgrimage authorities and the KPDYS.

An initial period of collaboration between the Association and sacred specialists is mentioned both by the Association's organizers and by Vyas ji. In recent years, however, the situation has changed, and the Association's activities are criticized by Vyas ji, who considers the circuits promoted by the KPDYS and other performers to be incorrect.[16] The processions, in fact, rarely perform the initial ritual, the *sankalpa*, at the Vyas Pith; moreover, they have been adapted to the territory and to participants, following a logic of convenience, instead of performing the sequences as given in previous guides. This means that the starting point is no more the Vyas Pith; instead, as I have observed myself, a priest usually pronounces the vow for pilgrims at the first stop of the procession, wherever that might be. The Vyas family, which still feels responsible for this ritual and of course derived advantages from it as well as obligations, is consequently excluded from officiating the *sankalpa*, and the space around the Vyas Pith is often now excluded from the living practice of pilgrimage.

Apart from a sort of simple pragmatism, which leads the processions to begin from the first stops of the sequences (and not from the Vyas Pith), and the will to keep alive the pilgrimage practice anyway,[17] surely the deviations of path are more deeply provoked by the spatial situation and management of the contested area by urban authorities and the consequent partial inaccessibility of the Pith itself. We have seen above that approaching the Vyas Pith is not easy for groups of pilgrims; in fact, even if formal permission is not really required to enter the area in groups, people have to cross a security check and then depend on the current policy of the security authorities, which changes constantly, according to festival dates, orders from higher authorities or even personal whims of particular officers. To be sure to enter the compound, therefore, the Association must formally ask for written permission from the District Magistrate and the Local Intelligence Unit (LIU) of the police. Bureaucratic procedures are far from irrelevant even to the *normal* practice of local pilgrimage; in fact, every procession has to be notified to the police stations (*thanas*) of the different areas involved in the circuits.

The required procedures to enter the main compound and reach the Vyas Pith are usually avoided by the Association, even though permissions are generally granted when they are followed correctly. In a few cases, however, the Association does go through the full process; for example, both Antargriha and Pancakroshi *yatras*, two highly textual, and thus symbolic processions for the city, are still performed according to the 'old rules' (*purani nyam se*) according to Gupta ji.[18] For these *yatras* initial and concluding rituals are still conducted at the Vyas Pith.

The other case in which formal permission is always requested is for having the *darshan* of Shringar Gauri on the occasion of a procession to a series of goddesses

90   Vera Lazzaretti

during Navaratri, twice a year. This is again a highly symbolic action as the back wall of the mosque, where the abode of the Goddess is identified, is at the core of various claims and security policy. This place, in fact, is considered to be the remaining part of a previously destroyed temple[19], which Hindutva groups wish to regain, and is entirely cordoned off from the living mosque. Access to and worship of the Goddess can indeed represent a dangerous and cyclically enacted re-appropriation of contested ground; this place is constantly the object of claims by Shiv Sena activists, who demand entry every year at the time of Shivaratri, a major festival in the city. Pilgrimage as the action of entering into a secluded space could easily become a symbol of conquest and be invested with communal and political meanings. In particular, the empty space produced by the current management is much more amenable to claims, such as those of Shiv Sena activists.

Regulated access to the contested space is pursued by the Association through bureaucracy with the intent, instead, of peacefully having *darshan* as part of a complete procession in the city's territory. This could be seen as a potential normalizing action downplaying the symbolic meaning of the underlying dispute and as an alternative to the current policy of restricted access. Through this form of worship and, for example, the insertion of Shringar Gauri in a wider cluster of deities, this inaccessible place could, instead, be transformed into a stop among many others, where shared religious ground could again become a living experience for pilgrims and the inhabitants of the city.

In terms of access to space, local participation and minimizing opportunities for outside actors to make claims on this space, the Association's activities clearly suggest a more sustainable pathway than the current arrangements. Such religious practice carries as well the capacity for development of the city and its shrines. Actions of tracing, performing and perpetrating spatial paths already shape the urban geography in a variety of ways; for example, by reviving and empowering a rich variety of minor shrines, which authenticate themselves by being part of local processions (Lazzaretti 2013).

Moreover, although the Association refers to the orthodox tradition of Karpatri ji, who for example acted against the admission of untouchables to the Vishvanath temple, today it gladly accepts pilgrims from all castes as well as foreigners like me to participate in their processions, thus being inclusive and naturally adaptable to social development. The experience of local processions is one that promotes a locally specific sense of community. Instead of being performed on specific days of the calendar, as previously prescribed, processions are now usually organized by the KPDYS on Sundays, so that ordinary workers as well can participate. Apart from being another deviation from past traditions, which is in fact criticized by the old authorities, the choice of Sundays for processions seems to promote the religious performances as also pleasure and leisure activities. The stress and strain of pilgrimage is indeed softened by a deep sense of enjoyment and, indeed, sharing, not just of an extraordinary experience, but also of ways of feeling togetherness while having the *darshan* of local divine places.

Processions are of course experienced as devotional and religious activities; however, they are also feasting times when various actors get together. In particular, lone women who usually do not wander around the city, are able to explore new devotional realities and share this experience with others. Walking for *darshan* to various deities, resting in the shrines' pavilions, singing devotional local songs and sharing all such activities, means performing a shared, specific and historically multi-constructed path in the urban territory. Such experience of attachment and belonging to the city and its many notable and minor shrines keeps alive knowledge of specific qualities and meanings of local places and deities.

In the footsteps of pilgrims, or alternative traces for sustainability

The dispute around the correctness of processions relies on different visions of place and of pilgrimage traditions and, in essence, pertains to contrasting ways of addressing and projecting religious heritage in the developing city.

On the one hand, actual 'traditional' sacred specialists, such as Vyas ji, feel their role as responsible for and representative of a place, whose significance is sanctioned by a never-ending and evolving transmission, both text-based and place-based, from the past. In this view, the power of place is inalienable as is the role of the sacred specialists in relation to it. The systematized processions in the last three centuries and the projection of the Pith as their starting place represented and were felt to be a necessary and natural implementation of past heritage in a new and different historical, political and religious context, just as the past glorification texts had been (Acri and Pinkney 2014, Smith 2007: 2).

On the other hand, urban authorities address the same space as just a section of the city to be managed according to wider considerations, including its 'protection'. As noted above, their official management policy heavily affects the space and communities' access to it. As far as religious heritage and its official management are concerned, it is evident here that 'the government's measures for protection may in effect serve as means of dispossession' (Hafstein 2007: 79), especially for local actors, such as sacred specialists. These actual performers, who in terms of ritual and spatial knowledge are heritage bearers for the city, are then detached from their natural space and removed from their roles.

Moreover, according to this view, religious heritage such as pilgrimage can be shifted and re-created by superimposed secular authorities who have the power to do so, unlike the pilgrimage performers themselves, the sacred specialists and unlike the minority group linked to this space, who are even more powerless. The current policy seems to be looking for appealing new forms of manufactured religious heritage, such as the construction of so-called traditional *pathshalas* and *dharmashalas* in the main compound. These projects seems to be based on the myth of the eternal Hindu pilgrimage city, whose danger and pervasiveness has received various critiques (Dalmia 1997: 59–62, Desai 2007: xxix, Dodson 2012: 1), and are more likely to attract tourists and pilgrims from far away destinations than addressing local places, inhabitants and their needs. Such projects rely on a specific (often 'Western', and mainly economic) conception of development which is far from locally sensible.

92   Vera Lazzaretti

Planning authorities seem to be rarely concerned with the potentials of local religious practice in terms of spatial sharing, local communities' visions of place enhancement and re-opening of secluded space to lively practices. Indeed, my contribution highlights the lack of a multivocal and inclusive concept of sustainability in the official management policy for the space addressed. If an abandoned and rejected space is produced, where local performance of pilgrimages is discouraged or diverted to the periphery and past authorities are left behind, such a no man's land would be far from a safe, shared and locally sensitive urban space and risks instead becoming a fecund field for external actors to make demands and assertions about rights of occupation. That would be the very opposite of a sustainable place for the city.

Within this picture, the KPDYS activities seem to have a constructive mediating role between the official projection of heritage and the actual bearers of this heritage, such as 'traditional' sacred specialists. The tradition of local processions emerges as one capable of adapting and engaging creatively with the exigencies that reshape the city's spaces. The KPDYS is constantly negotiating the challenge of borders and rules settled by urban authorities, in order to find innovative and adaptable ways of continuing the practice of pilgrimage. These actions could be seen as basic to the discourse on sustainability as something fluid, constantly negotiated and inclusive of opposed visions.

Actual local practices and performers, rather than superimposed official policy, emerge as powerful means of building and re-shaping sense of place, of belonging and of community. Planning for sustainability, therefore, should consider and be informed by the multiple actual religious heritages of specific places.

Notes

1 The word *pith*, from *pitha* in Sanskrit, has different meanings, such as seat, chair, stool or bench. It also indicates the religious student's seat or a royal throne, but also a wider space, such as a province or district, and even a sitting posture (www.sanskrit-lexicon. uni-koeln.de/monier/). In the language of sacred geography, *pith* has come to be known as mainly related to the geography and pilgrimage of the Goddess; in fact, the Shakti Pithas, usually canonized as 51 places all over the Subcontinent, are the notable abodes of the Goddess. In the current context, the term indicates a sacred place, where a God or Goddess dwells as inalienable presence. Consequently, the Vyas Pith seems to indicate the place where Vyas, both in his mythical and physical presence, sits as in his natural abode. It is a white stone seat, similar to a sort of throne actually, which is part of the pavilion pavement next to the Well of Knowledge and where the authority in charge is supposed to sit during the performance of rituals for pilgrims.
2 Vyasa in Sanskrit means 'compiler' and 'organizer'; as a proper name, it often appears as Veda Vyasa and indicates the mythical author of the Mahabharata and the Puranic corpus, where the bard also appears as a character. Vyas is also used as a title to indicate those Brahmans who recite the Puranas in public, and have knowledge about such texts and rituals related to sacred places. The Vyas family living at the Well of Knowledge adopted the name as title and as indication of their mythic lineage from Veda Vyasa.
3 Names and roles of the trustees can be found at the Trust website: http://shrikashiv ishwanath.org/.

4 See for example the city's profile in the Varanasi Development Authority (VDA) website: www.vdavns.org.
5 About local glorification traditions and religious history of the city previous to the KKh see Bakker 1996 and Bakker and Isaacson 2004.
6 For an overview of the main construction activities and sponsorships see Gutschow 2006: 32–38 and Desai 2012: 27–29.
7 Sarasvati 2001: 249.
8 For the life and works of Karpatri ji, see Pellegrini 2009.
9 For a full synopsis of Chapter 10 of the KR, see Gengnagel 2005: 83–89.
10 For a history of the Kashi Naresh dynasty, see Dalmia 1997: 64–94.
11 Personal communication with Kedarnath Vyas, March 2013.
12 Interview with P. N. Dubey, Additional Chief Officer of the Kashi Vishvanath Trust, March 2013.
13 Personal communication with Abdul Batin Nomani, mufti-e-shahar of Banaras and imam of the Gyan Vapi masjid, March 2013.
14 Personal communication with P. N. Dubey, Additional Chief Officer of the Kashi Vishvanath Trust, March 2013.
15 Interviews with members of the Tripathi family, previously in charge of the Kashi Vishvanath Temple, and with Abdul Batin Nomani, mufti-e-shahar of Banaras and imam of the Gyan Vapi masjid, March 2013.
16 Personal communications with Vyas ji, March and April 2012.
17 Interview with Uma Shankar Gupta, July 2011.
18 Interviews with him, March 2013 and 2014.
19 Vijayram Sen, author of the *Tirthamangala*, a text of 1757 that reports about his own trip to the city, observes the pilgrims worshipping the base of the mosque's wall; quoted by Desai 2007: 5.

References

Acri, A. and Pinkney, A. M. (2014) 'Reorienting the Past: Performances of Hindu Textual Heritage in Contemporary India'. *International Journal of Hindu Studies*, Vol. 17, No. 3, pp. 223–230.

AlSayyad, N. and Massoumi, M. (eds.) (2011) *The Fundamentalist City? Religiosity and the remaking of urban space*. Oxford: Routledge.

Appadurai, A. (1988) 'Place and Voice in Anthropological Theory'. *Cultural Anthropology*, Vol. 3, pp. 16–20.

Appadurai, A. (2001) *Modernità in polvere*. Roma: Meltemi.

Asad, T. (1983) 'Anthropological Conceptions of Religion: Reflections on Geertz'. *Man* (new series), Vol. 18, No. 2, pp. 237–259.

Assayag, J. (1997) 'Action rituelle ou réaction politique? L'invention des processions du nationalisme hindou dans les années 1980 en Indie'. *Annales. Histoire, Science Sociales*, 52e Année, No. 4, pp. 853–879.

Bakker, H. (ed.) (1992) *The Sacred Centre as the Focus of Political Interest*. Gröningen: Egbert Forsten.

Bakker, H. (1996) 'Construction and Reconstruction of Sacred Space in Varanasi'. *Numen* XLIII.1, pp. 32–55.

Bakker, H. and Isaacson, Z. (2004) 'A Sketch of the Religious History of Varanasi up to the Islamic Conquest and the New Beginning'. In: Bakker, H. and Isaacson, Z. (eds.), *The Skandapurāṇa*, volume IIA (Adhyāyas 26–31.14), *The Varanasi Cycle* (pp.19–82). Gröningen: Egbert Forsten.

94 *Vera Lazzaretti*

Bayly, S. (1999) 'Caste, Society and Politics in India, from Eighteenth Century to the Modern Age'. In: *The New Cambridge History of India*, IV: 3, Cambridge: Cambridge University Press

Beardslee, T. (2014) 'Whom does heritage empower, and whom does it silence? : Intangible Cultural Heritage and the Jemaa el Fnaa'. Paper presented in the panel 'Critical Ethnographies of Cultural Heritage in Mediterranean Cities' at the *5th Ethnography and Qualitative Research Conference*, University of Bergamo, 5–7 June 2014.

Beatley, T. and Manning, K. (1997) *The Ecology of Place: Planning for Environment, Economy and Community*. Washington: Island Press.

Bhardwaj, S. M. (1973) *Hindu Places of Pilgrimage in India. A Study in Cultural Geography*. Berkeley: University of California Press.

Brosius, C. (2005) *Empowering Visions. The Politics of Representation of Hindu Nationalism*. London: Anthem Press.

CABE and DETR. (2000) *By Design: Urban Design in the Planning System – Towards Better Practice*. London: Thomas Telford.

Carta, M. (1999) *L'armatura culturale del territorio. Il patrimonio culturale come matrice di identità e strumento per lo sviluppo*. Milano: FrancoAngeli.

Casey, E. S. (1996) 'How to Get from Space to Place in a Fairly Short Stretch of Time: Phenomenological Prolegomena'. In: Feld, S. and Basso, K. H. (eds.), *Senses of Place* (pp. 13–52). Santa Fe, New Mexico: School of American Research Press.

Cohn, B. S. (1987) *An Anthropologist among the Historians and Other Essays*. New Delhi: Oxford University Press.

Dalmia, V. (1997) *The Nationalization of Hindu Traditions. Bharatendu Harischandra and Nineteenth-Century Banaras*. Oxford: Oxford University Press.

Desai, M. (2007) *Resurrecting Banaras: Urban Spaces, Architecture and Religious Boundaries*. PhD thesis in Architecture, submitted to the Graduate Division of the University of California, Berkeley.

Dodson, M. S. (ed.) (2012) *Banaras. Urban Forms and Cultural Histories*. New Delhi: Routledge.

Eck, D. L. (1988) 'The Imagined Landscape: Patterns in the Construction of Hindu Sacred Geography'. *Contributions to Indian Sociology*. Vol. 32, No. 2, pp. 165–188.

Feld, S. and Basso, K. H. (eds.) (1996) *Senses of Place*. Santa Fe, New Mexico: School of American Research Press.

Freitag, S. B. (ed.) (1989) *Culture and Power in Banaras. Community, Performance, and Environment, 1800–1980*. Los Angeles, Oxford: University of California Press.

Freitag, S. B. (2008) 'Visualizing Cities by Modern Citizens: Banaras Compared to Jaipur and Lucknow'. In: Gaenszle, M. and Gengnagel, J. (eds.) *Visualizing Space in Banaras: Images, Maps and the Practice of Representation* (pp. 233–254). New Delhi: Oxford University Press.

Gayer, L. and Jaffrelot, C. (eds.) (2012) *Muslims in Indian Cities: Trajectories of Marginalisation*. New Delhi: HarperCollins Publishers India.

Gengnagel, J. (2005) '*Kāśīkhaṇḍokta*. On Texts and Processions in Varanasi'. In: Gengnagel J., Hüsken U. and Raman S., (eds.) *Words and Deeds. Hindu and Buddhist Rituals in South Asia* (pp. 65–89), Wiesbaden: Harrassowitz Verlag.

Gengnagel, J. (2011) *Visualized Texts. Sacred Spaces, Spatial Texts and the Religious Cartography of Banaras*, Wiesbaden: Harrassowitz Verlag.

Gupta, A. and Ferguson J. (1992), 'Beyond "Culture": Space, Identity and the Politics of Difference'. *Cultural Anthropology*, Vol. 7, No. 1, pp. 6–23.

Gutschow, N. (2006) *Benares. The Sacred Landscape of Varanasi*. Stuttgart/London: Edition Axel Menges.

Hafstein, V. Tr. (2007) 'Claiming Culture: Intangible Heritage Inc, Folklore©, Traditional Knowledge™'. In: Hemme, D., Tauschek, M. and Bendix, R. (eds.) *Prädikat "Heritage". Wertschöpfungen aus kulturellen Ressourcen*. Studien zur Kulturanthropologie/Europaischen Ethnologie. Göttingen: University of Göttingen.

Hirsch, E. and O'Hanlon, M. (eds.) (1995) *The Anthropology of Landscape. Perspectives on Place and Space*, Oxford: Clarendon Press.

Hüsken, U. (ed.) (2007) *When Rituals Go Wrong: Mistakes, Failure and the Dynamics of Ritual*. Leiden-Boston: Brill.

Kashikhanda (Skanda Purāṇa), with English translation, Tagare, G.V. (ed.) (1996). Delhi: Motilal Banarsidas.

Kashirahasya, Dubey, J.N. (ed.) (1984). Varanasi: Adarsha Prakashan Mandir.

Kirschenblatt-Gimblett, B. (2004) 'Intangible Heritage as Metacultural Production'. *Museum International*, Vol. 56, Oxford: Blackwell Publishing.

Lazzaretti, V. (2013) 'Banaras Jyotirlingas: Constitutions and Transformations of a Transposed Divine Group and its Pilgrimage'. *Kervan, International Journal of Afro-Asiatic Studies*, no. 17, pp. 1–20.

Mahadevia, D. (2001) 'Sustainable urban development in India: An inclusive perspective'. *Development in Practice*, Vol. 11 No. 2/3, pp. 242–259.

Marquart, V. (2014) 'Fragments of History: The Multi-Layers of Heritage in Istanbul'. Paper presented in the panel 'Critical Ethnographies of Cultural Heritage in Mediterranean Cities' at the *5th Ethnography and Qualitative Research Conference*, University of Bergamo, 5–7 June 2014.

Menon, A.G.K. (2005) 'Heritage conservation and urban development: Beyond the monument'. In: Tandon, R. (ed.) *Heritage Conservation and Urban Development* (pp. 1–7). New Delhi: INTACH.

Michaels, A. (2005) 'Samkalpa: The Beginning of a Ritual'. In: Gengnagel, J., Hüsken, U. and Raman, S. (eds.) *Words and Deeds. Hindu and Buddhist Rituals in South Asia* (pp. 45–63). Wiesbaden: Harrassowitz Verlag.

Michaels, A. and Mishra, A. (eds.) (2010) *Grammar and Morphology of Ritual*. Wiesbaden: Harrassowitz Verlag.

Motichandra (1985) *Kashi ka itihas*. Varanasi: Vishvavidyalaya prakashan.

Narayanan, Y. (2015) *Religion, Heritage and the Sustainable City. Hinduism and Urbanization in Jaipur*. London and New York: Routledge.

Patra, R. (2009) 'Vaastu Shastra: Towards sustainable development'. *Sustainable Development*, Vol. 17, 244–256.

Pellegrini, G. (ed.) (2009) *L'uomo e il sacro in India: Svāmī Karapātrī. Indoasiatica 5*, Venice: Venetian Academy of Indian Studies.

Prakash, G. (2007) 'Secular Nationalism, Hindutva, and the Minority'. In: Needham, A.D. and Rajan, R.S. (eds.) *The Crisis of Secularism in India* (pp. 177–189). Ranikhet: Permanent Black.

Rodman, M.C. (1992) 'Empowering Place: Multilocality and Multivocality'. *American Anthropologist*, New Series, Vol. 94, No. 3, 640–656.

Said, E.W. (1978) *Orientalism*, New York: Vintage Books Edition.

Santos, P.M. (2014) 'Crossed gazes over an old city: photography and the (de)construction of an heritage place'. Paper presented in the panel 'Critical Ethnographies of Cultural Heritage in Mediterranean Cities' at the *5th Ethnography and Qualitative Research Conference*, University of Bergamo, 5–7 June 2014.

Sarasvati, S. (2001) *Kashi Gaurav*, Varanasi: Dharma Sangh.

Sax, W. (2000) 'Conquering the Quarters: Religion and Politics in Hinduism'. *International Journal of Hindu Studies*, Vol.4, No. 1, pp. 39–60.

Sepe, M. (2013) *Planning and Place in the City: Mapping Place Identity*. New York: Routledge.

Sherring, M. A. (1868) *The Sacred City of the Hindoos: an Account of Benares in Ancient and Modern Times*. London: Trübner & Co.

Singh, R. P. B. (2002) *Towards the Pilgrimage Archetype. The Pancakrośi Yātrā of Banāras*. Varanasi: Indica Books.

Smith, T. L. (2007) 'Re-newing the ancient: the Kashikhanda and Shaiva Varanasi'. Special issue of *Acta Orientalia Vilnensia* 8, no.1 pp. 83–108.

Tuan, Y.-F. (1977) *Space and Place: The Perspective of Experience*. Minneapolis and London: University of Minnesota Press.

Varma, T. P. (1990) 'Tirthayatra: Fountainhead of Cultural Unity'. In: Dubey, D. B. (ed.) *Pilgrimage Studies. Text and Context*. Allahabad: Lallanji Gopal Editions.

Vyas, K. (1987) *Pancakroshatmaka jyotirlinga kashimahatmya evam kashi ka pracin itihas*. Varanasi: Khandelaval Press and Publications.

6 Recognising the spatial and territorial nature of religious communities in Colombo, Sri Lanka

Rohan Bastin

Introduction

The Sri Lankan commercial capital Colombo is a multi-religious city within a predominantly Sinhala Buddhist state. Through examples of certain religious edifices (hereafter structures) and practices, this chapter highlights the critical importance of a politics of recognition when it comes to identifying religious structures and their impact on the urban space in a city and country where much of the post-independence era has been marred by ethnic and religious conflict. A politics of recognition, as I call it, entails the capacity to acknowledge religious institutions and their communities and to explore the actual extent to which these entities can co-exist. Critical to such a process is a willingness to have one's common sense understanding of what is meant by religion challenged and possibly expanded. This is an issue for planners and developers just as much as for the general population, because urban planning and development are themselves so entangled – ideologically, socially and politically – that the act of recognition of religious structures must proceed through careful social and historical analysis and without the baggage of a priori notions regarding what a religious structure or practice comprises and how it might relate to other social institutions more routinely imagined as secular. At the heart of this is the understanding of how a religious structure elicits a spatial configuration and thereby interacts with other structures religious and otherwise. It is one thing, I suggest, for a planning or heritage consultant to map the city and note where the structures are; but quite another thing to understand how these structures interact and continue to create new meanings as well as new tensions and conflicts. Recognizing an Islamic bank, for example, is much easier than recognizing the religion in other banking systems whose seemingly secular existence is taken-for-granted as the normal order of things where the Islamic bank is deemed to be exceptional.

Acknowledging unofficial as well as official religious sites is a positive step for the politics of recognition tied also to a growing appreciation that much of what is taken for granted as 'religious' sits within a hegemonic discourse dominated by both Christian and modernist secularization concepts (Asad 2003). In a series of decadal surveys of the geographies of religion, Lily Kong (1990, 2001, 2010) charts the rise of the field of study, noting both the efflorescence after 2001 as well

98   *Rohan Bastin*

as a growing awareness of different kinds of religious site other than the usual official structures of church, mosque, temple, etc., and the growing appreciation for
multi-religious interaction (see also Hopkins, Kong and Olson 2013). Put simply,
a domain of human practice imagined by the modernisers to be waning and thus
easily ignored returns seemingly stronger and more diverse than ever, prompting
discussions of 'post-secularism' and the very welcome acknowledgement of prior
biases in approach (Cloke and Beaumont 2013). These are welcome developments, albeit developments the novelty of which is less evident to scholars working a long time in the field of religious interaction (Bastin 2002, 2005, 2012).

The approach pursued here thus resonates with recent work on 'grounded theologies, performative practices of place-making informed by understandings of
the transcendent' (Tse 2014: 202). Importantly, as Tse notes, such understandings
can be negative as much as positive. Moreover, they can be negative within a specific religious discourse such as a Sri Lankan Buddhist objection to the proximity
of a mosque, or negative within a meta-discourse such as developmental secularism concerning religious sites in general. Critically, though, these discourses can
both overlap and mutually enhance as part of a broader hegemony tied to political theologies and nationalism wherein certain discourses become dominant and
imagined as the bearers of heritage. In post-independence Sri Lanka, especially
through the years of civil war, Buddhism has attained such a position (De Silva-
Wijeyeratne 2014). In its commercial and erstwhile political capital, however,
the physical presence of Buddhism has been more muted for reasons explored
in the following description of multi-religion in Colombo. Through a far from
exhaustive account of the city's religious sites and an exploration of some religious festivals that emanate from and link these sites the paper explores the kinds
of issue the planner needs to be mindful of. An appreciation of history is critical.

Colombo: a colonial city

Colombo's old inner city is remarkable for a strong minority presence in the
population and built form, and a surprisingly weak Buddhist presence, given that
Buddhism is professed by roughly 70% of the population (see Table 6.1). As the
long-time commercial and political capital of the island,[1] the strength of Colombo's minorities reflects a number of historical factors including a long history of
European colonialism as well as a long history of Sinhala Buddhist kingdoms
whose political theology valued the agrarian social formation. Space prevents full
justification of this point other than to note the historical role played by Buddhist
temples and monasteries in landownership and agriculture (Gunawardana 1979)
informing a rural orientation that persists notwithstanding well over 150 years of
plantation capitalism. It is reflected, for example, in the way in which Sinhala
Buddhist deities are highly territorial with the entire island and within it the
various old kingdoms being divided amongst a plethora of guardian deities (Winslow 1984). Trade and traders have been ideologically and socially eccentric to
this system, with traders remaining external to the 'People of the Lion' or Sinhalese ethnic group and to the land-oriented caste order of the Sinhala Buddhist

Table 6.1 Population census data for district and division according to ethnicity

Region	Total number	Sinhalese	Sri Lankan Tamil	Indian Tamil	Sri Lankan Moor	Buddhist	Hindu	Muslim	Roman Catholic	Other Christian
Sri Lanka	20,263,723	75%	11%	4%	9%	70%	13%	10%	6%	1%
Colombo District	2,309,809	77%	10%	1%	11%	71%	8%	12%	7%	3%
– Colombo Division	318,048	25%	31%	3%	40%	19%	22%	42%	13%	3%
Gampaha District	2,294,641	91%	3%	0.5%	4%	72%	2%	5%	19%	2%
Kalutara District	1,217,260	87%	2%	2%	9%	84%	3%	9%	3%	1%
Combined districts	5,821,710 (29% of country)	84%	6%	1%	8%	73%	5%	9%	8%	3%

Derived from the 2012 Census of Population and Housing.[3]

100   Rohan Bastin

kingdoms. Through the colonial era, however, the situation began to change and this culminates with the grant of independence to the modern Sri Lankan state in 1948 (or Ceylon as it was then). Through democratisation starting in 1931, the 70% majority had become a highly significant voting bloc. Moreover, the Sinhalese ethnic group had transformed with the rise of entrepreneurial and urban working classes. Nonetheless, the colonial city of Colombo retained its minorities as a Sinhala Buddhist political and religious presence began to grow and be articulated through state institutions which have a dominant presence in the primate city.

The history of Colombo is very important, therefore, to understanding its religious configuration, because Colombo is very much a colonial creation. From 1505, it was a Portuguese fort and factory for processing spices, before being conquered by the Dutch East India Company in 1656 and ruled by them until 1796 when England annexed the Dutch territories. During this time, however, independent Sinhala Buddhist kingdoms remained, the most enduring of which was the Kandyan kingdom in the interior hill country which only fell to the British in 1815, but never lost the key Buddhist relics that had come to symbolise state power (Seneviratne 1978). This kingdom provided the model for a Sinhala Buddhist state and society that became an enduring concept through the latter stages of British colonialism wherein the British steadily granted autonomy to what Newton Gunasinghe (1990) calls subaltern elite – a bourgeois class of traditional elite landowners whose power and position derived from loyalty to the British – and to parvenu members of erstwhile subordinate castes, many not actually Sinhalese (but who became Sinhalese), who owed their position to participation in the colonial economy (Jayawardena 2000; Peebles 1995; Roberts 1982). Democracy, however, required a different kind of engagement with the general population, and from the first General Election of 1931 to the next, majoritarian politics and minority discontent began to dominate (Wickramasinghe 1995, 2006).

From minor grumbling over the use of the Kandyan Royal Standard (the Lion Flag) as the national flag at independence in 1948 to greater outcry over the official language policy in 1956, ethnic relations between the majority Sinhalese and minority Tamils deteriorated into violence that by the Colombo riots of 1983 had turned into a civil war. That war only ended in mid-2009 when the main Tamil separatist group, the Liberation Tigers of Tamil Eelam, was obliterated in a brutal military offensive in the north-east of the country. Over the quarter century that the war raged in the north and east, the city of Colombo was transformed as it became the site of terrorist attacks and the haven for Tamils fleeing the fighting, many continuing their flight out of the country altogether (Thiranagama 2011: 229), and the haven for Muslims forcibly expelled by the Tigers from Tiger-controlled areas in 1990. But these displacements are not what accounts for Colombo's minorities; rather the minorities could come to Colombo because of its history of a transient minority presence.

One of several river mouth, or ferry ports along Sri Lanka's west coast, Colombo rose to prominence during the Kōṭṭe period from the late 14th century when the Indian Ocean spice trade was thriving and the island's native plant cinnamon was

The spatial and territorial nature 101

a prize commodity. Muslims, Arab and Indian, dominated the marketplace and the sea, along with family-based trading corporations from south-west India such as the Alagakōnnara, which had married into the ruling family, becoming active patrons of Hindu-Buddhist temples along the way. The king of Kōṭṭe (which is close to Colombo) cautiously welcomed the Portuguese in 1505 and allowed them to establish a trading post at the mouth of the Kelaniya River, which later became a fort from which Portugal captured Kōṭṭe and much of the littoral by the 1590s (including the separate Tamil kingdom of Jaffna in the north). An independent Sinhala Buddhist kingdom remained in the interior, with kings ruling from their capital in Kandy having secured the highly prized Buddhist Tooth and Begging Bowl relics which had formerly been housed at Kōṭṭe's main temple a few kilometres upstream from the river mouth, the Kelaniya Temple (Walters 1996).

Kōṭṭe's King Dharmapāla (1551–1597) converted to Catholicism and ceded Kōṭṭe to Portugal in the 1580s. In 1591, he destroyed the Kelaniya Temple, and bequeathed its land to the Franciscans who built a church on the site (Perniola 1991: 117; Walters 1996: 65). While he also attacked other religious structures, Dharmapāla's religious fanaticism was tempered by pragmatic Portuguese concerns. For example, according to De Queyroz (1992: 736) writing in the 1670s, Muslims were tolerated in Portuguese territories on account of their role in trade and availability to serve on ships, which the Sinhalese were loath to do. By 1626, however, armed with a royal decree from Lisbon and growing pressure from different Catholic orders, the Captain General Constantino de Sa de Noronha evicted every Muslim from Portuguese territory. As De Queyroz (1992: 745) writes, the many that fled to the Kandyan Kingdom subsequently did much to improve that kingdom's trade.

The critical point for our purposes is that by 1626 Colombo was an exclusively Catholic town with temples destroyed and Muslims evicted. Prior to this, prior to the Portuguese, Muslims made a significant presence in the urban centres of the coast because of their trader status, but also because the local political system of Sinhala Buddhist kingdoms left commerce in the hands of minorities that either remained external to the system or articulated at the top among its 'stranger-kings' (Strathern 2009, 2010). For the latter, though, articulation entailed conversion to the dominant religion. Under the Portuguese that religion became Roman Catholic. It also became highly intolerant.

The Dutch ousted the Portuguese from Colombo after a bloody siege in 1656 whereupon they suppressed Catholic worship and required the subaltern elite – the *mudaliyars* – through whom the Portuguese ruled to convert to the Dutch Reformed Church (Peebles 1995: 100). Occupying Colombo as the capital of their colony for 140 years, Dutch religious intolerance lessened over time enabling the city and surrounds to become more diverse, including the strong Roman Catholic presence among the coastal fishing communities that migrated from the Tamil-speaking Fishery Coast in south India. And while the Dutch sought to conquer the interior kingdom of Kandy, the hill terrain and guerrilla-warfare techniques of the Kandyans prevented them. From the 1750s, meanwhile, the Kandyan king Kirti Sri Rājasiṁha (1747–1782) reformed the Buddhist *sangha*

102   Rohan Bastin

(order of monks) and incorporated the Tooth Relic in his capital's annual temple festival (Holt 1996; Seneviratne 1978); contributing to a model for Buddhist ceremony that would subsequently inform Buddhist revitalisation movements during the 19th and 20th centuries throughout the island. The *Navam Perahära* of Colombo's Gangaramaya Temple, for example, dates from the 1980s and deliberately brings "Kandy to Colombo" as it also borrows from the decorative wall design around its lake (Seneviratne 1999: 227) – the Beira Lake created by the Portuguese as a southern defence to Colombo Fort and later reclaimed by the British.

Kirti Sri Rājasiṁha's efforts to transform the religious dynamic of Kandy were driven in part by the antagonism of members of the Kandyan nobility for whom the Nayakkar dynasty to which Kirti Sri belonged represented a foreign and more specifically Tamil presence. The tension remained, notwithstanding Kirti Sri's efforts, and later intensified under the last Kandyan king, Sri Vikrama Rājasiṁha (1798–1815), who undertook a major transformation of his capital in the early 19th century by imposing spatially what James Duncan (1990) regards as a Hindu ideology of kingship celebrating the deity Śakra (a form of Indra, king of the gods) instead of the Buddhist celebration of Emperor Aśoka through public works like *stūpas* and *vihāras* (monasteries). The Kandyan system that later becomes a model of Sinhala Buddhist heritage evident, for example, in the architecture and land (actually waterscape) of the new Parliament at Kōṭṭe (opened in 1984) was thus a system redolent with its own tensions.

England annexed the Dutch territories in 1796 and by 1815 they had deposed the last Kandyan king and established island-wide suzerainty. While they did not require conversion to Anglican Christianity as a pre-requisite for *mudaliyar* status or position, the large numbers of Anglicans showing up in British census reports, especially for Colombo and the Western Province suggests the practice had become habitual. But religious revitalisation was gaining ground, with an active Hindu revival in the Northern Province preceding by roughly a quarter of a century the Buddhist revitalisation movements that grew amongst members of upwardly mobile caste groups exploiting both economic opportunities made available by colonialism and ethnic opportunities made available by the opening of the Kandyan economy and society (Bastin 1997; Malalgoda 1976). Primarily members of the *karāva, salāgama* and *durāva* castes, these new rich joined with the low country members of the superior *goyigama* caste to champion a new Buddhism through new orders (*nikāya*) of monks and new temples, albeit temples heavily focussie on rural locations where the bourgeoisie sought land (Gunasinghe 1990; Peebles 1995). Many came to live in Colombo, but they were extensively networked to the village and to the grand *walauwa* houses that resembled the English manor house, while being and/or becoming thoroughly enmeshed in plantation capitalism (Jayawardena 2000; Roberts 1982). Traditional roles and obligations to temples were linked to these houses with the temples of the old Kandyan kingdom providing the model. The critical point, then, is that the native urban elite were thoroughly embedded in the colonial plantation economy but at the same time closely articulated with the village and its manorial

The spatial and territorial nature   103

surrounds based in a system of caste and religion. Colombo and other coastal urban centres maintained their ethnic and religious eccentricity.

From the 1840s the plantation economy boomed with coffee followed by tea in the interior hill country, rubber in the foothills of the west and south-west and coconut products in the north-west. Colombo port expanded, especially after the opening of the Suez Canal in 1869 and the construction of railways that converged on the city. With new port developments in the early 20th century, Colombo's premier commercial status was complete and with the Dutch ramparts demolished the city grew. The Municipal Council, the first of its kind in Asia when it was created in 1865, busied itself with urban planning by draining a large section of Beira Lake (originally expanded by the Portuguese as a southern defence to the fort), widening streets and creating grids, enabling elite house construction in the old cinnamon plantations, and creating Victoria Park, around which the British built various social and sporting clubs, the Colombo Museum (opened in 1877) and elite Christian schools (Perera 1999; Schaffer 1998). Overlooking the other popular leisure spot Galle Face Green was the splendid Galle Face Hotel (opened from a grand Dutch residence in 1864 and subsequently expanded), while in Fort the Bristol and the Grand Oriental hotels accommodated the wealthy travelling between Europe and the Far East or Antipodes who could shop at the Cargill's and Miller's department stores.

At the same time, the city fringes filled with shanties, especially on the north side and along the river and canals, while the old narrow streets of Dutch settlement near Fort were occupied by migrant workers (Sinhalese and Tamil) as well as Muslim traders, who all added to the existing minority presence busy in the thriving plantation economy and expanding city. Mosques, churches (Catholic and Protestant) and temples (Hindu and Buddhist) were built or extended. The secular nature of British rule combined with the large number of ethnic and religious minorities moving into the city to ensure Colombo's multi-religious nature and its physical appearance where the whitewashed structures were not Buddhist stūpas but Greco-Roman colonial buildings like the Museum and Colombo Town Hall (opened near Victoria Park in 1927). Nearby and on the edge of what was once called Lipton Circus (after the famous tea planter-trader Sir Thomas Lipton) one finds the Cinnamon Gardens post office and a Baptist church facing the roundabout and 100m away the Devatagaha Mosque built on the site of a Sufi shrine created when the area was still heavily wooded. This one area, of Town Hall, mosque, Baptist church and post office built at a road junction named after arguably the country's most famous tea planter and merchant says a great deal about the city in the late 19th and early 20th centuries.

Population snapshot of Colombo and its neighbouring districts

The 2012 census data (Table 6.1) show the population figures for Colombo and indicate the relationship between Colombo and the peri-urban fringe. Consisting of 13 divisions, of which Colombo Division incorporates the old city, Colombo District is bound on the northern side by Gampaha District and to the south by Kalutara District. The table includes these districts both in order to reckon somewhat for urban sprawl and to highlight the contrast between the older inner city and the surrounding but now urbanising country-side that until the 1850s included many of the other divisions in what is now Colombo District. These other divisions are not included here for reasons of space and also because they neither illustrate nor contradict the general point that old Colombo was a minorities' town and that its urban growth has been rapid.

The Sinhalese speak the Indo-European language Sinhala and are predominantly Theravāda Buddhist throughout the country. However, along the coast in and around Colombo, large numbers of Sinhalese profess Roman Catholicism (hence the figures for Gampaha District of 91% Sinhalese and 19% Roman Catholic). The Tamils are Tamil-speaking with Sri Lankan Tamils having very long histories of domicile in the country while the Indian Tamils have closer historical connection to Tamil Nadu. They are not only indentured labourers or their descendants, but also *chettiar* traders renowned for Hindu temple and temple festival sponsorship in many Asian cities that grew in the British Empire (Rudner 1994). The Tamils are mainly Śaivite Hindu, but like the Sinhalese also include a proportion of Christians. The Sri Lankan Moors are Tamil speaking, but Muslim and primarily of Indian background.

The prevalence of Tamil language among the different minority groups especially the Moors reflects a number of historical points including the historical status of Tamil as a trade language. Related to this, the frequency of Tamil being spoken among the ostensibly Sinhalese Catholic fishermen of Colombo and the neighbouring districts (again, especially Gampaha) reflects Tamil's status as the traditional language of the sea (Stirrat 1988: 24). Tamil is, therefore, not prevalent simply because of the plantation era and the import of labour, or the migration of Tamils from their areas of traditional domicile in the north and the east. These are contributing factors. However, another factor is the long history of regional trade and with it the way in which such trade was subordinated or externalised in the Sinhala Buddhist kingdoms relative to irrigated agriculture and control of land, or more precisely, access to land through the social and political institutions of the kingdom (Gunasinghe 1990; Gunawardana 1979; Jayawardena 2010). In this system, *demala* (Tamil) has the capacity to be a metonym for immediate outsiders that can be qualified by other labels such as *marakkarar* (Tamil, ship people) now a pejorative loan word in colloquial Sinhala to describe Muslims. The point is that trade was ideologically external to the polity: how the political system imagined itself and defined its citizens.[2]

For the 13 divisions of Colombo District the representation by the majority Sinhalese (77%) and largest minority Tamil – comprising Sri Lankan Tamils (10%) and Indian Tamils (1%) – accord pretty much with the national proportion (75% and 11% respectively). However, in the old part of Colombo – the Colombo Division – the ratio is very different (25% and 31%). Including the peri-urban fringe (Gampaha and Kalutara districts), these proportions flatten dramatically; thereby highlighting the fact that the old inner part of Colombo

The spatial and territorial nature 105

is a major centre for the country's main minority groups of Tamils (31%) and Muslims (40%). What this reflects is the old situation wherein Colombo was a city for the minorities.

This situation for greater Colombo today not only differs from before, but varies on a daily basis with an estimated half-a-million people commuting into Colombo daily for work and access to resources, most of them from the neighbouring districts, but many travelling from as far away as Kandy and Matara, because Colombo remains such a commercial and administrative centre, while not being somewhere that people can easily occupy. Apart from some immigration from the war zones, especially after the expulsion of Muslims from Tamil Tiger-controlled areas in the early 1990s and the movement of Tamils away from the fighting, many hoping to treat Colombo as purely a transit centre through which to emigrate altogether (Thiranagama 2011: 229), the high numbers of minorities in Colombo Division reflect a long-standing minority presence. At the heart of this is the historical role played by minorities in trade. And closely connected to that feature is the historical role played by the majority Sinhalese in agriculture and land ownership and, with land and farming, how the Sinhalese came to be defined as an ethnic group (Gunawardana 1990). The minority presence is thus not simply a colonial product, but is emergent from long historical processes into which European colonialism was inserted (with, of course, its own extractive agenda).

These are, of course, sweeping characterisations that will require some qualification. For example, the strong Sri Lankan Tamil presence in Colombo derives from their role not in trade but the civil service (Bastin 1997). The Indian Tamil presence derives not only from trade but also from indentured labour (Peebles 2001). Finally, not all Sinhalese are farmers or ex-farmers. Indeed, many have made a niche as traders (although strikingly their Tamil roots roughly align with the Kōṭṭe/colonial era of the 15th and 16th centuries) (Roberts 1982). Nonetheless, the general propositions regarding trade and minorities as well as land and the majority have substance and will be explored further below.

Some Colombo religious institutions

Buddhism pervades Colombo as a function of its being practised by the majority of the country's population and, since 1956, the growing support for Buddhism by the state (including the grant of a 'foremost place' in the new Constitution of 1972 when Ceylon became Sri Lanka). Such pervasiveness is symbolised by the tower gateway at the land entrance to Colombo harbour. Built to commemorate the 2,500th anniversary of Lord Buddha's *jayanthi* (his death and release from existence) in 1956, the Buddha Jayanthi Chaithya is a *stūpa* or *dagäba* atop four tall concrete pillars forming a pointed archway on which the *dagäba* sits with a total height of roughly 75m. Easily visible from ships entering the harbour, the tower could also be seen from the shore in the years before the civil war, which led to the area around the port and navy headquarters becoming a high security zone. Like the Buddha statues that proliferated from the 1950s along many of Colombo's

106 Rohan Bastin

main roads and roads down south (Obeyesekere 1970) the Colombo Port tower aligned with the political mobilisation of Buddhism that took place in Sri Lanka after independence and especially in the Buddha Jayanthi celebrations in 1956 (Seneviratne 1999, Tambiah 1992). What this mobilisation led to is the creation of a Buddhist state. While the city remained multi-religiously plural, Buddhism began to pervade the governmental space with road-junction shrines, bo-trees allowed to grow and stay in place and statues of famous monks as well as Lord Buddha deliberately installed as spatial markers in a religious world where road-side and road junction shrines have been important for a very long time in towns as well as villages and for a variety of reasons that require further examination.

The first of these reasons is a matter of social access. In Hinduism, low castes were traditionally excluded from temples and obliged to make offerings at home, at the shrines erected on the temple walls, or, if permitted, at their own temples presided over by their own priests. Such shrines were themselves for lower order deities who were understood as being more accessible as they were more active in the world like the lower social strata themselves. While 20th century caste movements in Sri Lanka and elsewhere did much to transform the issue of temple entry, the spatial configuration of shrines and deities remain.

The second reason bears upon the first. Active in the world, the lower order deities stand more on the cusp between order and disorder, cosmos and chaos, divine and demonic. In Sinhala Buddhism and Tamil Hinduism, these deities' primary role is that of guardian, particularly in the zones of anomie where demons are thought to be active – the spatial and temporal junctures including cross-roads and cemeteries as well as dawn and dusk. Embodying themselves many of the demonic characteristics of their adversaries, the boundary deities highlight the way in which the pantheons stretching from the highest to the lowest give expression to a series of hierarchical transformations where the superior encompasses the inferior and the inferior is an aspect of the superior, albeit as a transform along a continuum from divine to demonic.

A further striking feature of this in the Sinhala Buddhist pantheon is the close association between deities and political geography (Winslow 1984) with certain deities known as the principal deity of a region granted a mandate by Lord Buddha to command a space in the manner of a noble. Vibhīṣaṇa is such a figure understood to be the regional guardian of the Greater Colombo area. The pious brother of the demon-king Ravana of *Rāmāyaṇa* fame, Vibhīṣaṇa's protruding canines attest to his demonic status, a status akin to a whole class of demon-deities (*dēvatāvā*) in both the Hindu and Buddhist pantheons. His contemporary worship is, however, poorly expressed, reflecting in part the presence of minorities, the absence for hundreds of years of a state-cult,[4] and urban migration by Sinhala Buddhists from other areas where Vibhīṣaṇa is relatively unknown. The result is that in Colombo, the local demon-deity is replaced by the more generic figure of Suniyam whose cult is more explicitly aligned with sorcery (Kapferer 1997: 58).

Road junction shrines are not, therefore, mere territorial markers declaring a space to belong to a particular religious community. They are actually instruments

The spatial and territorial nature   107

in the ordering of space and the control over the demonic. This is just as true for Roman Catholic shrines in Sri Lanka as it is for Hindu and Buddhist temples. It is best demonstrated for churches to the popular Saint Sebastian whose hagiography describes a 3rd century Roman soldier martyred by his emperor. In his churches, the saint is represented on the outside as the soldier and on the inside as the disarmed martyr shot full of arrows (which he miraculously survived only to be beaten to death subsequently). In this way, he is a soldier of Christ on the outside and an imitation of Christ on the inside. Like Saints George and Michael–the warriors who vanquish dragons (the Devil) – Saint Sebastian encapsulates the temporal and spiritual conquest and thereby represents excellently the Portuguese. The way he is represented and worshipped, however, reveal a powerful resonance with the two major and closely interrelated religions that the Portuguese set about eradicating. Unsurprisingly, their acts of destruction were routinely characterised as waging war on the Devil who had come to reside in the pagan idols and temples as if from citadels (see for example Bastin 2002: 1).

The spiritual conquest of the island by the Portuguese thus acted to reproduce a potent understanding within the cosmologies of the religions the Portuguese set out to eradicate. It is thus most striking that Catholic Church festivals commence with the planting and raising of a flag pole, just like the installation of the *kapa* in the Buddhist temple festivals (and the flag-raising in the Hindu temple festivals). Some mosques have also appropriated the practice of both festival and flag. Critically, what this means is that individual worshippers can make use of other people's deities and just as readily make an offering to a saint as to a *dēvatāvā*.

It also follows that just because these shrines have religious potency in the complex dynamics of their pantheons that they have no power in the seemingly secular domain of communal politics and spatial occupation. To imagine otherwise is to presume a thorough disconnection between the spatial configuration of a religious pantheon and the physical location of communities in space. It presumes a fortiori a thoroughly sociocentric perspective whereby the reality of physical social groups is acknowledged while effectively denying what these groups claim their spaces to comprise by way of invisible forces (as if a community with shared identity is not itself imagining itself ex nihilo). For sure, scepticism and agnosticism exist, within and between groups. Moreover, there are degrees of knowledge about pantheons, etc.

Nevertheless, it is extremely important to recognise that the religious or cosmological meanings that are possible in the configuration of pantheons and their spatial location in the city achieve considerably more than the legitimation of a communal identity.

Seen in these terms, then, the Buddha Jayanthi Chaithya is considerably more significant than it first appears. It is a state structure built by a government department in 1956. It commands the space of the harbour, the key point of access to the national economy and society that was for so long commanded by a Portuguese, a Dutch and then a British fort. It thus serves to overlay and embrace the total social field and give order to the disparate elements that make up the contemporary society.[5] And thus, just as the Tooth Relic was added to the Kandy

108   *Rohan Bastin*

Perahära, the addition of the Harbour temple encompasses the state and declares Buddhist sovereignty over the island's greatest commercial and political hub. That hub contains the minorities and their practices. The issue thus becomes an issue of 'cleansing'.

Put simply, can the Buddhist state accommodate religious diversity or must it remove the minorities? The broad answer to this question is that both accommodation and removal have occurred and that Buddhism was never the sole agent (recall the Portuguese conquest). In the final section of the chapter, I consider briefly one example, but before doing so note that the history of modern Colombo has been a history of territorial struggle between religious groups involving roadside shrines and statues Buddhist and Catholic as well as disputes and even riots over religious processions, drumming, amplified sermons and the call to prayer (Roberts 1990). The multi-religious space is both aural as well as visual.

Tamil Hindus in Colombo and the Vel Festival

Two principal areas of Tamil settlement in Colombo reflect key aspects of Sri Lanka's colonial history and plantation economy as these brought significant numbers of Tamils into the city from elsewhere in the island (mainly the Northern Province) and from south India. They are the Pettah, the old commercial hub immediately adjacent to the harbour and fort, and the late 19th century residential development on the south side of the city in the area known as Bambalapitiya. The Pettah is synonymous with south Indian traders including but not limited to the *chettiar* castes that have been active in the economy and religious life of the island for centuries while also playing a significant role in the expansion of the British Empire as bankers and providores (Rudner 1994).

In Pettah one *chettiar* group built a temple for the popular south Indian Hindu god Murugan in Sea Street, while another trader community, the Madras Palayakat Textiles Company, built their own temple in Main Street and were involved in the construction of a partner temple at Bambalapitiya adjacent to a temple for Ganeśa, the elephant-headed deity known as Murugan's wiser older brother (Cartman 1957: 123f; Clothey 1978, 2006). These temples served their local communities with the Bambalapitiya/Dehiwala area filling with educated Sri Lankan Tamils employed in the civil service and other white collar roles associated with colonial plantation capitalism.

Murugan's most famous shrine in Sri Lanka is at Kataragama in the remote south-east of the island. Popular with Sinhala Buddhists who worship Murugan under the name Kataragama Deviyo, the jungle temple is a major pilgrimage destination for both religions (Gombrich and Obeyesekere 1988) and a site that grew rapidly through the influx of south Indian plantation labour during the second half of the 19th century when the annual festival began to attract large crowds and the colonial authorities became increasingly concerned by outbreaks of cholera and typhoid. In 1874, entry to Kataragama was restricted to small district-specific quotas, prompting the *chettiar* owners of the Sea Street Murugan temple to stage their own festival procession from Pettah to Bambalapitiya.

The Colombo Vel Festival was thus created as an urban alternative to a jungle pilgrimage on account of colonial bureaucratic legislation concerning public health and the protection of plantation labour. It was created, moreover, with the participation of the *chettiars* working in hand with the Sri Lankan Tamil petty bourgeoisie working in the colonial bureaucracy. It is in this regard a thoroughly modern urban temple festival comparable with the markedly similar Thaipusam events staged (albeit at a different time of the year) in other colonial cities like Singapore, Kuala Lumpur and Penang (Clothey 2006).

Some 20 years after the commencement of Vel, the Main Street Murugan temple, the Kathiresan temple joined the event by staging its own procession from Pettah to Bambalapitiya departing a day earlier and highlighting the theme of *kāvadi* – the devotional dance performed with wooden pole roughly one metre long decorated with a crescent hoop on one side and peacock feathers at each end. More elaborate performances of this devotion (*bhakti*) include circular hoops attached to the devotee's body with metal hooks and even crane-like poles from which the devotee is suspended on hooks, their cheeks and even tongues pierced by brass spears – representations of the deity's main weapon, the *vel* (lance). *Kāvadi* dancing and hook-swinging fulfil individual vows made to the deity during the year and contribute enormously to the spectacle of the procession which connects the two areas of strong Tamil presence in the city. Specialist musicians and male transvestite dancers accompany the procession, which gives particular expression to the excessive spill-over of divine power (*śakti* – what the *vel* represents) transmuting into its demonic possibilities as the temple pushes its boundaries in order to encompass and reorder the cosmic space.[6]

Colombo's worst ethnic riots of July 1983 coincided with the festival and it was cancelled as Colombo Tamils' homes and businesses were attacked and several hundred people slaughtered in the streets as they were dragged from buses and cars. Many refugees left never to return leading to noticeable changes in the old areas of ethnic concentration. The temples were mainly spared the wrath of the mobs which, with copies of the electoral register supplied by members of the main pro-government public sector union, focused their attention more on property (often with the owners inside) and on public spaces. In the following years, the festival was held, but often with dramatically reduced crowds and little by way of participation in the processions by the troops of male transvestite dancers and high quality Indian Tamil musicians who used to give the processions so much of their carnival spectacle. Events focused more on the temple interiors rather than the public processions (Jeganathan 2000: 121–122). In 2004, the festival stopped altogether and has only been restored through active government support in 2010 – after the war.

The new Vel Festival displays the triumph of the Sinhala Buddhist State by elaborating an aesthetic more closely aligned with Buddhist temple festivals than the original. Kandyan dancers and musicians are now included, and prominence is given to the Sri Lankan President and his wife who greet the procession as it passes by their official residence. The carnival-like spirit of license of the old Vel Festival has abated, notwithstanding the continuation of self-mortification by

110   *Rohan Bastin*

individual devotees. And so just as the Kandy *Perahära* was Buddhicised in the 1750s by the inclusion of the Tooth Relic in the procession, and the Colombo Harbour was Buddhicised by a tower temple in the 1950s, the Vel Festival is being Buddhicised and incorporated within the Buddhist state in the aftermath of the separatist conflict. Colombo thus has the capacity to be multi-religious and able to celebrate its heritage of diversity. But it does so with one important caveat and that is the overarching and encompassing 'foremost place' of Buddhism in a state committed to fostering and protecting the majority religion. In more recent times, this process of capture by inclusion has been directed back to Muslims and this has occasioned violence in Colombo and elsewhere.

Conclusion

In this chapter, I have described Colombo's multi-religious nature, but made a case for the idea that some religions in the city have had or currently have an eminent position in respect to the other religions as they have enjoyed at different times a favoured relation with political power. This favoured relation has not always been a strict correspondence between state and religion, for as I showed during the Kōṭṭe period, the port was about commerce and commerce was in the hands of the Muslims, while the kingdom was Hindu-Buddhist and more concerned at the ideological level with being an agrarian state. The Portuguese Catholics transformed this situation by destroying temples and eventually evicting the Muslims. But then they gave way to the Protestant Dutch who themselves gave way to the increasingly secular bureaucratic British who created a colonial state and a native bourgeoisie that inherited power and a plantation economy as well as a religiously revitalised diverse society that has increasingly demanded that the majority religion be granted the foremost place. This has not been achieved easily or without bloodshed, because the foremost place for Buddhism in Sri Lanka entails the territorial capture of both space (and time – sound) within which the minority religions can exist and co-exist as long as they acknowledge and subordinate themselves to Buddhism.

Returning to the work of Kong whose research on the city of Singapore informs this chapter, she notes in her most recent consideration of the geographies of religion how scholars have broadened their typologies of religious spaces and religious practices to embrace institutions traditionally seen as non-religious. She thus develops a sense of the post-secular as more than simply a condition of religious revival or perpetuation of an enduring spirituality, but as the permeation of religion in new spheres of practice creating new forms of visibility to both social scientists and participants, as well as new forms of interaction in a human population that, as the 2009 World Development and Human Development reports note,[7] is becoming increasingly mobile and, with that mobility, increasingly urban. This leads to new challenges for urban planners, heritage managers and the broader aspiration that development can be sustainable. Notwithstanding reservations regarding sustainability, based as they are on the historical picture of

The spatial and territorial nature 111

Colombo's vexed history presented here, I have argued in this chapter that the starting point must always be the willingness to criticise our taken-for-granted assumptions about religious structures, how they happen, and how they interact.

Notes

1 Given the fact that the political capital since 1984, Sri Jayawardenepura, is actually now part of the growing Colombo Metropolitan Region, the change of political status is largely irrelevant.
2 The pattern is neither unique to Sri Lanka nor an indication of trade's economic unimportance (Dumont 1980: 165). Rather, it indicates the relative status of commerce, its eccentricity as Geertz (1980: 87) describes it for Bali, that highlights a recognition of the uncertainties of trade; a recognition expressed in Sinhala Buddhism in the close association between money, movable wealth, trade and the demonic (Kapferer 1997: 59).
3 Please note that only the main ethnic groups are included, in some instances missing about 1% of the total. The data are derived from the 2012 census. (www.statistics.gov.lk/PopHouSat/CPH2011/index.php?fileName=pop42&gp=Activities&tpl=3)
4 This state cult derived from the Kelaniya Temple where Vibhīṣaṇa worship was promoted during the Kōṭṭe period (Walters 1996).
5 Space prevents further elaboration other than to note two additional features of Buddhist overlay. The first is the celebration of each full moon (*poya*) as a religious holiday where alcohol sales are banned. Bars and restaurants may open, but only with any display items conspicuously hidden from view. The second is the most important *poya*, the Vesak Poya which celebrates Lord Buddha's *jayanthi*. The event is marked by Vesak card exchanges modelled directly on Christmas and the erection of giant electronically lit painted displays (again seemingly drawing upon Christmas) depicting Buddhist themes and creating a spectacular night-time display throughout the city, especially at the major road junctions. These are not permanent structures and so might escape the planner's eye. They are, nevertheless, extremely important territorialising features of the dominant Buddhist polity.
6 In *kāvadi*, the dancer imitates the antigod Surapadman who is the last surviving antigod from the battle for which Murugan was first created (Clothey 1978). All of the *asura* are devotees of Śiva, and so Surapadman carries two mountains as a form of worship on behalf of himself and his brothers. The hoop structures carried by devotees represent these mountains who in the condition of their vow embody the antigod/victim who is sacrificed (and reborn) by the god. The festival thus displays a very similar logic of divine encompassment over demonic chaos as what I describe for the roadside junctions.
7 Reshaping Economic Geography (World Bank 2009), Overcoming Barriers: Human Mobility and Development (UNDP 2009).

References

Asad, T. (2003) *Formations of the Secular: Christianity, Islam, Modernity*, Stanford: Stanford University Press.
Bastin, R. (1997) 'The Authentic Inner Life: Complicity and Resistance in the Tamil Hindu Revival', in *Sri Lanka: Collective Identities Revisited* (vol. 1, pp. 385–438), ed. Michael Roberts, Colombo: MARGA Institute.
Bastin, R. (2002) *The Domain of Constant Excess: Plural Worship at the Munnesvaram Temples in Sri Lanka*, New York and Oxford: Berghahn Books.

112 Rohan Bastin

Bastin, R. (2005) 'Hindu Temples in the Sri Lankan Ethnic Conflict: Capture and Excess', *Social Analysis* 49(1): 45–66.

Bastin, R. (2012) 'Saints, Sites, and Religious Accommodation in Sri Lanka', in *Sharing the Sacra: The Politics and Pragmatics of Intercommunal Relations around Holy Places*, ed. Glenn Bowman, New York and Oxford: Berghahn Books.

Cartman, Rev. J. (1957) *Hinduism in Ceylon*, Colombo: M.D. Gunasena.

Cloke, P. and Beaumont, J. (2013) 'Geographies of Postsecular Rapprochement in the City', *Progress in Human Geography* 37(1): 27–51.

Clothey, F. W. (1978) *The Many Faces of Murukan: The History and Meaning of a South Indian God*, The Hague: Mouton.

Clothey, F. W. (2006) *Ritualizing on the Boundaries: Continuity and Innovation in the Tamil Diaspora*, Columbia: University of South Carolina Press.

De Queyroz, F. (1992 [1930]) *The Temporal and Spiritual Conquest of Ceylon*, trans. Father S. G. Perera, New Delhi: Asian Educational Services.

De Silva-Wijeyeratne, R. (2014) *Nation, Constitutionalism and Buddhism in Sri Lanka*, Abingdon Oxon: Routledge.

Dumont, L. (1980) *Homo Hierarchicus: The Caste System and Its Implications*, complete revised English edition, Chicago and London: University of Chicago Press.

Duncan, J. S. (1990) *The City as Text: The Politics of Landscape Interpretation in the Kandyan Kingdom*, Cambridge: Cambridge University Press.

Geertz, C. (1980) *Negara: The Theatre State in Nineteenth-Century Bali*, Princeton NJ: Princeton University Press.

Gombrich, R. F. and Obeyesekere, G. (1988) *Buddhism Transformed: Religious Change in Sri Lanka*, Princeton, NJ: Princeton University Press.

Gunasinghe, N. (1990) *Changing Socio-Economic Relations in the Kandyan Countryside*, Colombo: Social Scientists' Association.

Gunawardana, R. A. L. H. (1979) *Robe and Plough: Monasticism and Economic Interest in Early Medieval Sri Lanka*, Tucson: University of Arizona Press.

Gunawardana, R. A. L. H. (1990) 'The People of the Lion: the Sinhala Identity and Ideology in History and Historiography', in *Sri Lanka: History and Roots of Conflict* (pp. 45–86), ed. Jonathan Spencer, London: Routledge.

Holt, J. C. (1996) *The Religious World of Kirti Sri: Buddhism, Art and Politics in Late Medieval Sri Lanka*, New York: Oxford University Press.

Hopkins, P., Kong, L. and Olson, E. eds. (2013) *Religion and Place: Landscape, Politics and Piety*, Dordrecht: Springer.

Jayawardena, K. (2000) *Nobodies to Somebodies: The Rise of the Colonial Bourgeoisie in Sri Lanka*, New Delhi: Leftword Books.

Jayawardena, K. (2010) *Perpetual Ferment: Popular Revolts in Sri Lanka in the 18th and 19th Centuries*, Colombo: Social Scientists' Association.

Jeganathan, P. (2000) 'On the Anticipation of Violence: Modernity and Identity in Southern Sri Lanka', in *Anthropology, Development and Modernities: Exploring Discourse, Counter-Tendencies and Violence* (pp. 112–126), eds. Alberto Arce and Norman Long, Abingdon, Oxon: Routledge.

Kapferer, B. (1997) *The Feast of the Sorcerer: Practices of Consciousness and Power*, Chicago and London: University of Chicago Press.

Kong, L. (1990) 'Geography and Religion: Trends and Prospects', *Progress in Human Geography* 14(3): 355–371.

Kong, L. (2001) 'Mapping "New" Geographies of Religion: Politics and Poetics in Modernity', *Progress in Human Geography* 25(2): 211–233.

The spatial and territorial nature   113

Kong, L. (2010) 'Global Shifts, Theoretical Shifts: Changing Geographies of Religion', *Progress in Human Geography* 34(6): 755–776.

Malalgoda, K. (1976) *Buddhism in Sinhalese Society 1750–1900: A Study of Religious Revival and Change*, Berkeley, Los Angeles and London: University of California Press.

Obeyesekere, G. (1970) 'Religious Symbolism and Political Change in Ceylon', *Modern Ceylon Studies* 1: 48–63.

Peebles, P. (1995) *Social Change in Nineteenth Century Ceylon*, Colombo: Navrang in association with Lake House Bookshop.

Peebles, P. (2001) *The Plantation Tamils of Ceylon*, London and New York: Leicester University Press.

Perera, N. (1999) *Decolonizing Ceylon: Colonialism, Nationalism and the Politics of Space in Sri Lanka*, New Delhi: Oxford University Press.

Perniola, V. (1991) *The Catholic Church in Sri Lanka: The Portuguese Period Volume II, 1566–1619, Dehiwala*, Sri Lanka: Tisara Prakasakayo Ltd.

Roberts, M. (1982) *Caste Conflict and Elite Formation: The Rise of the Karāva Elite in Sri Lanka, 1500–1931*, Cambridge: Cambridge University Press.

Roberts, M. (1990) 'Noise as Cultural Struggle: Tom-Tom Beating, the British and Communal Disturbances in Sri Lanka, 1880s–1930s', in *Mirrors of Violence: Communities, Riots and Survivors in South Asia* (pp. 240–285), ed. Veena Das, Delhi: Oxford University Press.

Rudner, D. (1994) *Caste and Capitalism in Colonial India: The Nattukottai Chettiars*, Berkeley, Los Angeles and London: University of California Press.

Schaffer, M. (1998) 'From Victoria to Vihara Mahadevi', in *Culture and Politics of Identity in Sri Lanka* (pp. 72–90), eds. Mithran Tiruchelvam and C.S. Dattathreya, Colombo: International Centre for Ethnic Studies.

Seneviratne, H.L. (1978) *Rituals of the Kandyan State*, Cambridge: Cambridge University Press.

Seneviratne, H.L. (1999) *The Work of Kings: The New Buddhism in Sri Lanka*, Chicago and London: University of Chicago Press.

Stirrat, R.L. (1988) *On the Beach: Fishermen, Fishwives and Fishtraders in Post-Colonial Sri Lanka*, Delhi: Hindustan Publishing Corporation.

Strathern, A. (2009) 'The Vijaya Origin Myth of Sri Lanka and the Strangeness of Kingship' *Past and Present* 203: 3–28.

Strathern, A. (2010) *Kingship and Conversion in Sixteenth-Century Sri Lanka: Portuguese Imperialism in a Buddhist Land*, Cambridge: Cambridge University Press.

Tambiah, S.J. (1992) *Buddhism Betrayed? Religion, Politics, and Violence in Sri Lanka*, Chicago and London: University of Chicago Press.

Thiranagama, S. (2011) *In My Mother's House: Civil War in Sri Lanka*, Philadelphia: University of Pennsylvania Press.

Tse, J.H. (2014) 'Grounded Theologies: "Religion" and the "Secular" in Human Geography', *Progress in Human Geography* 38(2): 201–220.

United Nations Development Program (2009) *Overcoming Barriers: Human Mobility and Development*, Human Development Report 2009, Basingstoke and New York: Palgrave Macmillan.

Walters, J.S. (1996) *The History of Kelaniya*, Colombo: Social Scientists' Association.

Wickramasinghe, N. (1995) *Ethnic Politics in Colonial Sri Lanka, 1927–1947*, New Delhi: Vikas Publishing House.

Wickramasinghe, N. (2006) *Sri Lanka in the Modern Age*: A History of Contested Identities, London: Hurst and Company.

114 *Rohan Bastin*

Winslow, D. (1984) 'A Political Geography of Deities: Space and the Pantheon in Sinhalese Buddhism', *Journal of Asian Studies* 43: 273–292.

World Bank (2009) *Reshaping Economic Geography*, World Development Report 2009, Washington DC: The International Bank for Reconstruction and Development / The World Bank.

Part II

Informality, marginalisation and violent exchange

7 Religious structures on traffic lanes

Production of informality in New Delhi

Surajit Chakravarty

Introduction

A curious phenomenon observed at numerous locations around New Delhi is for religious structures to be found *on* streets, that is, on the asphalt-paved traffic lanes that are intended for use by vehicles (also known as the 'carriageway'). Bottlenecks of traffic result, as one lane of the street is effectively lost, and regained only after passing the protruding structure. This chapter inquires how such anomalies occur within a city that is otherwise planned and managed according to modernist principles, indeed deriving its name from this distinction. These religious structures represent informality in the sense that they stand clearly in contradiction to rational systems of planning, but are tolerated nevertheless, and yet also continue to be a source of anxiety for the state. It is with this general understanding of the term – lived spaces and activities falling outside the State's standards and regulations – that this chapter approaches informality.

The common explanation is that as thoroughfares were widened over time, structures formerly at the edges began jutting into the streets. Since religious structures cannot be demolished, they were left as they were, even if it meant obstructing traffic. This explanation raises further questions. Why does the state allow religious structures to violate the scientific principles used to plan streets? Why are streets not redesigned to go around the structures? What do these contradictions tell us about the conception of modernity according to which we plan cities and run other branches of administration? Exploring these questions will contribute not only to finding solutions to the mundane problem of traffic jams, but also lead to a deeper understanding of informality in general.

This chapter analyzes informality as a condition (with historical and political contingencies) rather than simply a kind of activity undertaken by a kind of people. Further, building on existing knowledge, informality is reconceptualized as a process and tool employed by the state for strategic purposes. The religious sites studied here highlight the inability of the state to fit these artifacts within newfound systems of modernist planning. These ordinary spaces show how conditions of exception evolve to hide gaps between unresponsive policy-making and the real experience of everyday life. By understanding informality as a process, and contextualizing its evolution and political functions, this chapter offers a new analytical approach for both theoretical and policy purposes.

118 *Surajit Chakravarty*

Solving the traffic component of the problem has direct benefits for environmental sustainability (savings in carbon emissions) and public interest (fewer
accidents and shorter commute times), while broader lessons on informality could
potentially lead to gains in social and economic sustainability through improved
policy-making. Achieving sustainability in years to come will depend on how
well the phenomenon of informality is understood and addressed. Considering
that 67 per cent of the non-agricultural labor force in Indian cities is engaged in
the informal sector (Mitra, 2014), and millions live in informal housing, addressing informality in a humane and just manner is critical for attaining goals of
sustainability (AlSayyad, 2004; Briassoulis, 2001, 1999; Yeo and Heng, 2014). At
the very least, state agencies might acknowledge that proliferation of informality
is caused, in large part, by inept planning and implementation compounded by
ambivalence in dealing with divisive and difficult decisions.

Framework of analysis

Informal activities, though not explicitly illegal, lie outside the state's regimes
of enumeration, regulation and control. This may include a 'dizzying array of
phenomena' (Helmke and Levitsky, 2004, p. 726). Informality is a general style
of management and control, or even (as some would argue) a tool of governance,
that affects all aspects of urban life. Cities in South Asia deal with numerous
economic, social and spatial manifestations of informality. These have been studied primarily in the context of informal housing ('squatter' settlements, 'shanty
towns' etc.) and informal business practices (hawkers, weekend markets, uses of
sidewalks etc.). The study of informality itself, as an epistemological category, has
gathered momentum in recent years. It has become apparent that informality is
not simply a condition that arises due to underdevelopment, and 'cures' itself as
economic growth takes off.

The framework of analysis used in this chapter is predicated on three borrowed
insights. First, Bishwapriya Sanyal (1991) argues that the idea of *informality* is not
the same as the *informal sector*. There is a tendency for the two ideas to be col-
lapsed and used interchangeably, not without reason, but ultimately to the detriment of theoretical advancement. Second, Ananya Roy (2009) has argued that
informality cannot be reduced simply to *poverty*. The labor and housing practices
of those living in poverty often fall under the category of 'informal'. We must,
however, strive to examine informality as a structural condition rather than a
behavior pattern. Third, Neema Kudva (2009) emphasizes the importance of the
'everyday politics' (p. 1615) and 'political economy' of informality, and argues
for serious consideration of the 'space of localities' (p. 1625). Using a Lefebvrian
framework, Kudva argues that space not only contains, but also is generative of
informality. Thus *from space* one can attempt to read the conditions that create
informality.

This study of the state's contested relationship with places of worship focuses
on three religious structures in New Delhi. The selected cases are (1) Shahi Masjid Zabta Ganj on Rajpath, (2) Irwin Road Mosque on Baba Kharak Singh Marg

and (3) Auliya Mosque on the outer circle of Connaught Place near Minto Road. The three sites are all in the heart of 'Lutyens's Delhi', which was imagined as the new capital of British India, a demonstration of imperial power and of the potential of its modern-scientific administrative and engineering apparatus.

The selected sites enable a comparative study of their treatment first by the colonial government, and then by planning agencies in early independent India, and later by the neoliberal state. The structures continue to be stark examples of the ideas being discussed. It is only a matter of historic succession, and not preference on the part of the imperial government, that all three structures happen to be Mosques. Few Hindu temples, if any, existed on the site selected by Lutyens to plan New Delhi. It is also not a selection bias of the author. The phenomena reported in this chapter, are by no means exclusive to Islamic sites. Further, to be clear, the places of worship themselves (regardless of affiliation) are not responsible for any of the issues discussed. The purpose, rather, is to derive lessons from these sites about the challenges of managing urban space, particularly in developing countries, where informality (not least by way of religious sites and practices) plays an important role in everyday life. In this context 'informality' emerges as an arrangement that allows the city to function, albeit with various undesirable externalities such as public nuisances. Moreover, the problem with temples on traffic lanes is not simply one of traffic jams. The situation also reveals a more subtle problem of the state being incapable of recalibrating its response to society's needs, and of constructing its own modernity in the process.

The politics of informality is analyzed in this chapter, not just in the sense of sites and practices of informality being matters of political contestation, but also by way of informality itself being a tool of statecraft, used to achieve various symbolic and material objectives. The chapter approaches informality from a level of abstraction, with the hope of gaining insight applicable to a variety of situations. In particular the analysis is concerned with the emergence of informality, and the contests associated with conditions of exception. The conclusion offers an alternative reading of informality, one that neither exalts its limited economic successes as a touchstone of efficiency, nor decries its human suffering as a universal given, but rather calls for a nuanced understanding of the contests and motivations that create and sustain it.

Discontents of negative definitions of informality

Keith Hart (1973) is credited for coining the term 'informal' (AlSayyad, 2004; Kamete, 2013). Hart (2009, 2008) later explained that the term 'mirrored' Cold War politics, where 'formal' stood for state control and the 'informal' represented free market entrepreneurialism. This argument seems to contradict the fact that the term 'informality' is used widely in a pejorative sense, connoting lack of order, control, predictability and stability – all essential features of free markets.

> In theory, the term "formal" is taken to represent the ordered city – in terms of its urban and architectural shape as well as its cultural, economic, political

120 *Surajit Chakravarty*

and social organization – while the "informal" is understood as the opposite: the shapeless areas of the city where economic and socio-political structures particularly unstable and in which culture is characterised by its apparent incoherence

(Hernandez and Kellett, 2010, p. 1)

It is no surprise then, that (as Hart himself puts it) '"Informality" has come to be perceived as a threat to "private sector development"' (Hart, 2008, p. 18). Further, the strongest political associations of the idea of informality are with neither capitalism nor socialism, but rather with underdevelopment. Certainly, Hart's defensive statement about the presence of some aspects of informality in developed countries is true. But this is not the sense in which the term has been used to refer to features and practices of development, governance and urbanization in developing countries. Consequently, his attempt, ex-post, to locate informality in Cold War terminology, and particularly to align informality with liberty, remains unconvincing.

Hart's opinions are important because of his 'founding' association with the term informality. Informality has continued to be misinterpreted because of its 'negative' definition. The construction of the idea of informality not only presupposes 'the formal', but also relies on the formal for its own definition. If formal activities are those that can be controlled, measured and categorized in a consistent manner, then informality is that which lies outside such a scheme. The challenges and needs of the informal sector are always understood within a formal-normative framework. Much effort made towards promoting sustainability could be misdirected as a result of this problematic interpretation. The negative construction of informality impedes theoretical advancement in at least five significant ways.

First, the negative definition inhibits our ability to appreciate and understand informal activities as valuable, whole and legitimate in their own right. Maloney (2004), for example, argues 'that as a first approximation we should think of the informal sector as the unregulated, *developing country analogue* of the voluntary entrepreneurial small firm sector found in advanced countries' (p. 1160, emphasis added). The phenomenon of informality appears to have few intrinsic qualities except absence of rationality, typically interpreted as 'advanced', capitalist rationality. Sindzingre (2006) explains some of the epistemological problems that follow from conceptual ambiguity. For example, in describing the informal sector 'methods often construct the concept' (p. 6), that is, informality is measured using conceptual tools designed to interpret other phenomena. Further, the heterogeneity of informality is flattened by a one-dimensional reading (Sindzingre, 2006, p. 6).

Second, the negative construction forces us to view informality as a problem. Accordingly, the focus has been mainly on its experience and phenomenological aspects, along with economic implications and policy options to control and manage it. To an overwhelming degree, studies have tried to 'solve' informality, while relatively few have critically examined the politics of its evolution, materiality and treatment in discourse.

Third, the negative definition privileges one or another conceptualization of formality, often derived from the dominant ideology of the state at the time. There is a tendency to lose touch with the basic idea that 'formality' is a matter of legitimacy accorded by the state – a flexible, negotiable, political act. This distracts attention (at least in policy circles) from critiques of the so-called formal sector. The regime of rules and regulations, which defines formality in any activity or sector, may itself suffer from various flaws (such as lack of transparency, selective implementation, insider politics, revolving doors, corruption and the like). But rather than focus on economic and spatial relations that are actually sanctioned by law, the focus shifts to informality, often considered inherently problematic. Informality must not be viewed in isolation from the formal. Further, the role of state institutions in producing informality must be taken into account.

Fourth, even in appreciating the entrepreneurial spirit, creativity and efficiencies of the informal sector, studies tend to reproduce the formal-informal binary. Ann Varley (2013) finds that informality is often caught in 'binary entrapments' (p. 93), and stereotypical formulations such as 'unplanned', 'emergent', 'spontaneous', 'labyrinthine', 'rhizome' etc. There is a need, then, to problematize the negative definition of the informal, and ask critical questions about *informality* as a political condition and strategy.

Fifth, using the signifier 'informality' to describe the everyday life of the world's dispossessed peoples creates an ahistorical and depoliticized version of their struggles. It is important also to contextualize historically and politically the various administrative regimes of regulations, definitions and maps that are used to classify informality. Any sustainable development agenda dealing with the informal sector must recalibrate current assumptions regarding informality.

We can now turn to the case studies. The next section sets up the historical context of the planning of New Delhi, specifically the role of the munity of 1857. This is followed by an analysis of the three selected cases. The chapter concludes with an argument for understanding informality as politically produced disjuncture, engaging in particular with the work of Chakrabarty (2004) and Roy (2011, 2009, 2004).

Political space for religious monuments: British attitudes and aspirations after 1857

Indra Sengupta (2013) correctly posits that the East India Company's frugal attempts to preserve historical structures 'had much to do with the efforts of the company to legitimize its rule as the natural successor of the Mughal rulers of India' (p. 23). Sengupta finds George Nathaniel Curzon's appointment as Viceroy of India, in 1899, as a moment of significant change. In addition to fast-paced action, change in management structure and increased funding, Curzon is credited with selecting John Marshall to head the Archaeological Survey of India. John Marshall's *Conservation Manual* of 1923, which followed his efforts on the 1904 Ancient Monuments Preservation Act until today forms the basis of the heritage preservation policy in the country.

122 *Surajit Chakravarty*

Sengupta (2013) argues that John Marshall's work, too, was aligned with colonial narratives justifying imperial rule, by (1) contrasting 'landscapes of ruination . . . as a metaphor of general decline and death' (p. 27–28) with the progress and vitality of colonial rule, and (2) thereby confirming British custodianship of Indian heritage. 'Out of this emerged an authority over India's fate' (Sengupta, 2013, p. 28). Sengupta proffers an excellent analysis to explain colonial attitudes towards Indian heritage, but omits to account for the impacts of the 1857 mutiny on the British administration's perception of religious structures. Changes were well under way before Curzon's arrival.

Widespread rebellion against the British East India Company in 1857 was a turning point in Indian history. The immediate cause is understood to be the hurting of religious sentiments because of the use of ammunition covered with leather and laced with lard. The ammunition became symbolic of all the violence and imbalance of the East India Company's engagement with India. Since the animal products were drawn from both cows and pigs, they served to unite Hindu and Muslim soldiers against the insensitive and unjust outsiders. The mutiny, which took two years to suppress, changed British attitudes towards India. The governance of India passed into the hands of the British crown through the Government of India Act of 1858. Various 'reforms' were carried out after formal annexation, many with significant effects on urban space.

After the British took back Delhi from the mutineers, 'the loot, massacre, hanging, digging of houses and arresting of people started' (Sharma and Tewari, 2012, p. 304). Retribution caused fragmentation, restructuring and militarization of the city. Jyoti Hosagrahar (2005) reports that the British appropriated land and property within and outside the walled city, both to recover costs incurred during the mutiny and for redistribution to those who had remained loyal. 'When the British laid siege to Delhi in 1857, the city was purged of all its inhabitants' (Hosagrahar, 2005, p. 23). The properties, including traditional *haveli* residences, gardens and orchards, were arbitrarily subdivided before allocation, leading to changes in the fabric, use and design of space (p. 23).

A high priority was accorded by the British to make Delhi a safe place for the soldiers from 1860 (Sharma and Tewari, 2012, p. 318). Narayani Gupta's (1971) explanation of the militarization of space in Delhi reveals the anxieties of the imperial government after the mutiny. Impacts of the mutiny included expansion of military presence, establishment of a large cantonment in the heart of the city, confiscation and occupation of private land and demolition of large tracts of inhabited parts of the city (Gupta, 1971). In Gupta's assessment '[a]lthough the size of the army in Delhi was smaller than in other Punjab towns, the city functioned solely as a cantonment' (p. 63). The cantonment remained in place until 1910 when it was removed because it had become redundant to occupy the walled city in order to defend British occupation and military positions. Moreover there were greater monetary benefits to be had from both the sale of central land and from letting the new owners convert it into commercial use (p. 63).

The degree to which a seemingly small matter had perturbed the natives, and the scale of revolution it had galvanized was clearly a shock to the Company and to the British government back home. The administration responded by attempting to extricate itself from any situation where it might be seen as interfering with religion. One of the results of this effort was the Religious Endowments Act of 1863 (also known as Act 20 of 1863) – '[a]n Act to enable the Government to divest itself of the management of Religious Endowments'. The haste with which the change was made is evident from the fact (as noted in the 'Statement of Object and Reasons' contained in the text of the Religious Endowments Act of 1863) that the legislation was first presented as a Bill to the Legislative Council in 1860, that is, within two years of the British government taking control of India.

The 1863 Religious Endowments Act required the government 'to make special provisions respecting' religious buildings, and 'to prevent injury to and preserve buildings remarkable for their antiquity, or for their historical or architectural value, or required for the convenience of the public'. The Religious Endowments Act (1863) also repealed parts of two prior legislations – Regulation 19 of the Bengal Code (1810) and Madras Regulation 7 (1817). The repealed sections had previously allowed the Company to charge fees for executing maintenance repair works not only on religious sites, but also on public buildings, bridges etc. The two laws had also allowed 'appropriation of the rents and produce of lands granted for the support of Mosques, Hindu Temples and Colleges or other public purposes'. It is easy to comprehend why such a 'management' enterprise, a component of the Company's wider land revenue extraction system, might have appeared risky after 1857.

The Religious Endowments Act of 1863, along with Regulation 19 of the Bengal Code (1810) and Madras Regulation 7 (1817) appear frequently in government documents today as the supporting legislation for initiating historic preservation and architectural conservation in the country. It is true that the laws provide legal backing for such endeavors, but the narrative is not without degree of naiveté. The Archaeological Survey of India, for example, imagines the legislations as part of a 'cultural renaissance'.

Cultural renaissance of early nineteenth century witnessed enactment of the first ever antiquarian legislation in India known as Bengal Regulation XIX of 1810. This was soon followed by another legislation called as Madras Regulation VII of 1817. Both these regulations vested the Government with a power to intervene whenever the public buildings were under threat of misuse. However, both the Acts were silent on the buildings under the private ownership. The Act XX of 1863, was therefore enacted to empower the Government to prevent injury to and preserve buildings remarkable for their antiquity or for their historical or architectural value. (Archaeological Survey of India Bengaluru Circle, 2011).

Act XX (Religious Endowments Act) of 1863 may have legitimized preservation efforts, but to say that such was its main intent would be grossly overlooking the context of the legislation. The Central Public Works Department (2013), too, credits the same set of legislations without noting the roles these legislations played in colonial extraction.

In the years after the role of governing India was claimed by the British crown, it became accepted practice for religious sites to be left untouched in construction

124 *Surajit Chakravarty*

and improvement works. The respect accorded to religious sites can be seen as yielding at least four political benefits. First, as noted above, elaborate policies for preservation helped establish British custodianship of Indian heritage. Second, the events of 1857 had left the British jittery about hurting religious sentiments in India. Distancing British government from religious matters created a measure of security. Third, the British government had an interest in making a spectacle of inclusiveness, even if it was mostly symbolic, as a part of its ongoing mission of 'civilizing' the colonies. Fourth, pursuant of the 'divide-and-rule' policy utilized in India and other colonies, a heightened appreciation for the separate heritages of the two faiths was a small though not meaningless measure. Spatial manifestations of 'divide and rule' in New Delhi and elsewhere have been studied by Nicholas Roberts (2013), Carl Nightingale (2013, 2012) and Anthony Christopher (1988) among others.

The discussion so far sets the stage for examining Lutyens's design of New Delhi. The capital of India was shifted from Calcutta to Delhi in 1911. A new city was envisioned in Delhi, to serve as the capital, rich in symbolism, and an epitome of all the virtues of British rule in India. The next section presents an analysis of the treatment of existing religious structures within the new plan. It is argued that these were the first instances of informality within the built spaces of New Delhi.

Origins of the exceptional: religious monuments in the imperial capital

Three sites in the heart of Lutyens's New Delhi illustrate the idea of tolerant exclusion as practiced by imperial architects, and the ambivalence of planners in post-independence India. The three sites have been selected because of their prominent locations and because they are stark examples of the principles being described. As mentioned earlier, the fact that three Islamic sites were selected is only due to their existence in Lutyens's Delhi since before it was planned. Similar trends can be observed with numerous Hindu temples in other parts of the city.

Shahi Masjid Zabta Ganj, Rajpath

Zabta Ganj was a 'cluster of seven small settlements' (Khandekar, 2012) near the main axis of New Delhi. The villages were removed in the process of building the capital, but as per policy, the mosque, built in 1740, was left in place (Khandekar, 2012). The mosque enjoys an enviable location on protected land, looking onto a water channel and surrounded by well-maintained lawns. Its treatment, however, in the design of the axis connecting Raisina Hill with India Gate deserves closer scrutiny.

According to the Imam of the mosque (as reported by Khandekar, 2012) the site was an abandoned ruin until the late 1960s. It is safe to say, then, that the Lutyens's plan did not imagine an active role for the mosque, especially after the communities it served were relocated. The linear East–West axis (Kingsway, now known by its Hindi translation *Rajpath*) passed 70 meters North of the Mosque. Rajpath was buffered on both sides by lawns and artificial water channels running parallel to the street. According to the design, the mosque, on the Southern side of Rajpath, lay half inside the water channel (see Figure 7.1), making it abundantly clear that it was not part of the design.

With the luxury of laying the plan on a tabula rasa, various design alternatives could have been used to address the issue of the existing mosque in the path of an artificial water channel. The channel of water could have been divided into two sections on either side of the mosque, it could have been moulded around the walls of the mosque, or it could have been designed to pass to North or South of the mosque (a matter of about 10 meters). Figure 7.2 shows the mosque located partially in the channel. There is no doubt that the ambience is peaceful and also, to an extent, picturesque. But this immediately seems more of an accident when one considers the fact that the mosque is not buffered from the traffic, has received no special landscaping treatment and is not even aligned with the channel (as seen in Figure 7.3). If the intention was to accentuate the mosque aesthetically, this purpose would have been better served with more thorough treatment, such as a garden or by sculpting the water channel around the mosque.

The manner in which the space was designed, highlighting the mosque but only as a misfit, seems to have been a strategic choice, not for the benefit of the structure, but rather for the political symbolism it afforded. Although the Zabta Ganj mosque lies on a water channel and not on a traffic thoroughfare, it encapsulates the principles that were adopted in other instances. It is noteworthy that the strategy was followed also by other architects working with Lutyens. Examples discussed below show a similar pattern of places of worship left languishing at the margins of modernist geometries.

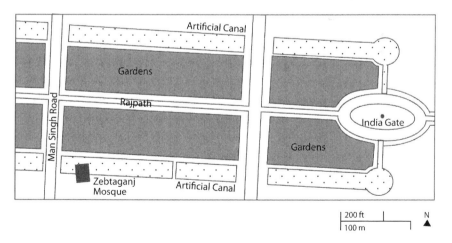

Figure 7.1 Zabta Ganj Mosque on Rajpath.

Figure 7.2 Picturesque setting of Zabta Ganj Mosque.

Figure 7.3 Mosque not aligned with the orientation of the channel.

Religious structures on traffic lanes 127

Auliya Mosque, Connaught Place outer circle near Minto Road

Connaught Place was planned as the commercial heart and main public space of New Delhi. Designed by architect Robert Tor Russell, its geometry of concentric circles pierced by long linear avenues, a central park, open vistas and colonnaded arcades could not have been more different from the inscrutable alleys and milling crowds of Shahjahanabad.

An existing religious structure, Auliya Mosque, near the outer circle of Connaught Place (Figure 7.4), presented a design challenge. Auliya Mosque could have been neatly incorporated into the new construction by allowing the mosque to occupy a nook or corner within it. Alternatively, the circular form could have been interrupted, and continued on either side of the mosque, to promote its integration into the structure. For the imperial architects, the integrity of their modernist geometry was crucial for the import of the underlying symbolism. Auliya Mosque was 'incorporated' into the design to the extent that it was not demolished, but instead it was allowed to stand at a distance of 10 meters from the nearest structure, protruding into the thoroughfare, bearing the distinct appearance of being tolerated but not wanted, or at least not readily a part of the overall scheme of things.

Figure 7.5 shows the Auliya Mosque located between the structures of the outer circle and the carriageway of the adjacent street. Figure 7.6 shows the point at which space of faith meets the space of flows. The corner was made to appear normal through the addition of a wide sidewalk (used as parking space), which narrows significantly next to the mosque.

Irwin Road Mosque, Baba Kharak Singh Marg

The Irwin Road Mosque is one of several significant religious structures (including the Hindu temple *Hanuman Mandir*, the Sacred Heart Cathedral, and the Sikh temple *Bangla Sahib*) that are all located within a 1-kilometer stretch of Baba

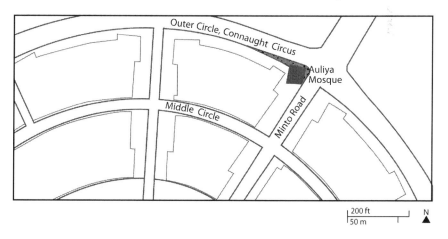

Figure 7.4 Auliya Mosque, Connaught Circus.

Figure 7.5 Auliya Mosque between the structure and the street.

Figure 7.6 Parking space.

Kharak Singh Marg (formerly known as Irwin Road). The street connects the General Post Office to Connaught Place. Irwin Road was aligned in such a manner that one of the corners of the mosque lies on the carriageway (Figure 7.7). In order to avoid the structure of the mosque the street would need to bend around the protruding corner, or be laid at a slightly different angle. But instead the street was laid out as an absolutely straight line, with the mosque simply sitting in the way of oncoming traffic. The street loses an entire lane at its narrowest point (Figure 7.8)

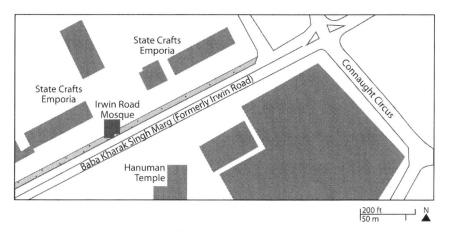

Figure 7.7 Irwin Road Mosque, Baba Kharak Singh Marg.

Figure 7.8 Sidewalk designed to ease the appearance of protrusion.

Figure 7.9 Lost traffic lane reappears.

adjacent to the mosque, creating a traffic bottleneck, and other accident risks as people take evasive measures to avoid driving straight into the mosque. The lane reappears, quite abruptly, on the other side of the structure (Figure 7.9). This part of Lutyens's plan was also executed by Robert Tor Russell.

General observations

Very little effort was made to actively integrate these structures into the design of the project. The old structures seem to stick out from the new superimposed design, like outmoded anomalies. They serve no special design function and look out of place. Worse still, in designing the modern city around these structures, their own requirements were not considered. Very little attention was given to aspects of either aesthetics or social needs of the religious structures left standing. For example, there was no isolation from traffic, no sense of enclosure through landscaping, and no special provisions for activities to flow out naturally into the surrounding areas. Further, due to their awkward location, some of these places of worship have no sense of place, and can only hope to play a truncated role in the community, which, in any case, had long been relocated. In short the planned city was not planned around these uses, but rather let them sit where they were, tolerated but invisible, as symbols of the generosity and civility of the empire, and its tolerance and acceptance of Indian culture and indigenous values. Carl

Nightingale (2012, 2013) analyzes Lutyens's work in New Delhi in the context of planned segregation in the colonies. He argues that

> [t]he plans' broad avenues, looming palaces, and elaborate racial zoning systems were intended to function as arrogant disquisitions on the contrast between the backward splendor of the East and the cutting-edge progressivism of the West.
>
> (Nightingale, 2013)

It appears as though the religious structures were invisible to the designers. These buildings only served as ostentatious displays of 'inclusion' in the most superficial sense. In hindsight, they can be read as strong statements of *exclusion through exception*. Lutyens's own racist and supremacist attitudes are well-documented (King, 1976; Ridley, 2003; Varma, 2010). This oft-cited quote tells much about the 'syndrome' afflicting 'imperial perceptions' in the design of New Delhi as in wider politics (Chakravarty, 1991, 1986).

> The natives do not improve much on acquaintance. Their very low intellects spoil much and I do not think it possible for the Indians and whites to mix freely and naturally. They are very different and even my ultra-wide sympathy with them cannot admit them on the same plane as myself.
>
> (Lutyens, as quoted in King, 1976, p. 238)

One wonders, then, whether Lutyens was referring to rodents when he opined that the old city's walls helped 'protect New Delhi from the rats of Old Delhi' (Lutyens, as quoted in Jain, 1990, p. 74).

Lutyens has his admirers who point to the elegance and sensitivity of his designs. Monica Juneja (2011), for example, not incorrectly, appreciates the avoidance of overtly religious symbols in New Delhi's architecture. But this is where it is important to keep in mind James-Chakraborty's (2014) Foucauldian cautionary note derived from a study of early scholarship on New Delhi: 'the romantic engagement with style suffused with the haze of nostalgia . . . obscured the often very ugly realities of colonialism and its legacy' (p. 2). One must bear in mind the acts of violence that underpin the construction of New Delhi. David Johnson (2010), for example, in an account of the processes of land acquisition in clearing the site for New Delhi describes how communities were uprooted by 'colonial mechanisms of domination and subordination' (p. 91). Analyses of the design of urban spaces that eschew political factors tend to fetishize aesthetics. An abundance of this mode of thinking presents an ongoing challenge to both research and education in the fields of urban planning and architecture.

As with the two sites discussed before, the Irwin Road Mosque reflects the architects' desire to make the colonial capital a fitting monument to the empire's glory, power and permanence, and to make emphatic pronouncements, through design, in support of the modernizing and civilizing influence of the empire. As symbols go – and the construction of New Delhi is rife with symbolism at many levels – one

132 Surajit Chakravarty

might also argue that the practice of isolating religious sites in the middle of New Delhi without engaging with them through design, also reflected the imperial perspective of Indian culture as fundamentally incompatible with modernity. Exotic artifacts were allowed to stand by and witness proper planning, as streets and neighborhoods were laid out all around them, highlighting the stark contrast between native religious practices and the modern urbanism of the empire.

It is axiomatic, however, that Lutyens and his collaborators would interpret Delhi in this manner. But the more relevant part of the production of informality lies in the transfer of institutions from British to independent India. Even after independence, and in almost seven decades since, Delhi has not attempted to review the flaws of imperial architecture and planning, and to amend the city according to the needs of its residents. Instead, assuming a sanctimonious outlook towards Lutyens's Delhi, administration has normalized the irrational and outmoded.

Exceptional spaces, existential issues: religious structures after independence

To be clear, the intent here is not to blame the colonial period for today's conditions of informality. The objective, rather, is to conceptualize informality as the exercise of power to create exceptional conditions towards political ends. This is equally possible in any kind of state.

Figure 7.10 shows a schematic that summarizes the state's responses to planning near religious monuments and places of worship. The image on the left shows the interpretation of the colonial government. The monument (shown as a square) crosses over the edge of the street and on to the carriageway, directly in

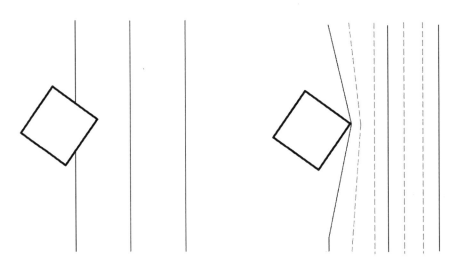

Figure 7.10 Colonial (left) and post-independence (right) interpretations of protecting religious structures.

Religious structures on traffic lanes 133

the way of moving traffic. As discussed above, imperial architects allowed such configurations in their designs for specific symbolic purposes to do with the colonial leitmotif. The image on the right shows how the independent Indian state responded to planning concerns on the same sites. To begin with the sites were left untouched for decades. Relatively recent (post-liberalization) sensitivities regarding city image, branding and marketing, as part of broader strategies of the neoliberal urbanism, brought new attention to old problems. The planners then proceeded to cover up the aberrations through facile design interventions, trying to smooth the edges (quite literally) and manufacture an appearance of control to replace the image of ineffectual administration.

Rather than make the requisite financial and political investment to bend the straight imperial boulevards, Delhi tried to mould the sidewalks in such a manner that the structures protruding on the carriageway might *appear* to be minor misalignments. Further, as the city continued to grow, many more religious structures (mosques *and* temples) found themselves on the carriageway. As streets were widened, these religious structures were allowed to occupy parts of the street, obstructing traffic and adding to the chaos on the street. Figure 7.11 shows another Hindu temple located well in front of the line where adjacent properties end, and effectively on the carriageway. There is not even a proper sidewalk between the temple and the speeding trucks. Traffic bottlenecks are common at this spot because three lanes worth of traffic is forced to pass through two lanes of

Figure 7.11 Temple on carriageway creates traffic bottleneck.

space in front of the temple. Figure 7.12 shows another similar situation. Here we can see the edge of a sidewalk skirting around the temple structure, and a white line clearly marking the space of traffic. Once again, we see the street becoming narrow and then wider. Figure 7.13 shows a Muslim shrine, again located on the street, in such a manner that approaching drivers are forced to merge into a single lane of traffic.

What does this evolution in the treatment of Delhi's religious structures tell us about the idea of informality? The state's approach to this ordinary issue on mundane urban sites reveals a kernel of postcolonial governmentality. The state is able neither to take a stance overturning pre-independence practices, nor to appropriately define the needs of the contemporary city. Caught between the weight of history, the challenges of everyday urban management, and the aspirations of 'world city' status, the state clumsily muddles through its compromises, cobbling together solutions that keep the city moving, if only just. In this case the politics of informality involves a wide range of constraints and motivations, not least path dependence, lack of resources, desire and compromise.

Menon (2000) astutely points out that planners have not been able to shake 'the "aura" of Delhi' (p. 147). For Menon, Lutyens's

> design for the new capital was deeply inflected with intimations of its imperial glory . . . After independence, continuing the pursuit of these urban

Figure 7.12 Lost lane of traffic opens up after temple structure.

Figure 7.13 Shrine on carriageway, one lane lost.

and architectural intentions became an article of faith with the planners of Delhi.

(Menon, 2000, p. 147)

Scholarship and practice have both not done enough in Delhi to create a critical distance with regards to the city's spaces. In a sense, the act of preserving places of worship, to respect religious sentiment, is certainly not an undesirable or unjust objective. The practice of preservation in a manner that it becomes a nuisance to everyday public interest illustrates the challenges of governance in postcolonial cities, in particular administering spaces and practices that exist in between different rationalities and definitions of normal.

Informality as disjuncture and exception

The character of informality is path dependent. AlSayyad argues that 'the urban informal sector is not a new or a novel phenomenon. Rather it becomes important with the rise and maturity of a formal sector' (AlSayyad and Roy, 2004, p. 5). It follows, then, that an analysis of the formal sector is essential for fully comprehending that which falls outside it. Informal settlements, informal economic activities, or informal labour practices, are contingent outcomes that depend on various factors, not least of which is how the state uses exceptional conditions.

136 *Surajit Chakravarty*

As polities transition from subject colonies to independent-modernist nations (with either religious or secular leanings), to networked-neoliberal states, informality becomes increasingly layered with meaning. It is not appropriate (for both epistemological and policy purposes) to consider all spaces and practices thought of as 'informal' as part of a single group of less-than-hundred-per cent-legal activities, far less so in a globally uniform sense.

The treatment of religious structures on Delhi's streets indicates that informality is not simply a condition of 'the informals' (to borrow a term used before by De Soto in 1989). Asef Bayat (1997, 2000) critiques various one-dimensional readings of informality.

> Although the prevailing perspectives (survival strategy, urban social movements and everyday resistance) provide useful angles to view the activism of the urban subaltern, they do, however, suffer from some major drawbacks. The latter are reflected in the essentialism of the "passive poor", reductionism of the "surviving poor", Latino-centrism of the "political poor" and conceptual perplexity of "resistance literature".
>
> (Bayat, 2000, p. 553)

Varley (2013) also critiques 'heroic' interpretations of informality, including those that celebrate and (arguably) to some extent romanticize notions such as 'community', 'resistance', 'transgression', 'architectural existentialism', 'improvisation', and 'ecological virtues' (p. 91). In light of this critique of the scholarship on the agency of the informals, and in view of the findings from this study, it would be useful to understand informality as a set of practices that exist outside those structures and institutions that have been accorded legitimacy by the state, though not necessarily in contravention of laws and regulations.

What is deemed legitimate depends on what the state is able to control, and sees value in controlling. If we work with this definition, then new avenues open up for investigating the politics of informality. Why and how do some activities – economic, social, architectural, or of any other kind – come to be recognized as formal while others remain informal? This approach calls into question existing structures of formality, rather than viewing informality as the problem. It also lays explanatory emphasis on the disjunctures, which can be caused as easily by state action as by the agency of 'the informals'.

Daniela Fabricius (2008) argues that informality is 'the urbanity that takes place between the ruins of the Modernist city and the entropic expanses of the postmodern city' (p. 8).Vanessa Watson (2009) considers informality a largely postcolonial phenomenon.

> [T]he fact remains that in most of these regions the planning systems in place have been either inherited from previous colonial governments or have been adopted from Northern contexts to suit particular local political and ideological ends. The need for planning systems to be pro-poor and inclusive has therefore not been given much consideration.
>
> (Watson, 2009, p. 2260)

Varley (2013) locates the disjuncture farther back. '[T]he barrios do not lack form. Their form should be understood, rather, as defying the forms of both the colonial city and the deluded utopia of modern urban planning' (Varley, 2013, p. 89). Citing Chatterjee (2006), Rao (2006) argues that

> [i]llegality and informality thus tug at the normative roots of the state, leading to an arena charged with violence of and toward the governed. These forms of violence are staged around the paternalistic welfare policies of the state designed to placate and manage populations whose civic, political and social rights are patently out of sync.
>
> (p. 680)

New conceptions of sustainable cities will have to engage with the critique of 'violence towards the governed' (Rao, 2006, p. 680) and find suitable responses. It would help to reorient our perspective on informality. For Hernandez and Kellett (2010), 'the term formal represents a spatial abstraction created in order to disavow other forms of space conceived within or outside it' (p. 2). It leads to a split in the society and space creating an appearance of 'parallel realities' (Simone, 2001) or distinct temporalities (Mehrotra, 2010). Although these formulations approach the issue from different perspectives, they seem to agree fundamentally that informality is a kind of mismatch, break or gap between plans and realities of everyday life, particularly those of different periods. *In a more abstract sense, informality is a disjuncture between regimes of regulation and realities of everyday life.* In this light, it is problematic to continue thinking of informality as the lack of formality. Such an approach tends to fetishize socially constructed regimes of 'formality' as natural, logical and inevitable. An important departure offered by this perspective is that it holds responsible, at least partially, structural flaws for the proliferation of informal conditions.

It would be useful, then, to conceptualize informality as a disjuncture in the norms of successive governance strategies (or paradigms, or ideologies). Informality is a mismatch between pre-existing spaces and practices, and overlaid institutions representing successive dominant ideologies (imperialism, modernism, capitalism, nationalism etc.). In other words, informality is produced when systems and institutions designed to sustain any given ideology, are unable to integrate some of the spaces and practices on which they are overlaid. Informality is the failure of precepts of formality to engage and integrate that which is alien.

'Exception' is particularly potent for analyzing informality and its relationship with sustainability. Conceptually, exception may not only be caused by structural flaws, but also it might be created strategically, as has been argued by Ananya Roy (2011, 2009). According to Roy, the neoliberal state deliberately 'unmaps' territories so that it can derive political value, as needed, from conditions of both legality and illegality. Formality of this kind, created by deliberate state in/action could be far more hurtful to public interest, particularly those living at the margins of state-sanctioned formality.

In fact, some would argue that 'exception' potentially can become a permanent condition, which makes it easier to control spaces and communities. Ali

138 *Surajit Chakravarty*

(2010), in the context of citizenship regimes, calls this condition 'permanent impermanence'. For Yiftachel '[g]ray spaces are neither integrated nor eliminated, forming pseudo-permanent margins of today's urban regions, which exist partially outside the gaze of state authorities and city plans' (2009, p. 243). Roy (2009) and Yiftachel (2009) concur on the increasingly 'permanent' nature of the informal conditions under neoliberal governance regimes, which sharply contradicts common official narratives of poverty alleviation and economic mobility. This calls into question how we interpret and analyze narratives of sustainable development.

The condition of exception is the result of the negotiations between the actions of the state and the agency of people at the margins of the legalities of housing and labor. There can be multiple political motivations behind exceptional conditions, and in the ways in which these conditions are imagined, built, and hidden. These motivations depend on the needs of the state, and are not necessarily confined to colonial or postcolonial governments. As noted above, the neoliberal state has developed efficient mechanism with which to extract value from informality, but informality cannot be assumed to begin with neoliberalism. Informality, in diverse forms, existed well before the neoliberal state. The latest set of machinations of the state, based on the most recent dominant ideology, must not preclude other stories and representations of the phenomenon of informality.

Being able to exist in a state of exception is a reflection of power, just as being forced to exist in a state of exception could be a reflection of its lack. In the Indian polity, religious beliefs and practices of large numbers of constituents, invests places of worship with tremendous power, and thus with the ability to exist in a state of exception. It is not merely that these places are 'unplanned' (for political profit), or that the state is incapable of planning them. These places reflect power relations and contestations in the Indian secular democratic system, as they did as special sites under the protection of the British Empire in earlier times.

The present study of religious structures on New Delhi's streets indicates that both formality and informality are constructed with the support of state designation and implementation. To an extent the agency of those at the margins of formality is able to influence actual outcomes. Informality, however, is not made only by 'the informals', but rather produced by complex negotiation between agents and subjects of the governing ideology.

Concluding comments

It would be apposite to conclude with a brief discussion regarding avenues for further research. Studying informality as a separate, self-contained, homogenous and globally uniform phenomenon is fraught with danger. As Ananya Roy (AlSayyad and Roy, 2004) warns us, imagining informality as a 'mode' or archetype implies a degree of 'coherence' (p. 5), whereas 'the organizing divide is not so much that between formality and informality as the differentiation that exists within informality – that which marks off different types of informal accumulation and informal politics' (p. 5). To liberate informality epistemologically it is important to challenge and problematize the 'formal' and examine its production and evolution. Such analyses would facilitate a more nuanced and robust understanding of other instances and kinds of informality (not least those related to labor, industrial production, retail trade and housing).

Gautam Bhan (2013) agrees that planning in Delhi 'produces and regulates illegality' (p. 59). For Bhan, however, there is no option but to allow plans, regardless of their failures, to mediate the governance of space. These plans must become the sites for political contest and citizenship claims. In order to do so, however, future scholarship and professional practice must also address Dipesh Chakrabarty's critique of scholarship in India as suffering from a 'paralysis of imagination' (2004, p. 25), an assessment which applies to urban planning and architecture just as much as it does to history or social science (not least because of the vast overlaps between the fields).

> The problem is . . . that we do not have analytic categories in our aggressively secular academic discourse that do justice to the real, everyday, and multiple connections that we have to what we, in becoming modern, have come to see as nonrational.
>
> (Chakrabarty, 2004, p. 26)

Rather than consider informality a poorer version of formality, there is an urgent need to disassemble edifices of meaning, and indeed of perspectives, that are no more than lingering vestiges of colonialism. These have been further invested with meaning, since independence, by the modernist utopianism of the developmental state, and the more recent politics of neoliberal growth machines. Modernity remains an incomplete project because of the State's uncritical reliance on borrowed indicators and signifiers of modernity. Future scholarship on informality, and more generally on the production of space (in Lefebvre's sense), must strive to conceptualize urbanism and everyday life using terms of reference that are grounded in local realities.

This chapter has used religion mainly as a proxy for exploring and developing the concept of informality. But the study also shows how spatial meanings and manifestations of religion are serious planning issues in pluralistic multicultural societies. Contested religious spaces in today's cities reveal anxieties of the state. The way to find balance and sustainable practice is through dialogue and communication. Covering up matters (literally, at times, as discussed in this chapter) can only lead to administration disconnected from everyday life.

References

Archaeological Survey of India Bengaluru Circle. (2011). Legislations. Accessed on March 15, 2014, from http://asibengalurucircle.org/legislations.html

Ali, S. (2010). Permanent impermanence. *Contexts* (Spring), 26–31.

AlSayyad, N. (2004). Urbanism as a "new" way of life. In Roy, A. and AlSayyad, N. (Eds.) *Urban Informality: Transnational Perspectives from the Middle East, Latin America, and South Asia* (pp. 7–30). Oxford: Lexington Books.

140 *Surajit Chakravarty*

AlSayyad, N. and Roy, A (2004). *Prologue/Dialogue*. In Roy, A. and AlSayyad, N. (Eds.) *Urban Informality: Transnational Perspectives from the Middle East, Latin America, and South Asia* (pp. 1–6). Oxford: Lexington Books.

Bayat, A. (1997). Un-civil society: The politics of the 'informal people'. *Third World Quarterly, 18*(1), 53–72.

Bayat, A. (2000). From 'dangerous classes' to 'quiet rebels': Politics of the urban subaltern in the global south. *International Sociology, 15*(3), 533–556.

Bhan, G. (2013). Planned illegalities. *Economic & Political Weekly, 48*(24), 59–70.

Briassoulis, H. (1999). Sustainable Development and the Informal Sector: An Uneasy Relationship? *Journal of Environment and Development, 8*(3), 213–237.

Briassoulis, H. (2001). Sustainable development – The formal or informal way? *Environment and Policy, 29*, 73–99.

Central Public Works Department. (2013). *Handbook of Conservation of Heritage Buildings*. Accessed on March 15, 2014, from http://cpwd.gov.in/Publication/ConservationHertBuildings.pdf

Chakravarty, S. (1986). Architecture and politics in the construction of New Delhi. *Architecture + Design, 11*(2), 76–93.

Chakravarty, S. (1991). *The Raj Syndrome: A Study in Imperial Perceptions*. New Delhi: Penguin Books.

Chakrabarty, D. (2004). *Habitations of Modernity: Essays in the Wake of Subaltern Studies*. Chicago: University of Chicago Press.

Chatterjee, P. (2006), *The Politics of the Governed: Reflections On Popular Politics in Most of the World*. New York: Columbia University Press.

Christopher, A.J. (1988). 'Divide and Rule': The Impress of British Separation Policies. *Area*, 233–240.

De Soto, H. (1989). The informals pose an answer to Marx. *Washington Quarterly, 12*(1), 165–172.

Fabricius, D. (2008). Resisting representation: The informal geographies of Rio de Janeiro. *Harvard Design Magazine, 28*(Spring/Summer), 4–17.

Gupta, N. (1971). Military security and urban development: A case study of Delhi 1857–1912. *Modern Asian Studies, 5*(1), 61–77.

Hart, K. (1973). Informal income opportunities and urban employment in Ghana. *Journal of Modern African Studies 11*, 61–89.

Hart, K. (2008) 'Between Bureaucracy and the People: A political history of informality', DIIS Working Paper no 2008/27, Copenhagen: Danish Institute for International Studies.

Hart, K. (2009). On the informal economy: The political history of an ethnographic concept. *Working papers CEB, 9*.

Helmke, G. and Levitsky, S. (2004). Informal institutions and comparative politics: A research agenda. *Perspectives on Politics, 2*(4), 725–740.

Hernández, F. and Kellett, P. (2010). Introduction: Reimagining the informal in Latin America. In Hernández, F., Kellett, P. W. and Allen, L. K. (Eds.), *Rethinking the Informal City: Critical Perspectives from Latin America* (Vol. 11, pp. 1–22).

Hosagrahar, J. (2005). *Indigenous Modernities: Negotiating Architecture and Urbanism*. New York: Psychology Press.

Jain, A.K. (1990). *The Making of a Metropolis: Planning and Growth of Delhi*. New Delhi: National Book Organization.

James-Chakraborty, K. (2014). Beyond postcolonialism: New directions for the history of nonwestern architecture. *Frontiers of Architectural Research, 3*(1), 1–9.

Johnson, D. A. (2010). Land acquisition, landlessness, and the building of New Delhi. *Radical History Review*, *2010*(108), 91–116.

Juneja, M. (2011). Global Art History and the 'Burden of Representation'. In Belting, H., Birken, J. and Buddensieg, A. (Eds.), *Global Studies: Mapping Contemporary Art and Culture* (pp. 274–297). Stuttgart: Hatje Cantz.

Kamete, A. Y. (2013). On handling urban informality in southern Africa. *Geografiska Annaler: Series B, Human Geography*, *95*(1), 17–31.

Khandekar, N. (2012). A spot of shining white. *Hindustan Times*. November 18. Accessed from www.hindustantimes.com/india-news/newdelhi/a-spot-of-shining-white/article1–960771.aspx on January 10, 2014.

King, A. D. (1976). *Colonial Urban Development: Culture, Social Power and Environment* (p. 180). London: Routledge & Kegan Paul.

Kudva, N. (2009). The everyday and the episodic: The spatial and political impacts of urban informality. *Environment and Planning A*, *41*(7), 1614–1628.

Maloney, W. F. (2004). Informality revisited. *World Development*, *32*(7), 1159–1178.

Mehrotra, R. (2010). Foreword. In Hernández, F., Kellett, P. W. and Allen, L. K. (Eds.), *Rethinking the Informal City: Critical Perspectives from Latin America* (Vol. 11, pp. xi–xvi). London: Berghahn Books.

Menon, A. G. K. (2000). The contemporary architecture of Delhi: The role of the state as middleman. In Dupont, V., Tarlo, E. and Vidal, D. (Eds.), *Delhi: Urban Space and Human Destinies*. New Delhi: Manohar.

Mitra, A. (2014). Urban informal sector in India. *Yojana*, October. Special Issue: Informal Sector, 4–7.

Nightingale, C. H. (2012). *Segregation: A Global History of Divided Cities*. Chicago: University of Chicago Press.

Nightingale, C. H. (2013). The Segregation Paradoxes. Mas Context, Issue 17, Spring. Retrieved September 15, 2014, from www.mascontext.com/issues/17-boundary-spring-13/the-segregation-paradoxes/.

Rao, V. (2006). Slum as theory: The South/Asian city and globalization. *International Journal of Urban and Regional Research*, *30*(1), 225–232.

Ridley, J. (2003). *Edwin Lutyens: His Life, His Wife, His Work*. London: Pimlico/ Random House.

Roberts, N. E. (2013). Dividing Jerusalem: British urban planning in the Holy City. *Journal of Palestine Studies*, *42*(4), 7–26.

Roy, A. (2009). Why India cannot plan its cities: Informality, insurgence and the idiom of urbanization. *Planning Theory*, *8*(1), 76–87.

Roy, A. (2011). Slumdog cities: Rethinking subaltern urbanism. *International Journal of Urban and Regional Research*, *35*(2), 223–238.

Roy, A. and AlSayyad, N. (Eds.). (2004). *Urban Informality: Transnational Perspectives from the Middle East, Latin America, and South Asia*. Oxford: Lexington Books.

Sanyal, B. (1991). Organizing the self-employed: The politics of the urban informal sector. *International Labour Review*, *130*(1), 39–56.

Sengupta, I. (2013). A Conservation Code for the Colony: John Marshall's Conservation Manual and Monument Preservation Between India and Europe. In Falser, M. and Juneja, M. (Eds.), *'Archaeologizing' Heritage? Transcultural Research – Heidelberg Studies on Asia and Europe in a Global Context*. Berlin Heidelberg: Springer-Verlag.

Sharma, R. A. and Tewari, M. (2012). *Delhi: Biography of a City*. Aakar Books: Delhi.

Simone, A. (2001). Between ghetto and globe: Remaking urban life in Africa. In Tostensen, A., Tvedten, I. and Vaa, M. (Eds.), *Associational Life in African Cities: Popular Responses to the Urban Crisis*. Nordiska Afrikainstitutet: Stockholm.

142 *Surajit Chakravarty*

Sindzingre, A. (2006). The relevance of the concepts of formality and informality: A theoretical appraisal. *Linking the Formal and Informal Economy: Concepts and Policies* (pp. 58–74). Oxford University Press, Oxford. Retrieved from www.oecd.org/dac/governance-development/37791314.pdf

Varley, A. (2013). Postcolonialising informality? *N-AERUS XI: Urban Knowledge in Cities of the South*.

Varma, P.K. (2010). *Becoming Indian: The Unfinished Revolution of Culture and Identity*. New Delhi: Penguin Books India.

Watson, V. (2009). Seeing from the South: Refocusing urban planning on the globe's central urban issues. *Urban Studies*, *46*(11), 2259–2275.

Yeo, S.J. and Heng, C.K. (2014). An (extra)ordinary night out: urban informality, social sustainability and the night-time economy. *Urban Studies*, *51*(4), 712–726.

Yiftachel, O. (2009). Critical theory and 'gray space': Mobilization of the colonized. *City*, *13*(2–3), 240–256.

8 Animals and urban informality in sacred spaces

Bull-calf trafficking in Simhachalam Temple, Visakhapatnam

Yamini Narayanan

The deep red pottu[1] smeared across the forehead of the male calf had started to bleed in the rain, appearing as a premonition of a dark gash slicing his face. He stood still, patiently with three other baby males at the foot of the 1000 steps that mark the ascent to the Simhachalam Temple in Visakhapatnam city, Andhra Pradesh. Simhachalam is the second most venerated Hindu temple in the state after the Tirumala Tirupathi Devasthanam, which in turn is regarded as one of the holiest Hindu sites in the world. Each calf was decorated with a garland of drenched flowers and holy basil or glittery red ribbons. Following possibly a painfully squashed ride in the backseat of an auto-rickshaw or even a long trek from a nearby village in the peri-urban conurbation of Visakhapatnam, the baby male calves had been, briefly gods, before being donated by their owners to Simhachalam. Ribs protruded painfully from the ribcage of each calf. I reached out to rub one calf's back to find it sodden with rainwater. I did not know that calfskin could soak up wetness that heavily.

There was not a trough of water or a blade of hay nearby; three of the calves fell hungrily upon a large branch of ripe bananas I offered. One small calf hung back in misery refusing even to smell the fruit. He caught scent of my extended hand and desperately suckled it for a couple of minutes before turning his small head away in disappointment; he did not even yet have teeth. A young man who had accompanied me from a local animal shelter gently prised open the baby's mouth and managed to force in three mashed bananas. This calf at least was almost certain to die slowly from heartbreak and starvation. It was only nine in the morning, and these calves would be joined by more donated male calves through the day, up to even 200 calves a day on auspicious occasions. At the end of each day, an independent animal rescue team with a large transfer bus will take the calves away to few acres of greenery in the outskirts of Visakhapatnam where they will join close to 1200 such other rescued cattle, the numbers increasingly daily. Up to 40 per cent of the youngest babies will die without their mother's milk and body warmth, both essential to the survival of young cattle. These are the 'lucky' male calves. Four years ago, they would have been sold en masse by the Simhachalam Temple on a weekly basis to slaughterhouses in Visakhapatnam, owned by Hindus as well as Muslims for a generous profit to the temple.

(Field notes, November 2014)

Introduction

The various states of informality and the challenges in managing informal growth in Indian and other South Asian cities substantially complicate the task

144   Yamini Narayanan

of planning 'sustainable cities' for urban development authorities. Most of the growth in the developing nations of South Asia takes the form of various states of informal growth and development, blurring and complicating the lines between formal and informal, legal and illegal, and black and white. Informal development in its manifestations in the more traditional sense of unorganised labour (Davis 2006), the destabilisation of notions of real estate and property ownership (Cruz 2007) as well as Ananya Roy's (2005) framing of the informal as a conscious, strategic, even a 'planned' product of formal planning is indeed the face of urban growth itself in India. Developing countries depend on the large scale of the informal in their cities to sustain high growth rates and rapid neoliberal development. Many of the tensions of informality revolve around issues of oppression, exploitation and powerlessness of the poor subaltern groups in the city, and their struggles to claim agency and rights to livelihoods and self-determination through subverting formal norms of claiming space.

Religion plays a crucial role in the neoliberal growth meta-narrative of developing nations. Neoliberal development, especially in developing nations almost always occurs at the intersection of religion and devastating violence (Bulankulame 2013). Religion is utilised as a means of dismantling democratic governance and equitable social structures, and privileging instead, intensive, large-scale – and violent – exploitation of labour and natural resources. Religion can enable a 'state of exception', which condition is required to sanction violence on the labour and bodily resources of the poor, women, nonhuman animals and natural resources (Crockett 2014). Informality in developing cities intersect closely with religion in various forms (Davis 2006) and can be a means of oppression, as well as agency for subaltern groups who may utilise religion for assertion strategies in identity politics in claiming spaces (like slums) otherwise deemed unregulated (Bhatewara and Bradley 2013).

In all cases, informality hitherto has unquestioningly referred to activities, conflicts, labour resources and tensions relating to human citizens of cities. However cities are spaces of distinct micro-climates with immense biodiversity with a wide range of nonhuman animal users occupying and claiming habitats. In addition to urban wildlife, city spaces are utilised for the farming, transportation and slaughter of several domesticated animals for human consumption. Many domesticated animals in Indian cities such as cattle are also regarded as sacred icons in the dominant Hindu worldview.

In this chapter, I introduce a new paradigm of informality that scrutinises the ways in which animal citizens occupy, utilise and are utilised in cities. I suggest that nonhuman animals occupy spaces of informality in the city as they are not recognised as political entities with agency and capacity to resist, and the right to self-determination. In particular, I focus on cattle, a meta-animal where every part of their bodies is reduced as products of consumption. Cattle are a common sight in Indian cities, frequently scavenging toxic urban waste for their survival before they are illegally slaughtered in India or transported abroad for killing. India is as one of the world's largest suppliers of dairy, beef and leather. Cows and bulls in particular are simultaneously vital capital commodities, large-scale utilisers of arable land, methane emitters and sacred Hindu icons, standing for *dharma* or righteousness itself.

I use the case of the practice of male calf donation to the iconic Simhachalam temple in Visakhapatnam city in Andhra Pradesh state in India to show that urban governance in Indian cities collaborate with Hindu religious spaces, sites and representatives to support the informality that enables the violence-ridden trafficking and slaughter of unwanted male calves. Formal urban development authorities play a crucial role in the brutalisation of cattle, specifically bull-calves, the globally acknowledged 'waste product' of the dairy industry. In India, slaughter of cows and bulls is largely prohibited by laws inspired by Hindu religion. However for neoliberal capitalism to continue its path of profit accumulation through the commodification of cattle, I argue that Hindu religion itself is made complicit in cattle slaughter.

Religion as well as neoliberalism tend to deploy animals for strikingly similar purposes: human identity construction; community building through the use of animal symbols; mobilisation and assertion of power; and prominently of course, the use of animals' bodies for consumption. Formal urban development, I suggest, is one major actor in lubricating the profitable union between religion and neoliberalism by overtly as well as covertly providing logistical support and/or turning a blind eye to illegal spatial and mobility practices that involve animals. Sustainable development, an efficiency-driven development paradigm that ostensibly stands for equity is fundamentally anthropocentric, and does not extend its scope across species. If sustainable development planning in Indian and other South Asian cities does not address the admittedly overwhelming challenge of formal development's role in supporting the oppressive forms of informality, it risks being complicit in perpetuating, rather than eliminating violence, inequality and suffering.

The example of the trafficking and slaughter of the Simhachalam bull-calves using religious 'donations' to temples as a smokescreen illustrates how religion and urban planning intersect to enable animal cruelty and the violence done to them, to support neoliberal growth for humans. The practice of male calf donations to Hindu and even Jain and Buddhist temples serve as one of the largest concealments for the violence of the dairy, veal and leather industries in India. India is the world's largest producer of milk, and almost singlehandedly holds up the cattle agri-business (Narayanan 2015b). In India, dairy rather than beef or any other cattle product is directly linked to the slaughter of cattle (Narayanan 2015b). Cities throughout India and their conurbations are implicit in providing the transportation infrastructure, routes and spaces necessary for the transportation and slaughter of animals. Religious and secular planning dimensions dovetail around the ethical concerns on the utilisation of cattle, where they may both mutually reinforce humane or inhumane treatment of domesticated animals in Indian cities. Though cities and urban governance cannot be held solely responsible for cruelty shown to bull-calves unwanted for dairy, they nonetheless play a critical role in animal abuse – and as this chapter argues, can instead choose to strengthen animal protection in urban spaces.

146 *Yamini Narayanan*

The planned future trajectory of Visakhapatnam's development is in stark contrast to its inherited precolonial histories and rituals. Visakhapatnam is Andhra Pradesh state's second largest city with a population of almost two million (Census of India 2011). More than 44 per cent of households of the city are located in slums (UNEP 2014), making the ambit of informality nearly equal to formal development of Visakhapatnam. In early 2015, Visakhapatnam was among the 100 cities selected by the Prime Minister's office to be conceptualised and planned as a 'Smart City', wherein real-time data will manage urban problems that have been conceptualised as sustainability issues such as traffic and transportation (Newman and Kenworthy 1999), sanitation and waste-management, and safety (Narayanan 2012). Advanced communications technologies are pivotal in this project, and the models of a 'Smart City' are the modern metropolises of Singapore, Hong Kong and Dubai. These visions of a smart, sustainable city do not even consider nonhuman citizens, whose welfare risks further neglect as the city indeed grows through their exploitation.

The chapter seeks to understand the bull-calves as objects of informality as well as located in spaces of informality. The motivations for calf-donations are beyond the purview of this chapter. As such, the chapter has sought material and views from 'expert' respondents to understand the issue, in other words, interviewees who have professional insight into the intricacies of this issue, namely, animal activists and urban planning officials from the Greater Visakapatnam Municipal Corporation (GVMC) and the Visakapatnam Urban Development Authority (VUDA).

The chapter is structured as follows: in the next section, I discuss the religious profiling of the cow and the bull in Hinduism, which provides a useful context to understanding how the male progeny of these sacred animals are regarded. In the third section, I analyse the intersections of religion as a component of informality, and sustainable development as a component of formality in enabling animal exploitation for neoliberal growth. In the final analysis, I argue that planning inclusive, safe cities for animals, scrutinising the informal spaces they occupy in the city and their invisibility in formal planning frameworks is vital to conceptualising of sustainable cities in India, and religion is a vital concept in framing this analysis.

Cattle as pillars of Hindu civilisation

Of all animals and birds that have held divine statuses historically and currently, cattle, especially the cow and the bull in native Indian *zebu* breeds arguably occupy the most definitively sacred position. The religious deification of the cow, and at the same time, the commodification of her male child as dispensable and a 'waste' are starkly at odds with the respect and love that is to be accorded to Mother Cow. Mahatma Gandhi took the view that cow protection stands for the 'protection of the whole dumb creation of God'. 'Cow protection is . . . not about protecting *only* the cow' but is indeed a trans-species ethic (Narayanan 2015b); certainly it includes the young of cattle.

Animals and urban informality 147

To provide a context for the brutalisation of young male cattle, I highlight three dimensions to the status of the adult cow and to some extent the bull: one, the Hindu mythological status of the cow/bull as the symbol of human morality. Two, I examine the communalisation of the cow as sacred as a way of right-wing Hindu assertion politics, and the othering of Muslims/low-caste Hindus. This social othering is also reflected spatially. Illegal cattle slaughterhouses which vastly outnumber authorised abbatoirs by the thousands in every Indian city, tend to be located in poor Muslim and low-caste Hindu ghettoes. Last, I discuss the spurt in animal activism that emphasise the welfare and rights of cattle regardless of their religious significance to any community.

The cow is renowned for her sacred status in Hinduism though the early Vedic references to the cow are not in purely sacralised terms; the early Vedas discuss the practical utility of the cow and other cattle in agriculture. Cow slaughter in *yajnas* (sacrifices) are also discussed in the early Vedic texts, which link cow sacrifice to the smooth running of the universe itself. Korom (2000) writes that the 'One thing that we can discern from the portrayal of the cow during this period is that she was identified with the totality of the universe'. Lord Krishna equates the cow and/or the bull to the Universe itself in the *Bhagvad Gita,* one of the central texts of Hinduism. He further pronounces that the relationship between the cosmic cow/bull and the Universe is centrally dependent on dharma or human morality. Dharma can also be variously understood as 'duty', 'law', 'righteous conduct', 'justice', or 'ethics' (Flood 1996: 52). This dharmic relationship between the cow and the human is further clarified in a temporal context. The Hindu concept of time is understood to be cyclical (as opposed to linear) with several Mahayugas (or great time cycles), each containing four smaller rotating time-cycles viz., (1) Satya yuga or the Age of Truth/Golden Age; (2) Treta Yuga or the Silver age; (3) Dvapura Yuga (Bronze age); and (4) Kali Yuga or the Dark Age.

During the progress through these eras, dharma is symbolised by the bull standing initially on four legs implanted on all four corners of the Universe. The cosmic bull of dharma loses a foot in each epoch as human morality is increasingly lost until he is left standing on just one foot in the last Age of Kali. The Lord predicts the breakdown of dharma or righteousness/morality/ethical duty among humanity in the Dark Age, which most Hindus believe currently is in progress. After the eventual collapse of the bull towards the end of the Kali Yuga, the Lord in his final avatar as Kalki comes to destroy the world, in order to make way for a new and morally renewed world order, and the start of the next cycle of a great time-cycle. The bull and the cow epitomise the suffering of cattle and all animals because of the breakdown in human morality.

However it was Mahatma Gandhi's invocation of the cow (who he termed 'a poem of pity') as a symbol of non-violence, and his appeal for vegetarianism and cow-protection as sacred Hindu duties, that the sacred status of the cow was well and truly cemented. The cow, for Gandhi, served as a meta-narrative for compassion, mercy and pity towards all life forms, including and especially non-humans which were incapable of representing for mercy and justice. For Hindus and

148 *Yamini Narayanan*

indeed for all humans, he regarded cow-protection as an inviolable duty, which problematic task he acknowledges.

The historical status of the cow in India combined with Gandhi's non-violence reinforced the case for a total prohibition on cow-slaughter, even as notably, Gandhi himself was against enforced prohibition. His reason however was his concern for the consequences of Hindu fundamentalist interpretations of cow-protection for non-Hindus, especially the Muslims. He was alarmed that labelling beef consumption an offensive 'Muslim' act and by extension, a marker of Muslim identity would actually pose a greater risk to the cow. While Gandhi expresses his anguish at cow slaughter and maintained that he could not yield his stand on the matter, he nonetheless was clear that by no means did the ethic of cow-protection morally empower Hindus to impose their will on the Muslims or other consumers of meat. Cattle continue to be at the heart of human identity politics of power and privilege as the slaughter prohibition in India is seen as a manipulation of a Hindu high-caste ethic imposed on low-caste Hindus as well as Muslims.

Indeed, Maharashatra and Haryana states' recent criminalising of beef clearly points to communal prejudices rather than cattle welfare, as dairy is a greater cause of cattle slaughter in India than beef (Narayanan 2015b). The dairy industry supports the veal industry and the cruelty meted out to baby male calves. Hindus are among the highest consumers of dairy in India as milk and ghee are used for eating as well as in religious rituals. Shiva temples in Jaipur city alone for instance, use several million litres of milk annually to bathe their idols (Sharma 2013). The Hindu right's emphatic link of beef rather than dairy with cow slaughter demonstrates that the political status of the cow as sacred in Hinduism, and the likening of cow's milk to mother's milk ultimately means that human identity politics rather than animal welfare in its own right centres around the holy status of the cow.

These social and sectarian tensions are also enacted spatially. Illegal cattle slaughterhouses of various sizes and capacities can generally be found throughout Indian cities but tend to be concentrated around poor Muslim areas and ghettoes (Contractor 2012; Miller 2010) and spaces of informal growth such as shantytowns. The Dharavi slum settlement in Mumbai is a stark example of low-caste Hindu and Muslim spatialities that contain slaughterhouses and tanneries. Chigateri (2008) is concerned that cow protection, based substantially on upper-caste notions of social purity/pollution can indeed intensify violence and 'injustice' against low-caste Hindus such as the Dalits or the former untouchables who work directly in the tanning industry.

In more recent times, cattle welfare has surfaced as explicitly an animal rights issue above all else, regardless of religious, caste, economic, political or other implications. In an article titled *The Force of Falsity*, animal activist Amit Chaudhery (2014), the president of People for Animals-Gurgaon rejects the objections of Muslim and low-caste Hindus on their 'right' to slaughter cows, and launched a strong attack on the framing of the cow-slaughter prohibition as 'nutritional necessity', 'religious freedom' and the undermining of 'personal liberty'. Emphasising the cow slaughter cannot be sanctioned for appeasement of any religious

Animals and urban informality   149

group, nor cattle made a sacrifice in negotiating Hindu–Muslim relations, Chaudhery (2014) provides graphic descriptions of the torture meted to bull calves in particular during transport and slaughter to make a case against cattle trafficking:

> At birth all calves are separated from the mother and allowed just enough milk to survive if they are female and none if they be male. Enterprising cowherds sever the heads of calves and tie them just near the rump of the cow to create the illusion of her calf as she turns to watch while they milk the udders. The *pashu melas* [cattle fairs] at Fatehabad, near Hissar in Haryana and Sonpur in Bihar among several other places present this common and sadly acceptable sight. In fact men ply the severed heads, renting them out by the hour. Between garbage, polythene and severed heads India gets her milk and milk products. I have commonly found male calves with legs precisely broken at the joints (they cannot be mended) and rendered immobile so that in the wee hours butchers can lift them into cattle trucks.

The religious profile of cattle and its multiple implications for human identities and meaning-making is deeply interwoven with their economic status. In the next section, I provide an overview of the Simhachalam case study, by locating the ways in which a state of informality is carefully produced by formal planning and governance in Visakapatnam city and its conurbation, to facilitate the transportation, trade and slaughter of the temple bull-calves for profit-making and capitalist growth.

Male calf donation in Simhachalam Temple, Visakhapatnam city

The 1000-year old Simhachalam temple, built atop a hill 20 kilometres outside of central Visakhapatnam city in Andhra Pradesh is a rare architectural wonder of South India's medieval era of the Chola dynasty. The temple is dedicated the fourth incarnation of Lord Vishnu, the Varaha-Narasimhan, the man-lion, who descends to earth to protect his devotees from the evil ruler Hiranyakashipu. The temple receives thousands of pilgrims every day. In the sanctum sanctorum or the 'womb' of the temple, the idol of the Lord is covered thickly with sandalwood paste, almost forming a little hillock, thus anointed as an act of piety. During the festival of Chandanaotsavam during the months of May and June, the sandalwood anointing ceremony is celebrated on a large, spectacular scale, and the temple receives millions of devotees, not just from within Visakhapatnam or even Andhra Pradesh, but from throughout western and north-western India and even beyond.

Alongside the pageantry and beneath the perfume of sandalwood, an inauspicious ritual is carried out in thousands under the name of auspiciousness and devotion. Families of pilgrims donate one or more baby male calf, sometimes only days or weeks-old to the temple as offerings. During peak festival season, the Simhachalam temple receives tens of thousands of bull-calves which used to

150   *Yamini Narayanan*

be sold en masse to slaughterhouses annually prior to recent intervention efforts from animal activist groups (VSPCA 2013). Male calves are globally regarded as a 'waste product' of the dairy industry, and it is accepted that they are slaughtered soon after birth for veal, calfskin or to dispose off an economic liability. In India, where the cow and her kin are directly venerated as divinity, dairy farmers in Andhra Pradesh have come up with a particularly innovative technique of unburdening themselves of male calves which is, in one fell swoop economically efficient, as well as ostensibly pious – routing the pathway to the slaughterhouse *via* temples, and donating bull calves to Hindu temples across the state. Suparna Baksi Ganguly, the vice president of Compassion Unlimited Plus Action writes (Animal People Online 2004), 'The villagers can't support the bull calves, so they donate them to the temples instead of selling them directly to butchers. Donating bull calves to a temple is a euphemism for sending them to slaughter'.

The Simhachalam case demonstrates the ways in which the 'donations' place the calves and the act of their trafficking in the informal, unregulated spaces of the city, and outside of the purview of formal governance, but only with the strategic compliance of formal planning. Major and minor arteries are used for animal transportation of these male calves, and illegal slaughterhouses operate in the thousands throughout the city and the Visakhapatnam conurbation. The trafficking of the bull-calves also emerges as an urban issue in other ways including public health and hygiene which are threatened by unregulated butcherhouses.

Animal activist and rescue organisation, the Visakha Society for the Care and Protection of Animals (VSPCA) was the first animal rights society in the state to bring attention to the cruelties committed against young male calves in the name of piety. In 1996, animal activist Pradeep Nath, the founding director of the VSPCA embarked on a long and ongoing legislative and activist battle with the temple authorities at considerable risk to life and limb, to forbid the forcible climb to the hill-temple endured by the young calves, and to ban the Simhachalam temple from auctioning off its donated calves to butchers. The temple awards the contract for the disposal of the temple-calves to the auctioneer with the highest bid. In an interview, Nath described the intricate nexus between the temple authorities, the butchers who'd bid for the calves, and the silent city governance in quietly enabling illegal transportation and slaughter of the bull calves:

> They [the devotees] take the baby male calves 1000 steps atop the Simachalam temple hill, and leave them there in the hot sun, 45 degrees. Every week, anything between 50–200 calves are stolen from their mothers, [during] peak festival season, 1000s of calves per day. Per day, May, June is the worst. They are crying and bleating for their mother. And then they [this time the butchers] bring them down 1000 steps again, what madness is this. These temple-calves end up in restaurants and cafes as veal, and are sold to butchers throughout the city. Temple is hand in glove with the cow mafia. We have rescued some 700 calves. . . . Supposing a calf is donated on Monday, he will be taken to slaughterhouse on Saturday, otherwise he is dying there [in the temple itself]. They get no milk, no water, they are just starving there. When

you bring them to the temple, you know they are going to die. Either in the slaughterhouse or from starvation.

The calves arrive in the temple via several major and minor arteries within the city, and from livestock markets that are located in the peri-urban areas outside Visakhapatnam, such as Nakappali, Kothavalasa, Jogulapalen, Tuni, Vepada and Alamanda, which are more than 200–250 km outside the central city (see Figure 10.2). The devotees who bring the calves to the temples typically are poor, small-scale dairy or agricultural farmers who live in the peri-urban and rural areas in the states of Andhra Pradesh, Orissa and even West Bengal, as well as from the metropolitan cities of Hyderabad, Visakhapatnam and Vijaywada, among others. The transportation of the calves occurs in what Yiftachel (2012: 153) refers to as 'gray space' debunking modernity's 'false dichotomy' of reinforcing categories such as 'legal' and 'criminal', 'fixed' and 'temporary' etc. While the transportation of the calves is not illegal, the methods of carriage are illegal: usually squashed into a small auto-rickshaw or mini-vans overcrowded with other calves and/or humans, or made to walk long miles to the temple leaving them even weaker and feebler. Further, the urban planning authority deliberately turns a blind eye to the ultimate purpose of calf transportation, and in this way, produces and reinforces informality, choosing to accept the pretension of calf donation for religious piety.

Figure 8.1 A weeks-old donated male calf stands abandoned at the bottom of the 1000 steps to the Simhachalam Temple.

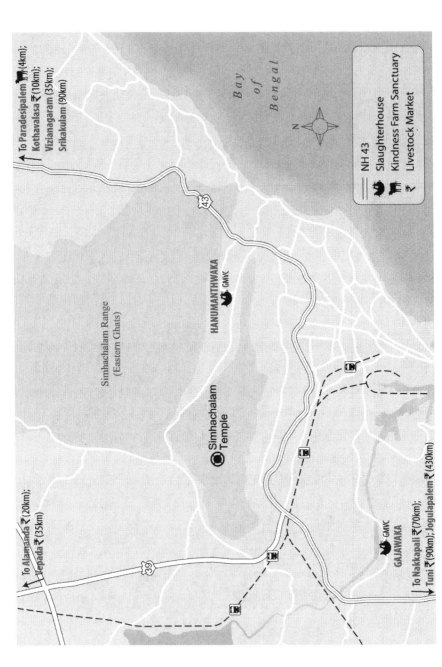

Figure 8.2 The Simhachalam Temple and the peri-urban areas in Visakhapatnam district wherein the bull-calves are trafficked between the temple, livestock markets and slaughterhouses.

The Andhra Pradesh Prohibition of Cow Slaughter and Animal Preservation Act, 1977 places a total prohibition on the slaughter of cows and calves, including bull-calves. As such, the slaughter of the temple-calves is illegal. However raids by activist groups in the three legal slaughterhouses operated by the Vishaka Urban Development Authority (VUDA) at Gajwaka and the two at Hanumanthwaka reveal routine slaughter of young cattle. Both animal activists as well as municipal veterinary officials from VUDA estimate that there are over 200 illegal slaughterhouses in every district around Vishapatnam and over a 1,000 unauthorised, unregulated slaughterhouses within the city itself. Some of these have a capacity to slaughter only one or two animals per day. Inspections at slaughterhouses revealed that for all intents and purposes, the methods of slaughter, issues of hygiene and violations of animal cruelty acts are as problematic as in illegal slaughterhouses. These spaces as well as the modus operandi of the slaughterhouses fall under VUDA's purview.

Hindu temples and state Devasthanam Departments or the temple administration bodies in Indian cities have come under fire in the last decade for their covert role in cattle slaughter role in the country, and in colluding with these slaughterhouses. The Jai Gopal Karodia Foundation filed a case in the Madras High Court, charging a number of stakeholders, principally the Chief Minister's Office of Tamil Nadu state, the Tamil Nadu Religious and Charitable Endowments Department as well as cattle donors of conniving together in the sale of donated male calves to a slaughterhouse, which falsely represented itself as a religious organisation for cow welfare. This case was iconic in exposing the religious coating and structures that was vital in supporting – as well as obscuring – the grisly realities of India's dairy and cattle industries. In 2004, the Madras (now Chennai) High Court declared that kine donated to Hindu, Jain or Buddhist temples must not, for any reason whatsoever, be auctioned off or sold to contractors; instead, they must be sent to a *goshala* which is monitored through health and safety inspections by independent animal welfare organisations every two months.

The VSPCA was successful in their lobbying efforts to ban the sale of calves by the temples to contractors in April 2013. Nonetheless, the temple's involvement in covertly smuggling calves continues. In May 2013, the Simhachalam temple superintendent was taken into custody by the police for colluding with the local tribal groups to smuggle 12 baby male calves out of the temple's *goshala* at night (The *Times* of India 2013b). Earlier in the same month, after the festival of Chandanotsavam, between 5 and 50 calves were found dead by trampling and suffocation every day in the tightly packed *goshala* of Simhachalam Temple, which housed more than 1200 male calves (The Times of India 2013a). These deaths were only noticed because of the smell of decomposition emanating from the *goshala*. The temple authorities caused great consternation when it was discovered that they were in fact digging more burial spots in preparation for more calf deaths at the Ramanna Cheruvu village on the Simhachalam-Andarapuram road where they moved the dead calves (The Times of India 2013a).

While the practice of calf donation has endured several hundreds of years, what is noteworthy is that a practice that is regarded as immoral as per Hindu

154 Yamini Narayanan

religious norms and illegal as per animal cruelty legislations, continues to occur through the complicity of modern formal governance. The calf donation is a clear example of informality which is, as Chakravarty (2015) notes in this volume, 'spaces and activities falling outside the State's standards and regulations'. Informality is implicitly – but not explicitly or *formally* – sanctioned by the state. Indeed, Chakravarty (2015) reconceptualises informality 'as a process and tool employed by the state for strategic purposes'. By the anthropocentric nature of most urban planning priorities, animals may be argued to exist at the 'periphery' or 'the space in between . . . never really bought under the auspices of the logic and development trajectories that characterize a centre' (Simone 2010: 14). The trafficking of animals and the thousands of illegal slaughterhouses in the city occur outside the purview of formality as the subjects of brutality are not recognised as having rights. Animals may be regarded as occupying 'gray spaces' (Yiftachel 2012), spaces of exception in Indian cities, and are untouched by the protection and infrastructure that formal planning may provide.

The smuggling and slaughter of the temple calves is aided in significant part by spaces and zones of informality within which animals exist in cities and throughout conurbations, whose safety and interests have been hitherto unimportant to the dominant urban development planning discourse. Sustainable development is a stated priority of the GVMC but is understood almost entirely in terms of efficiency, in transportation and mobilities etc. (UNEP 2014). Sustainable development is however not analysed in terms of informality in the city even though up to two-thirds of the city spaces are not yet formally planned, even as they fall within the jurisdiction of the GVMC (UNEP 2014). An analysis of the intersections of religion as a factor of informality, and sustainable development as a factor of formality reveals how this framework aids the exploitation of urban animals like cattle.

Below I discuss how Hindu religion and sustainable urban development can both be used to maintain and reinforce this status quo of informality and zones of exception to formal planning protocols, continuing to exclude cattle rights and welfare. However both religion and sustainable development make a moral call for equality and environmental protection, and must be part of the conceptualisation of cities as inclusive, peaceful and stable spaces, moving away from the commodification of animals towards a posthumanist worldview that sees human–animal relationships in cities in more mutually interconnected and independent ways, rather than exploitative.

Problematising 'religion' and 'sustainable development' for animals: considerations for informality

In recognition of the fact that planning is by no means the exclusive or legitimate purview of *planners* alone, the case for informality to be understood in nuanced ways beyond 'illegal', 'unplanned' and 'ungovernable' has gained increasing traction (Briassoulis 1997, Luz 2015, Roy 2005, Yiftachel 2009). The sites and structures of informal space and economies in developing cities are in fact an irreplaceable complement to the formal economy (Davis 2006, Neuwirth 2011), and formality and informality are in a constant state of mixing (Briassoulis 1997) to produce urban spaces, structures, ecologies and engagements. In the expanded scope for informal development as a legitimate, albeit formally ungoverned, form of planning, the case for religion in particular to be understood as a force in shaping informality in the 'South-East' has been recognised as imperative to shift from the privileging the planning theoretical frameworks of the 'North-West' in understanding urban realities in developing cities (Yiftachel 2006). Luz (2015: 1) calls for the critique of religion to consider 'the plethora of religious manifestations' that determine urban spaces 'mostly through informal spaces and gray spacing the city's landscape'. The lack of engagement with religion in understanding informality is a 'blindspot' (Luz 2015: 1) in understanding the urban experiences and struggles of 'marginalized groups'. Among this cohort, I have suggested, are large populations of non-human animal species.

Sustainable development's engagement with informality itself has been weak at best. In one of the first analysis of sustainability's links with environmental sustainability, Helen Briassoulis (1999: 225) notes the 'negative effects' of formal development on 'environmental resources and receptors', which is identifies as 'land, air and water ecosystems'. While she does refer to 'ecosystems' and refers to the perils of deforestation, soil erosion, water contamination etc., among other ecological issues, she notes the effect on no sentient life forms except humans. Consistent with all analyses of informality to my knowledge, nonhuman animals and birds are entirely invisible, falling outside the spectrum of considerations of formality, but also, incredibly, informality!

In this section, I identify two distinct narratives of informal and formal planning that engage to produce and sustain neoliberal growth – religion as an influential category of informality, and sustainable development as a planning priority of formal planning. My focus in particular here is to analyse how Hindu and sustainable development conceptualise and understand 'nature' in general, and animals in particular, thus jointly enabling their utilisation in carefully planned spaces of informality. These insights can be a useful starting point to understanding how environmentalism and environmental in/justices may operate in spaces of informality.

Hinduism as well as sustainable development are generally associated with positive outcomes for environmental welfare and protection. Yet conceptually and empirically, both notions have fallen short of ecological preservation. A closer scrutiny of how nature – particularly sentient life forms – are understood in religion and secular development reveals the problematic dimensions of environmentalism as driven by these lens. I suggest that both these concepts risk objectifying nature – as sacred resource and capital resource respectively – and objectification, regardless of purpose or process, is inherently a violent process.

Nature features prominently and positively in Hindu mythology. Hinduism conceives of the human relationship with nature as that of the *sishya* or the disciple, to the *guru* or the master: 'nature acts precisely as the human guru does; proposing through words and by example a path leading to insight and

156 *Yamini Narayanan*

realization' (Klostermaier 1989: 320). Hinduism's contribution to sustainability may be argued to come from the fact that it locates human beings *within* nature. Ecofeminists and ecophilosophers have long complained that human beings tend to disassociate themselves from the natural environment as 'superior' to it (Shiva 1993). However, as part of its spiritual practice, Hindu spirituality, in fact, elevates nature to a higher status than humans [as their *guru*], and thus makes care and respect for nature a spiritual duty.

Animals in particular also have a prominent place in Hinduism as sacred, revered and indispensible to the gods or even, as gods themselves. The first 4 of the 10 incarnations of Lord Vishnu each took a nonhuman form (consistent with biological evolution) as fish, tortoise, boar and man-lion. In addition to the bull and the cow, the cobra and the monkey are also worshipped directly as divinity. Further, a number of animals appear in mythological tales and pictorial depictions as the *vahanas* or the vehicles of gods – the mouse for Lord Ganesha, Nandi the bull for Lord Shiva, and the Goddess Kali rides on the lion/tiger.

All of this has lead to a widely regarded perception of Hinduism as a 'nature religion', as ecologically friendly, in harmony with the environment, and as a protector of Mother Earth. Bron Taylor (2010: 5) describes nature religion as 'an umbrella term to mean religious perceptions and practices that are characterized by a reverence for nature and that consider its destruction a desecrating act'. However by no means are nature religions or various forms of such religiosity – *'natural religion, nature worship, nature mysticism, and earth religion'* (Taylor 2010: 5, emphasis his) uniformly or universally benevolent in their attitudes and approaches towards nature; they can also be explicitly violent in their treatment and exploitation of nature, especially animals, in the name of worship and piety. Catherine Albanese (1990) makes a crucial distinction between nature as sacred and nature as a *sacred resource*; in the latter case, the value of nature based on its *utility* can drive violence against nature. Domination of nature can be an inherent part of the religious practices of what can also be regarded as nature religions.

In its growth-driven utilisation of nature, sustainable development is also arguably a process rife with violence, even as it claims lofty aims of ecological and social justice. Sustainable development as a concept is focussed on maximising efficiency such that neither the environment nor economic development may be compromised. Sustainable development is inspired by eco-efficiency, which fundamentally continues to focus on economic growth; in this strand of environmentalism, nature is not valuable *for itself* but to the extent that it can sustain maximum capital growth (Guha and Martinez-Alier 2000). Sustainable development is cognisant of the fact that continual economic growth on a planet with finite resources is, as Herman Daly (1973) put it, an 'impossibility theorem'. Sustainable development theories predominantly regard the environment as an economic good, albeit finite. Nature is typically understood in terms of 'natural resources' or 'nature capital', rather than 'Nature' (Martinez-Alier 2002: 11).

Ultimately, sustainable development prioritises human-centred development, and this meta-narrative carries over in the conceptualisation of sustainable cities. The city's reliance on its natural ecology is usually understood in terms of resources universally acknowledged as finite such as air, water and land/forest resources. However the city also relies significantly on animals for its growth, throwing into relief questions about not only human utilisation of animals but also about human destruction of the natural habitats of urban biodiversity. The continuing concern with human-centred urban development has resulted in a wide range of human-animal conflicts in urban spaces where nonhuman animals are usually frontline casualties over the struggle over resources, which includes, centrally, their bodies. Industrialised farming of animals has reinforced the perception that domesticated animals that the city relies upon, notably, are *not* regarded as finite, and hence, sustainability as a development concept feels no burden of protecting them as they are seemingly *infinite resources*. Indeed, the scale of mechanised factory farming and animal husbandry of widely consumed animals such as cattle, pigs and poultry have allowed widespread use and flagrant wastage of these animals and animal products.

As 'modern' concepts, both religion and sustainable development as frameworks for urban development in India need to be used cautiously. Historian C.S. Adcock (2010: 297) points to the modernity of religion as a concept, and expresses scepticism in using 'religion' as a valid critical concept to understand the socio-cultural context of the cow in India in its entirety. Nonetheless, it remains urgent to reconceptualise these notions, rather than disregard them as they are conceptually and empirically used to utilise animals. Critical engagement is vital, and sustainable city development thus not only has the challenge of considering religion as an analytical category but to understand the notion in its vernacular context, motivations and explanations. In the last section, I outline some broad challenges that urban development needs to consider to reposition its role as one significant actor in the human use of animals, environmental sustainability, and ecological and social justice in Indian cities.

Conclusion: cattle protectionism and safe cities for animals – a case for urban planning

The rights and status of cattle and other animals in cities is a multifaceted planning issue that requires, at the least, participation and contribution from a number of human actors including ecologists, theologians, veterinarians, community development practitioners, urban planners and stakeholders in the animal slaughter trade. This diversity of stakeholders indicates the multiple ways that cattle issues may be understood, and the need for consensus through participatory and democratic approaches. Missing in this list of participants are nonhuman animals themselves. Unrecognised as stakeholders in conceptions of sustainable cities, nonhuman animals occupy the ultimate 'periphery' of urban spaces, even as cattle, and the spaces and infrastructure of cities are actively utilised to support neoliberal growth. The commodification of high-value animals like cattle is aided by the sacralisation of these animals in India. While the issue of animal sentience, rights and welfare is by no means solely the concern and responsibility of urban development authorities, they remain a vital player whose roles have been thus far largely unacknowledged. However these complicated intersections need to be understood, and below I outline a few approaches that planning in India may begin to explore in this context in order to start the challenging process of reconceptualising sustainable cities from a trans-species worldview.

One of the first tasks for planning is recognise animals as stakeholders in sustainable cities with agency and the capacity to resist. Animal rights activist and scholar Dinesh Wadiwel (2015: 20) argues that far from being passive recipients of human violence, birds, animals and fish in fact do actively 'resist' their abuse at human hands. If it is accepted that animals have agency, then democratic planning is required to respond in a just manner. Planning is already faced with the creative challenge of facilitating inclusiveness through deliberative democracy approaches as a way of incorporating human cultural, social, political and gendered diversity. Scholars of environmental politics (Dobson 2007) as well as ecofeminists (Shiva 1993) have advocated frameworks for ecological democracy, to include the 'views' of non-human nature, and to redress the anthropocentrism of current democratic systems. According political agency to animals is vital for and recognising animal resistance to their killing/exploitation as political resistance, are useful starting ways for planning to think of sustainable cities in India and globally that are inclusive across species.

Two, in protecting multi-species diversity in cities, conservation biologists have emphasised the need for conceptualising a range of models documenting the varied nature of human/non-human animal relationships in cities as well as the complexity of interactions between other species (Jokimaki et al. 2011). Strong collaborations need to be developed between urban landscape planners and conservation biologists in order to preserve the natural environment that is so vital to a sustainable city (Jokimaki et al. 2011). Protecting the rights of animals to their natural habitat will make the urban environment and the micro-climate more livable as animals depend directly on the environment for their survival (as do poor women). Enabling positive and flourishing relationships between humans and nonhumans through spatial planning is also a creative way of restoring the much-lamented lost nature-human connection.

Three, planning has to urgently address and extend the concerns of Indian feminists (Narayanan 2012, Puri 2005) about violence against women (VAW) in moving transportation and in urban spaces to violence involved with the movement of animals, and the spaces of their destruction. The abduction, molestation, rape and even the murder of women in the 'privacy' of moving transport in Indian cities has been well documented, and these concerns extend to the trafficking of animals across large urban and peri-urban spaces. Planning can also no longer afford to ignore its complicity in supporting unlawful activities such as illegal slaughterhouses within its purview. Urban development authorities need to incorporate spaces for city *goshalas* or retirement homes for 'unusable' cattle, particularly near dairy farms where slaughterhouses typically abound.

This brings us to the fourth and an overarching challenge for planning that cuts across all of the above concerns: its multifaceted engagement with religion – scriptural, textual and popular interpretations. In India, planners need to acquire

Animals and urban informality 159

multi-religious literacies to be able to deal with issues of spatial access, privilege, safety and rights in their entirety for pluralistic community (Narayanan 2015a). This no less true while planning safe cities for animals. The reality nonetheless is that planning requires pragmatic approaches, and religious frameworks thus far have not yielded easily to policymaking. However akin to the aims of applied anthropology that aims to move the discipline beyond ethnography to practical field practices, Korom (2000) recommends an 'applied theology' or 'a theology that is aimed at solving problems' to address some of India's most pressing as well as volatile environmental problems. In cities, the nature of such application may be best discussed jointly by theologians, planners and welfare animal activists. Planning's collaborations with a range of religious and secular scholars, actors and representatives is thus clear, in its quest towards sustainable Indian cities.

Note

1 The red dot on the forehead worn in Hindu communities, symbolising the third, all-seeing eye.

References

Adcock, C. S. 2010. Sacred cows and secular history: cow protection debates in colonial north India. *Comparative Studies of South Asia, Africa and the Middle East*, 30 (2): 297–311.

Albanese, Catherine, L. 1990. *Nature Religion in America: From the Algonkian Indians to the New Age*. Chicago: University of Chicago Press.

Animal People Online. 2004. 'Why cattle "offerings" prevail where cow slaughter is illegal'. www.animalpeoplenews.org/04/5/cattleOfferings5.04.html (26th December 2014).

Bhatewara, Zara, and Tamsin Bradley. 2013. 'The people know they need religion in order to develop': Religion's Capacity to Inspire People in Pune's Slums. *The European Journal of Development Research* 25 (2): 288–304.

Briassoulis, Helen. 1999. Sustainable development and the informal sector: an uneasy relationship. *The Journal of Environment and Development* 8 (3): 213–237.

Bulankulame, Indika. 2013. 'Convictions beyond the bomb: Interplays between violence, religion and development in Sri Lanka'. In *International Development Policy: Religion and Development*, ed. Giles Carbonnier. New York: Palgrave Macmillan. 192–206.

Census of India. 2011. 'Visakhapatnam'. www.census2011.co.in/census/city/402-visakha patnam.html (11th August 2015).

Chakravarty, Surajit. 2015. 'Religious Structures on Traffic Lanes: Production of Informality in New Delhi'. In *Religion and Urbanism: Reconceptualising Sustainable Cities for South Asia*, ed. Yamini Narayanan. London: Routledge.

Chaudhery, Amit. 2014. 'The Force of Falsity'. www.strays.in/index.php/2014/11/the-force-of-falsity-by-amit-chaudhery/ (23rd November 2014).

Chigateri, Shraddha. 2008. 'Glory to the Cow': cultural difference and social justice in the food hierarchy in India. *South Asia: Journal of South Asian Studies* 31 (1): 10–35.

Contractor, Qudsiya. 2012. '"Unwanted in My City": The Making of a Muslim Slum in Mumbai'. In *Muslims in Indian Cities: Trajectories of Marginalisation*, eds. Laurent Gayer and Christophe Jaffrelot. New Delhi: HarperCollins Publishers India.

160 *Yamini Narayanan*

Crockett, Clayton. 2014. 'Sketch for a Political Theology of In-debted Nations'. Presented at the Violent Nations: 1984's Othering of Sikhs. Hofstra University, New York.

Cruz, Teddy. 2007. 'Levittown Retrofitted: An Urbanism Beyond the Property Line'. In *Writing Urbanism: A Design Reader*, eds. D. Kelbaugh and K. McCullough. New York: Routledge.

Daly, H. E. 1973. *Toward a Steady-state Economy*. San Francisco: W.H. Freeman.

Davis, Michael. 2006. *Planet of Slums*. London and New York: Verso.

Dobson, Andrew. 2007. *Green Political Thought*. London: Routledge.

Flood, G. 1996. *An Introduction to Hinduism*. Cambridge: Cambridge University Press.

Guha, Ramachandra, and Juan Martinez-Alier. 2000. 'The environmentalism of the poor and the global movement for environmental justice'. In *Recht auf Umwelt oder umwelt ohne recht?* ed. Werner G. Raza. Frankfurt: Brandes und Apsel.

Jokimäki, Jukka, Marja-Liisa Kaisanlahti-Jokimäki, Jukka Suhonen, Philippe Clergeau, Marco Pautasso, and Esteban Fernández-Juricic. 2011. Merging wildlife community ecology with animal behavioral ecology for a better urban landscape planning. *Landscape and Urban Planning* 100 (4): 383–385.

Klostermaier, K.K. 1989. 'Spirituality and Nature'. In *Hindu Spirituality: Vedas Through Vedantas*, ed. K. Sivaraman. London: SCM Press Ltd.

Korom, Frank, J. 2000. Holy cow! The apotheosis of zebu, or why the cow is sacred in Hinduism. *Asian Folklore Studies* 59 (2): 181–203.

Luz, Nimrod. 2015. Planning with Resurgent religion: informality and gray spacing of the urban landscape. *Planning Theory and Practice* 16 (2): 278–284.

Martinez-Alier, Juan. 2002. *The Environmentalism of the Poor: A Study of Ecological Conflicts and Valuation*. Cheltenham: Edward Elgar Publishing.

Miller, Sam. 2010. *Delhi: Adventures in a Megacity*. St. Martin's Press.

Mishra, Manjari. 2008. 'Illegal cattle trade funding terror'. http://timesofindia.indiatimes.com/india/Illegal-cattle-trade-funding-terror/articleshow/3554048.cms (24th January 2015).

Narayanan, Yamini. 2012. Violence against women in Delhi: a sustainability problematic. *Journal of South Asian Development* 7 (1): 1–22.

———. 2015a. *Religion, Heritage and the Sustainable City: Hinduism and Urbanisation in Jaipur*. Oxford: Routledge.

———. 2015b. 'Criminalising Beef, Not Dairy'. www.thehinducentre.com/the-arena/current-issues/article6982147.ece (20th April 2015).

Neuwirth, Robert. 2011. *Stealth of Nations: The Global Rise of the Informal Economy*. New York: Pantheon Books.

Newman, P. W. G., and J. Kenworthy. 1999. *Sustainability and Cities: Overcoming Automobile Dependence*. Washington, DC, and Covelo: Island Press.

Puri, Jyoti. 2005. Stakes and States: Sexual Discourses from New Delhi. *Feminist Review*, 83 (1), 139–148.

Roy, Ananya. 2005. Urban Informality: Toward an Epistemology of Planning. *American Planning Association. Journal of the American Planning Association* 71 (2): 147–169.

Sharma, Anil. 2013. 'Religion and environment: water for the gods – now being conserved in temples'. http://religion.info/english/articles/article_610.shtml (13th May 2013).

Shiva, Vandana. 1993. 'The Impoverishment of the Environment: Women and Children Last'. In *Ecofeminism*, eds. Maria Mies and Vandana Shiva. Halifax, Nova Scotia: Fernwood Publications.

Taylor, Bron. 2010. *Dark Green Religion*. Berkeley: University of California Press.

The Times of India. 2013a, May 15. 'Calves offered to Simhachalam temple found dead'. http://timesofindia.indiatimes.com/city/hyderabad/Calves-offered-to-Simhachalam-temple-found-dead/articleshow/20057450.cms (15th December 2014).

———. 2013b, May 21. 'Seven held for cattle theft from Simhachalam temple goshala'. http://timesofindia.indiatimes.com/city/visakhapatnam/Seven-held-for-cattle-theft-from-Simhachalam-temple-goshala/articleshow/20162900.cms (15th December 2014).

UNEP. 2014. 'Promoting Low Carbon Transport in India'. www.unep.org/transport/low carbon/PDFs/LCMP_Vizag.pdf (7th May 2015).

VSPCA. 2013. 'Simhachalam Calves: 2013 Update – 12 Months of Liberation for Thousands of Male Calves'. www.vspca.org/programs/calves.php (5th January 2015).

Wadiwel, Dinesh, Joseph. 2015. *The War Against Animals*. New York: Brill Rodopi.

Yiftachel, Oren. 2012. 'Critical Theory and "Gray Space": Mobilization of the colonized'. In *Cities for People, Not for Profit: Critical Urban Theory and The Right to the City*, eds. Neil Brenner, Peter Marcuse, and Margit Mayer. Oxford and New York: Routledge. 150–170.

9 Karachi – a case study in religious and ethnic extremism

Implications for urban sustainability

Claude Rakisits

Introduction

When one thinks of Karachi, one thinks of a very violent city. And, on the whole, one would be right to think so because violence of all types has been rampant in the city more or less since the mid-1980s. In many ways, it has become the natural order of things, something the residents of Karachi have not so much come to accept but have adapted to (Gayer 2014b: 4). Of course, it was not always like that. In the 1940s, Karachi was referred to as the 'Paris of the East'; it was the cleanest city on the subcontinent (Verkaaik 1994: 33). And in the early 1960s, Jackie Kennedy, flanked by Pakistan's president, Field Marshal Ayub Khan, drove through Karachi in an open top convertible, an event which today is almost impossible to imagine actually happened. Unfortunately, all this has changed beyond recognition.

Today Karachi is not only confronted with the usual problems of South Asian megacities – uncontrolled and unplanned urban growth; permanent slums; lack of amenities; insufficient adequate housing; no proper access to running water for millions of Karachiites; high level of unemployment and underemployment; lack of a mass transit system; insufficient number of schools and medical facilities – but this bad situation has been severely compounded by sectarian and ethnic violence, armed religious extremism and terrorist activity. The pervasive and widespread violence has also contributed to the increasing ghettoization of Karachi along ethnic lines. The hardening of ethnic barriers and the deepening of ethnic differences, which comes with spacial segregation, have further compounded the sustainability of this megacity and have affected the equitable distribution of limited urban resources. Accordingly, the combination of the different types of violence, the widespread ghettoization and the lack of amenities, infrastructure and socio-economic services for the bulk of the Karachiites has made large parts of the city virtually ungovernable. Put differently, the city's organisational capacity and its finite resources instead of being deployed to promote a sustainable city are effectively being diverted to promote ethnic conflict and sectarian extremism and expand the position of Jihadists and terrorists. Surprisingly, despite the enormous challenges noted above, Karachi still delivers more than 25 per cent of the country's gross domestic product, 54 per cent of central government tax revenues,

Karachi – a case study 163

70 per cent of national income tax revenue and 30 per cent of industrial output (Yusuf 2012: 4).

I will argue that Karachi's lack of sustained development – that is the effective, efficient and equitable distribution of resources – is directly linked to poor urban governance which itself is a consequence of poor governance at the national and provincial levels. Moreover, the lack of sustained and planned development in Karachi is compounded by a poor security apparatus, that is, an incompetent, ineffective and poorly trained and funded police force. This weakness is exploited by the various violent actors which further compounds the security situation, making it that much more difficult to break the vicious circle of violence and poor sustainable development. Unfortunately, given that Karachi is effectively a microcosm of Pakistan – and I do not see a dramatic improvement of the security situation in Pakistan in the near future, there is little likelihood that the federal and provincial authorities will be able to make any significant headway in improving the sustainability of Karachi. This is assuming that there is the political will to do so.

Unfortunately, if anything, inter-sectarian and inter-ethnic violence will most likely worsen, as will terrorist acts, thus deepening the ghettoization of the city and compounding the socio-economic conditions of millions in the process. These consequences will further deepen the governance problems of Karachi. Accordingly, the sui generis nature of Karachi's varied urban problems means that one cannot seek solutions to Karachi's sustainability problems strictly through socio-economic measures, but rather along three separate tracks: law and order, political and sustainable projects.

This chapter is divided into four sections. In the first section, the Setting, I discuss the historical and present drivers, particularly the impact of the different waves of migrants, which have led to Karachi being what it is today, particularly the ghettoization of many of its neighbourhoods. The second section examines the different types of violence – inter-ethnic, inter-sectarian and Jihadist – and how these tend to re-enforce each other and compound the governance and sustainability of the city. The third section, the ghettoization of Karachi, seeks to validate some of the urban theories to this case study. The final section makes some policy recommendations on the security, political and sustainability fronts which would need to be considered if Karachi is to become a more viable megacity.

The setting

At the time of Partition in 1947, Karachi was not a big city with less than half a million inhabitants. However, the sudden influx into Karachi of hundreds of thousands of *Muhajirs*, Urdu-speaking Muslim migrants from India-to-be, over a very short period of time under very difficult conditions to say the least – many having witnessed horrendous massacres in their migration to Pakistan – has left physical and psychological marks on the city which cannot be sufficiently stressed.

164   *Claude Rakisits*

Put differently, in many ways, Karachi has never recovered from the chaotic and exponential growth it went through. The growth of the population was phenomenal: a 369 per cent increase between 1941 and 1961 (Gayer 2014b: 23). However, not only was there a massive numerical change but the religious make-up of the city also went through a radical make-over. In 1941, over 50 per cent of the population were Hindu and 42 per cent were Muslims. By 1951, the city was 96 per cent Muslim (Gayer 2014b: 23). And compounding these demographic changes was the change in the language spoken in Karachi. In 1941, 61 per cent of the population of Karachi claimed Sindhi to be their mother tongue, whereas by 1951 over 50 per cent claimed Urdu to be their mother tongue, but only 8.5 per cent declared it to be Sindhi (Boivin 2002: 182). This radical change in the ethnic composition of the city would have far-reaching consequences further down the road, particularly with regard to who could have a greater claim to 'ownership' of Karachi.

The *Muhajirs'* overwhelming political dominance of Karachi's political landscape did not last very long, however, having to compete with new arrivals from other parts of the country. In the 1950s and 1960s, waves of migrants from other parts of the country, particularly from the Punjab and Khyber Pakhtunkhwa (former North West Frontier Province) where many poor peasants had been adversely affected by the Green Revolution, had settled in Karachi (Verkaaik 1994: 36). The next big migrant wave came as a consequence of the Afghan War (1979–1989). The arrival of four million Afghan refugees in Pakistan had an economic knock-on effect of pushing many Pashtuns out of the north-western part of the country and into the urban centres, including Karachi. The war also led to about a million Afghans coming to Karachi (Gayer 2014b: 24). Unfortunately, with these new migrants came guns and drugs smuggled from the Afghan–Pakistan border, often assisted by corrupt officials (Nawaz 2008: 361). One cannot sufficiently stress the significance of this period on the subsequent development of the culture of violence in Karachi. Compounding this violence has been the natural tendency of the new arrivals to Karachi to seek housing close to their brethren, thus creating ethnic ghettos. Finally, over the years there has been a steady stream of migrants from all over Pakistan seeking a better life in Karachi after having suffered droughts, floods and earthquakes (Ahmed 2014). And, of course, there are the thousands of victims of the aftermath of the many counter-terrorist operations in the north western part of Pakistan.

Karachi is the fastest growing city in the world with a population of around 21 million, making it the third largest city in the world, almost on par with Beijing (Kugelman 2014a: 2). This is only an estimate because there has not been a national census since 1998. In 2011, there was a limited one – House Listing Operation, which took a sample of living conditions throughout the country for socio-economic development plans. So needless to say, Karachi's exact population, let alone its ethnic break-down, remains a highly controversial issue with many potential political ramifications (Gayer 2014b: 25). Regardless of its exact size, it is uncontroversial that this makes Karachi the largest megacity in South

Asia, followed by Mumbai (12.5 million) and Delhi (11 million) (Census of India 2011, Provisional Population Totals).

Unfortunately, Karachi also has the dubious honour of being the most violent of the world's megacities (Gayer 2014b: 5). According to the Human Rights Commission, over 10,000 people were violently killed in the last 10 years, with 3,200 killed in 2013 alone (Mallet and Bokhari 2014). The motives for these killings are not always clear, but invariably, they are the result of gang warfare over turf competition, criminal activity, inter-sectarian violence, explosions (including hand grenade attacks) and killings by police and other security authorities (Sigal 2014: 1). It is important to note that these killings do not include the victims of terrorist acts, such as the attack on Karachi airport in June 2014 by the Pakistani Taliban in which more than 30 people were killed.

Compounding an already difficult living environment is the question of inadequate and insufficient accommodation for the majority of the people, particularly for the poorest segments of society. As a result, there is an acute problem of squatter and unplanned settlements. This is the result of successive national and provincial governments' inadequate response to the needs of the poor since the time of Partition. In order to deal with this lack of official housing, people have turned to living in *katchi abadi* (residential areas unofficially developed on state land), which are effectively slums. These are controlled by slum lords, corrupt officials, political heavies and other unsavoury characters. Ironically, it is the existence of these *katchi abadi* which has prevented mass-scale riots in protest for the lack of housing (Ahmed 2014). Accordingly, the city administration has turned a blind eye to this urban phenomenon.

Going hand-in-hand with the lack of proper housing is the lack of sufficient proper amenities, such as running water, access to electricity, closed sewers and public toilets, in the poorer, working-class neighbourhoods of Karachi. These decrepit conditions are nothing new and go back to pre-Partition days. For example, Lyari, which was the oldest settlement in Karachi whose original inhabitants were Sindhi fishermen and Baloch nomads, was completely neglected for infrastructure development under the British colonial administration. This policy continued post-Partition, with the priority being to assist with the resettlement of the *Muhajirs* and to develop new neighbourhoods for these Urdu-speaking migrants. Even after those legitimate early resettlements requirements were met, successive national and provincial government have continued to ignore the basic needs of Lyariites (Gayer 2014b: 129). So today, over 65 years after Partition, Lyari, which is Karachi's densest neighbourhood, is an utterly appalling urban environment, rife with poverty, criminality, violence and despair.

A few figures will illustrate the state of neglect of large parts of Karachi. Only 35 per cent of the 75,500 new housing units needed every year are provided, whether by the formal or informal sectors; over 40 per cent of the water supply is controlled by the 'tanker mafia'; and 45 per cent of the electricity is illegally obtained by syphoning off from regular electric cables (Gayer 2014b: 38). Today, 30,000 people die every year in Karachi because of contaminated water (Kugelman 2014a: 17). This toxic mix of deprived living surroundings, high unemployment

166 Claude Rakisits

and high population density in a multi-ethnic setting has provided the ideal conditions for three types of violence – inter-ethnic, inter-sectarian and Jihadist – to thrive in Karachi. Quite often these three categories of violence have an additional layer of criminality to them (Gayer 2014b: 123–162). Needless to say, because of the criminal gangs' inherent vested interests their support of the violence further weakens the governance of Karachi and sets back the sustainable development of the city. It is this issue of violence that I will now turn to.

Different types of violence

Inter-ethnic

Violence between the different ethnic groups is not a new phenomenon. As we noted above, it started upon Partition with the arrival of hundreds of thousands of *Muhajirs* and the consequent displacement of the local Muslim population, notably the Sindhis. This created tension between these two groups which has persisted ever since and has regularly flared up over the last six decades. This tense relationship between the 'sons of the soil', the Sindhis, and the migrants, the *Muhajirs*, was further complicated with the arrival of more migrants from other parts of the country, mainly Pashtuns, Punjabis and Baloch. Accordingly, the Sindhis and the newer migrants have all increasingly contested the *Muhajirs'* claim that Karachi is their city (Gayer 2014b: 27–29). This is particularly so given that the *Muhajirs'* birth rate is dropping and the number of internal migrants moving into Karachi has steadily been increasing over the last 30 years. So while the *Muhajirs* remain the single largest ethnic group, around 45 per cent of Karachiites, their relative position vis-à-vis the Pashtuns has eroded over the years. And, as noted above, while no one knows the actual size of each ethnic group, it is estimated that about 25 per cent of Karachi's population is Pashtun, making it the largest Pashtun city in Pakistan (Saleem 2010). This diminished demographic strength has fuelled among *Muhajirs* a sense of insecurity and, accordingly, their principal political representative, the Muttahida Quami Movement (United National Movement – MQM), has increasingly used violent tactics to protect its political position in Karachi (Gayer 2014b: 109–111). The MQM's founder, Altaf Hussain, stresses that the *Muhajirs* are a distinct ethnic group like the other ones in Pakistan and, accordingly, their interests have to be protected. Today, it is estimated that the MQM has about 10,000 armed men, with another 25,000 in reserve, making it the largest armed group in Karachi (Husain 2012).

The first violent inter-ethnic clashes in Karachi were in 1985 between Pashtuns and *Muhajirs*. The clashes were so violent that the army had to be brought in to bring it under control. The unrest lasted for months; it was a turning point in inter-ethnic relations. The next significant inter-ethnic dispute was in 1988, when Sindhis and *Muhajirs* clashed violently in Hyderabad and in Karachi. The MQM's armed wing got involved in this clash, and did so when it flared again in 1990, in which 130 Sindhis were killed. These violent clashes were an important factor in the eventual dismissal of the Benazir Bhutto government in 1990

Karachi – a case study 167

(Ziring 2003: 215–216). In 1992, the military, which was getting worried that the MQM was becoming a state within a state, launched 'Operation Clean Up' to degrade the MQM. And with the help of the police and paramilitary forces this lasted until 1996. Hundreds of MQM fighters were killed (Siddiqi 2012:106). The military has not returned into Karachi since then. Under the regime of General Musharraf, a *Muhajir* himself, the MQM felt less threatened. And under the Pakistan Peoples Party (PPP), the MQM was safe as well given that it was part of the ruling governing coalition in Islamabad (2008–2013). It was under Prime Minister Nawaz Sharif's previous administration that the military went into Karachi, so he may well be tempted to launch an operation in the future not only to tackle the MQM but also, as I will discuss later, to hunt down the thousands of Taliban militants hiding in Karachi. It is interesting to note that the MQM leadership suggested in August 2013 that a military administration be imposed on Karachi to stop the bloodshed. As noted above, a military solution was tried in the 1990s, and it resolved nothing; it only froze the political situation and did not deal with the long-term sustainability issues of the city. Needless to say, no one at either the federal or provincial level has entertained this latest idea (Desk 2013).

So what we have witnessed over the last 50 years is a steady deterioration in inter-ethnic relations in Karachi, leading to a very high number of deaths. Increasingly the different ethnic groups, through their respective political parties or groupings, that is, the PPP representing Sindhis, MQM representing *Muhajirs*, the Awami National Party (ANP) representing the Pashtuns, and the Peoples Peace Committee (PAC) representing the Baloch, have had armed clashes among each other. According to a 2012 report by the Unites States Institute of Peace, the armed wings of the PPP, MQM and ANP are the main perpetrators of urban violence (Yusuf 2012: 3). Some of these confrontations have effectively been pitched battles. A consequence of these violent clashes is that members of the different ethnic groups have had to find refuge in their 'own' ethnic neighbourhoods, further compounding the ghettoization of Karachi.

These inter-ethnic clashes are essentially about two fundamental issues: first, protecting the ethnic group's neighbourhood from encroachment from other ethnic groups, as well as trying to expand into other neighbourhoods. This is inevitable given that the number of new migrants coming into Karachi is greater than there is available living space in that specific ethnic neighbourhood. It is in the process of trying to break into new neighbourhoods that political parties turn to criminal elements, often indirectly, to assist them achieve their aims. The heavy-handed tactics used by the criminal groups include blackmailing, racketeering, extortion and kidnapping. According to the Citizen Police Liaison Committee, 166 people had already been kidnapped by mid-2014. This is a dramatic increase in the number of cases given that the first time kidnapping cases exceeded the 100 mark was in 2010 (Nasir 2014). These tactics inevitably lead to bloodshed and much personal despair.

The second issue is about political representation for the respective ethnic groups at the national and provincial levels. In this regard, the *Muhajirs* have done very well given their actual numbers. At the national level, following the

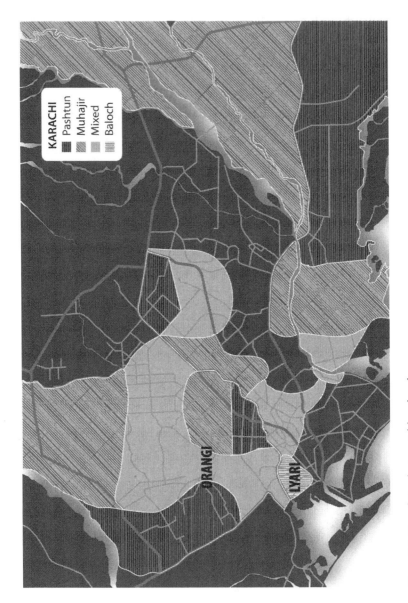

Figure 9.1 Karachi's ethnic neighbourhoods.

2013 elections the MQM won 16 of the 18 Karachi federal seats, having lost one to Imran Khan's Tehreek-e-Insaf party (PTI) and one (Lyari) having remained with the PPP. Put differently, the MQM managed to obtain the fourth largest number of seats in the National Assembly. At the provincial level, the MQM won 33 of the 42 Karachi seats, giving it 30 per cent of all the provincial seats. Moreover, even though the PPP had a majority in its own right in the provincial assembly following the 2013 election, it brought the MQM into the government, giving it two ministerial portfolios. On the other hand, the ANP did very poorly in the 2013 elections, failing to yet again obtain any Karachi seats and losing its only two provincial seats to the MQM and PTI. It is these electoral discrepancies between actual demographics on the ground versus federal and provincial seats which has led to increased tension and violence between the ethnic groups in the streets of Karachi. Unfortunately, this type of violence has been compounded with sectarian violence which in many ways is even more shocking.

Inter-sectarian violence

Much of the recent sectarian violence in Karachi can trace its origins back to the days of General Zia-ul-Haq's regime when he embarked on his Islamisation program and Pakistan became a frontline state, hosting the *mujahedeen* fighting the Soviet forces in Afghanistan. And while there had been inter-sectarian violence before that, particularly in the early 1950s and in 1969–1970 against the Ahmadiyah, a Muslim community which does not believe that Mohammad is the ultimate prophet, it was in the 1980s that sectarian violence significantly increased. Zia's Islamisation program set the religious tone by clearly favouring the fundamentalist school of thought, the one pursued by the Jamaat-i-Islami. More importantly, it was under his 11-year tenure that the number of *madrasas* (religious schools) expanded exponentially. In 1971 there were only 20 *madrasas* in Karachi and most of them were from the more tolerant Barelwi Sunni school of thought. However, today there are some 1800 *madrasas*, with the bulk being affiliated with the more hard-line Deobandi Sunni school of thought. Almost all of these latter ones were built under General Zia's watch (International Crisis Group 2007: 5). However, just as important as Zia's religious policy settings was the arrival on the scene after the end of the Afghan war of former *mujahedeen* who had fought the Soviet troops. These were battle-hardened and ideologically driven men who would use their jihadist 'skills' to oppose all religious groups which did not agree with their vision of the world.

Most of the sectarian killings in Karachi, which are now almost a daily occurrence, are executed by Deobandi groups whose principal targeted killings are Shia, but also Barelwi Sunnis and Sufi followers. The two principal culpable organisations are the Sipah-e-Sahaba Pakistan (The Army of the Companions of the Prophet-Pakistan – SSP) and the Lashkar-e-Jhanvi (LeJ). Working closely together, as well as with criminal elements, they have been involved in killing hundreds of Shias in Karachi since 1994 (Gayer 2014b: 176). Both these organisations were banned by the Pakistan government in 2001 because of their violent

170 *Claude Rakisits*

and illegal activities. Accordingly, the SSP re-branded itself as Ahle Sunnat Wal Jamaat (The Organisation of the Followers of the Tradition – ASWJ) which was itself banned in 2012. Both ASWJ and LeJ, which have a common origin and whose home base is Punjab, have had training bases in Afghanistan since the late 1990s. Their *madrasas*, mosques and training camps across Pakistan are conduits for foot soldiers, arms and funds from Punjab to other parts of the country, including to Karachi (International Crisis Group 2009: 7). ASWJ is on a major recruitment drive in Sindh, and because of its nation-wide network of some 4,000 *madrasas* has managed to recruit some 25,000 new members from around Karachi (Imtiaz and Walsh 2014). ASWJ and LeJ have been specifically targeting Shia doctors and lawyers on a regular basis with the aim of driving them out of Karachi. In the last few years, already thousands of doctors have left and migrated to other countries where life is safer. As for lawyers, many have real fear for their lives, as many of them who have taken up criminal cases against ASWJ and LeJ have been gunned down (Ur Rehman 2011). The Shia community has itself also established an organisation to counter the LeJ, the Sipahe Mohammed Pakistan (SMP), which is the armed wing of the Shia party, the Tehrik Nifaz-e-Fiqh Jafria (TJP), later changed to Tehreek-e-Islami after President Musharraf banned the TJP in 2002. While the SMP did retaliate as well with targeted assassinations of ASWJ and other Deobandi leaders, it has never been that active in Karachi (International Crisis Group 2007: 10).

The followers of the Barelwi Islamic jurisprudence school of thought have in turn established the Sunni Tehrik (the Sunni Movement) (ST) in 1990 to try to reverse the Deobandis' control of so many of Karachi's mosques (International Crisis Group 2007: 11). While the ST does not promote violent jihad, it has nevertheless used strong-arm tactics to protect the interests of the Barelwi community (Gayer 2014b: 165). Aside from being adherents of two different Islamic schools of thought, SP is different to the SPP in two fundamental ways: first, SP has no grievances with the Shia community; and, two, SP has no known links with Jihadist groups in Afghanistan and Pakistan because all of them are Deobandis. Let me now turn to the analysis of the Taliban, the most virulent and fastest-growing Jihadist group in Pakistan, and how it has managed to embed itself in Karachi.

Jihadist

The presence in Karachi of the Taliban, known officially as the Tehreek-i-Taliban Pakistan (TTP), is a relatively recent phenomenon compared to the sectarian groups which have been there since the 1990s. In December 2007, the TTP was founded bringing loosely together about 30 different Jihadist groups based in Pakistan's tribal areas which are inhabited by the Pashtuns. Until then the militant problem was largely limited to the north-western part of the country. Trouble really only started to spread around 2009 when the Pakistan army launched major operations in the Swat Valley and South Waziristan to dislodge the TTP. The consequence of these operations and subsequent ones was that it generated

Karachi – a case study 171

hundreds of thousands of refugees, many of whom sought safety in Pakistan's cities, including Karachi. Not surprisingly, these Pashtun refugees sought shelter with family and friends living in the Pashtun areas of Karachi, thus further reinforcing the ghetto nature of the social space. Hiding and moving unnoticed among those refugees were many TTP fighters trying to avoid being captured by security forces. Subsequent waves of internal refugees caused by floods, natural disasters and violence brought more fugitive TTP fighters to Karachi.

While their early presence went largely unnoticed, today the TTP's presence is obvious and growing fast. Based on the expertise of the police, analysts and Pashtun elders, it is estimated that most Pashtun neighbourhoods of Karachi are now under partial or complete control of the TTP (Ur Rehman 2014). Put differently, the TTP 'controls or dominates' a third of Karachi with an estimated 8,000 fighters as of 2012 (Kugelman 2014b). Some officials believe their numbers could be as high as 15,000 (Craig 2014). In any case, we can expect this figure to have increased, and certainly will in the wake of the military operation in North Waziristan launched in mid-2014. The TTP has managed to dominate such large areas of Karachi by ruthlessly suppressing any opposition to its writ. Using a tactic employed in the tribal areas, it targets the Pashtun political leadership. Accordingly, it has assassinated some 80 ANP leaders and office bearers (Ur Rehman 2014). It is only a matter of time before the TTP moves against the MQM. And in a demonstration of effective cross-fertilisation with extremist sectarian groups, the TTP working closely with the LeJ, has established a parallel system of justice (Gayer 2014b: 187). Despite its professed opposition to crime, the TTP has cynically turned to criminal elements to raise funds through bank heists, kidnappings and extortion (Ur Rehman 2014). The Taliban's armed tactics have been so effective that either police presence is minimal or some neighbourhoods, such as Manghopir at the edge of Orangi Town, are simply no-go areas for the police (Gayer 2014b: 187). As a consequence there has been a deepening of the ghettoization of the Pashtun neighbourhoods. Ironically, the growing presence of militants, coupled with diminishing police security, has provided an opportunity for criminals to increase their trade in kidnapping, extortion and robbery (Craig 2014).

The Taliban's success in expanding its territorial presence is that much more remarkable given that the TTP is not a monolithic organisation. Quite the contrary, it is highly factionalised, and those divisions are reflected in the way the TTP has carved up Karachi in roughly three 'fiefdoms' (Khattak 2014). Despite these internal differences, the TTP has managed to achieve two of the main reasons for its presence in Karachi: first, it raises funds which it sends back to the tribal areas to assist its brethren fight the Pakistani security forces; and, second, it recruits foot soldiers who are then sent back to the tribal areas to swell TTP ranks. It is important to note that most of the Deobandi *madrasas* around Karachi are attended by Pashtuns which provide the TTP with a ready pool of young recruits and funds (International Crisis Group 2007: 6). And, as Khan (2012: 577) argues, young people join militant organisations because violence brings a sense of self-worth to the recruits. And in this case the ethnic factor strengthens this pull.

Ghettoization

Turning to the literature on social-spacial segregation, and noting the discussion above, it is evident that the ever-present and growing violence at all levels and perpetuated by many different groups, whether ethnic, sectarian or Jihadist, has turned Karachi into 'zones of unsettled sovereignties and loyalties' (Gayer 2014b: 50). And as state security agents are increasingly unable or unwilling to perform their role in these ghettos, non-state actors are filling the vacuum in maintaining order within their own discreet areas (Gazdar and Mallah: 2013). But while these ghettos display a certain degree of internal stability, it is when planned districts, generally inhabited by *Muhajirs*, encroach into slums or unplanned neighbourhoods, e.g. Lyari inhabited by Sindhis or Orangi mainly by Pashtuns, that there are violent clashes. Accordingly, these brutal inter-ethnic encounters reinforce the ethnic barriers, confirming the argument by Raman and Dempsey (2012: 427) that the physical layout of the different ethnic neighbourhoods has an influence on the social interaction and in turn reinforces the ghettoization of Karachi. And this ghettoization or as Gayer (2014b: 28–29) puts it, the creation of a 'patchwork of partitioned ethnic urban space' has hardened the different ethnic and religious groups' position on issues of importance to each group. Complicating the urban picture has been the Talibanization of Karachi's Pashtun ghettos. Put differently, and using Massoumi's (2011: 227) framework as applied to Peshawar, Karachi, or at least parts of it, is 'an enclaved city fragmented and divided by the exclusionary and regulatory practices of the Taliban'. Accordingly, given the religio-political practices of the Taliban and the spacial strategy it uses to impose its authority, one could define those Talibanized neighbourhoods as constituting a 'fundamentalist city' as broadly characterized by AlSayyad (2011: 15).

The socio-economic impact of the ghettoization and Talibanization of Karachi has been deeply troubling at three levels for the people of the affected areas, particularly in the older parts of the city. At the personal level, no individual is safe from the ever-present violence. One needs to be constantly vigilant, even when going about doing routine tasks, such as shopping or taking the bus to school. Fear for one's life, one's family and for one's property is constant (Gayer 2014a). This simply compounds the already wretched and miserable human conditions many Karachiites have to endure. At the religious level, Sufis and Shiite, especially doctors and lawyers, are constantly being targeted. And while there has not been ghettoization on a sectarian basis, these religious communities need to be constantly on the alert. At the commercial level, many businesses have left the neighbourhoods which have witnessed the greatest violence, whether criminal, ethnic or sectarian. This has led to a decline in commercial activity and has thus further compounded the marginalization and ghettoization of poor urban areas. Compounding the economic costs is the fact that many employers prefer not to hire people living in the more violent neighbourhoods for fear that these workers may not always be able to come to work. This in turn further impoverishes the already neglected neighbourhoods and hardens the ethnic boundaries (Gayer 2014a).

Not surprisingly, these different manifestations of violence have directly affected investment and commerce as neither potential domestic nor international businessmen are going to invest in an unsecure place. According to the chairman of the All Karachi Trade Association, an estimated 20,000–25,000 businesses have left the city and the economic loss amounts to about $10 million a day (Santana 2012). This in turn means that the government collects less revenue from taxes which it desperately needs to build up the city's decrepit infrastructure. This lack of adequate urban development, notably in services and capital infrastructure, compounded by violence, in turn means more businesses will move out which means further loss of revenue for the government. And so with this vicious circle, the ghettoization of Karachi deepens.

Let me now turn to the policy implications of this multi-faceted violence, ghettoization and lack of sustainable development and examine what the national and provincial governments would need to do if they are going to make Karachi a sustainable city, which can contribute more effectively and efficiently to the socio-economic life of Pakistan.

Stabilizing and sustaining Karachi

The task of transforming Karachi into a sustainable city into the future will be made that much more difficult to achieve because of the high level of violence on so many fronts. However, if the relevant authorities are to make any headway, they would need to follow a three-pronged approach. First, they would need to secure Karachi and improve the appalling law and order situation before they can embark on executing major new public infrastructure projects. The second prong would be political, that is the need to have all major players involved in Karachi to agree on a number of critical measures to break the political stalemate. And third, in parallel with the political track, there would be a need to address the sustainability requirements which would make Karachi a more bearable urban environment to work and live in, that is, embark on executing major public infrastructure projects such as a mass public transport system, and improving existing decrepit ones, such as schools, hospitals, sanitation system and roads. I will now turn to the security dimension.

Securing Karachi

First and foremost, Karachi's police force needs to be strengthened and better equipped and it needs to be depoliticised. The size of the police force is simply too small. It is roughly the size of New York City's even though Karachi's population is three times bigger (Craig 2014). Compounding the issue is that about a third of the force is on protection duty of VIPs, such as judges, businessmen and politicians, thus further reducing the force's deployable capability. Only about half of the 3,000 to 4,000 officers deployed at any one time have bulletproof vests. And their working conditions are poor, with the police stations generally dilapidated (Santana 2014). Given these conditions, there are serious doubts that the law enforcement authorities are in a position to check the violence. Accordingly, increasing the number of police officers on the beat, providing better training and more funds and ensuring the officers have proper equipment would assist combat the city's criminal and terrorist scourge.

174   *Claude Rakisits*

The problem for the police is that, in addition to being out-gunned by heavily armed and better-equipped gangs of criminals and terrorists, it is hamstrung by what it can do because the police force is highly politicised. According to the inspector general of the Sindh police, more than 40 per cent of the city's police have been recruited on political grounds (Yusuf 2012: 22). As a result, action is not taken against the hard-core criminals, extortionists and land mafias who are connected with political parties (Kaleem and Khan 2011: 60–61). And if they do arrest some of these individuals, political connections get them released (Husain: 2012). Instead, the police pursue softer targets such as members of the ST and SSP (Gayer 2014b: 181). Compounding this politicisation is the highly corrupt nature of the police force, thus further diminishing its trustworthiness vis-à-vis the people it is meant to protect from criminals (Ul Hassan 2013). The de-politicisation of the police force would be critical to address the city's violence. Re-instating Police Order 2002, which would allow the Inspector General of the Sindh police to make all the police appointments, would end the present system in which the provincial government makes all appointments above deputy superintendent (Yusuf 2014: 22). This system is completely abused politically, with the government distributing the police appointments on the basis of political necessity rather than organisational requirements.

Unfortunately, this weak and ineffective police force in Karachi is compounded by an equally poor criminal justice system. Without going into too much detail, some of the major flaws to the system are: a lack of successful prosecution of arrested individuals, a large backlog of cases, a lack of a witness protection program, a poor evidence-gathering capability, and under-staffed and under-resourced courts (Yusuf 2012: 23–24). This too needs to be completely overhauled so that an eventual reformed police force's work does not get undermined by a poor judicial system. Unfortunately, the poor state of the judiciary in Sindh province is not unique to that province; it is a governance issue repeated in other provinces and at the national level.

However, one security measure which could be implemented relatively easily and at little cost to the treasury while bringing results relatively quickly would be to set check-points at all entrances into Karachi. For the best results, these check-points would need to be staffed and controlled by the army, one of the few national institutions on the whole not yet contaminated by the political parties. At these check-points all new entrants into Karachi could be registered into a national monitoring data system. Such a system if properly managed would make it more difficult for potential recruits, whether for criminal or Jihadist organisations, to slip into Karachi unnoticed.

Grand political accord

Just as important as securing Karachi is the need to correct the political imbalance between actual ethnic numbers and political representation at the national and provincial levels. Until this critical governance issue is corrected there will be no long-term solutions to Karachi's sustainability problems. One of the most obvious ways to do this is to finally conduct the long-delayed national census, the last one having been conducted in 1998. In December 2013, the government of Prime Minister Nawaz Sharif agreed to hold one in time for the 2018 general elections, as this would determine the formation of the electoral constituencies. If this census does finally take place and is conducted in a transparent and honest way, it will allow not only to discover the true demographic strength of the various ethnic groups but to accordingly redraw the electoral constituencies. As noted above, it is estimated that the *Muhajirs* make up about 45 per cent of Karachiites and Pashtun about 25 per cent. Of course, these are only guestimates, but even if these are correct, these numbers are absolutely not reflected in the number of parliamentary seats, both at the provincial and national levels. The ANP, the Pashtuns' political party, has no seats in the Sindh provincial assembly and no Karachi representation in the National Assembly. The MQM has the lion share by far of the Karachi seats in both chambers. This lack of equitable representation means that government funds for urban development and social services have been skewed in such a way as to being directed principally to *Muhajir* neighbourhoods (Yusuf 2012: 27). This perpetuates the ghettoization of Karachi and further fuels ethnic tensions. Hopefully, a new census and a subsequent new demarcation of the electoral seats would correct this unfair electoral representation.

Armed with the actual ethnic demographics, the political parties should then establish a Karachi City Commission (KCC) which would be independent from the provincial government and whose membership would reflect the city's true ethnic numbers. In consultation with the national government, the Sindh provincial government should raise a new city tax on businesses and the revenue that it would raise would only be used for the urban development of the city, such as on roads, hospitals, schools, parks and public transport, not for general provincial expenditure. Such a tax would help provide greater fiscal certainty for the city administration. All decisions on major developmental projects would be taken by the newly established KCC on a two-third majority basis, forcing the different ethnic groups to work together to ensure everyone eventually benefitted from the funds raised. It would effectively be a power-sharing arrangement.

Making Karachi sustainable

If Karachi is made more secure through greater political dialogue, the setting up of security check-points, and a more equitable distribution of developments funds following the holding of a census, then the city administrators could more credibly turn their attention to making Karachi more sustainable for the future. From reading the above, it would come as little surprise to anyone to learn that Karachi never went through a systematic urban planning process (Kugelman 2014b). However, in January 2007, the City District Government of Karachi (CDGK) put out its Master Plan for the Development of Karachi 2020 (KMP 2020). It is very comprehensive and deals with all aspects of urban life and what is required to make Karachi a sustainable city. Unfortunately, there was virtually no public consultation in its development (Khuro and Mooraj 2010: xi). It is also very ambitious and most of its goals are quite simply unachievable. For example, it aims to have 100 per cent of Karachiites connected to the sewerage system and receiving solid waste collection services by 2020. Today just over 50 per cent of residents are enjoying these services. Nevertheless, it is the only plan on the table and therefore one cannot dismiss it out of hand. It could form the basis of more limited projects in the future.

Given the limited space available, I will focus on only one aspect of the plan, one that I believe is probably one of the most important: implementing a mass transit. Out of the millions of cars clogging up the streets of Karachi, only 6 per cent qualify as public transport. And the state of this limited public transport is extremely poor. Put differently, 40 people fight for every seat (Aligi 2011). Karachi is one of the few megacities not to have a mass transit. But KMP 2020 puts forward two. One is the Karachi Circular Railway, which would serve about 700,000 passengers per day, and is expected to be 50 kilometres long and cost $1.58 billion. The Japanese International Cooperation Agency (JICA) will provide the entire funding for the project through a soft loan repayable over 40 years. While this mass transit will be welcomed by some, it will not be going through the centre of the city. So the poor, who are most in need, will lose out. And the middle class which owns most of the cars clogging the city roads will not have an alternative mode of transport. It remains unclear when the project will actually begin but the date for completion will be anytime between 2017 and 2022 (Ali 2013). The second mass transit project is the Green Line Bus Project which will cost 15 billion rupees and which the federal government has agreed to cover the cost in full. It would be 22 kilometres long, and it would link Surjani Town in the north of the city with the city centre. While the federal government has given the go-ahead, there is no date for its completion (Samar 2014). If these projects do eventually go ahead, they will provide some relief to the commuting Karachiites, albeit only to a fraction of them. The mass transit system would eventually have to be substantially more extensive to make a significant difference to a majority of commuters. Importantly, a mass transit system would help break the lock Pashtuns have on the urban transport system and, hopefully ease inter-ethnic turf wars.

Conclusion

The city of Karachi is a microcosm of Pakistan. Accordingly, and as I argued, while urban improvements can be made to Karachi, these will not be sustainable over the long-term unless there are fundamental improvements to the quality of governance and the overall security situation in Karachi *and* at the national level. In parallel with the security issue, this is an opportunity for Prime Minister Sharif to show political and economic leadership in trying to address some of Karachi's major structural problems discussed above. However, given that the prime minister's PML-N has no political power in Karachi (no federal seats and only three provincial seats), it is unlikely that the federal government will expend more than the minimum of its limited funds and political capital on addressing the city's massive structural needs even though this would be in the national interest.

The growing Taliban threat in Karachi – possibly bigger than in the tribal areas – could bring the secular parties, notably the PPP, MQM and ANP, closer together to fight a common enemy. However, if they were unable to do so when they were all three part of the PPP-led national coalition (2008–2013) in Islamabad, it is unlikely to happen today. But, even if such a political understanding could be generated, it is no guarantee that there would be peace down the road. The disorder in Karachi has been manageable because it is in none of the actors' interest to see the city descend into utter chaos. Moreover, there has been an understanding that ultimately the state would intervene to prevent this from happening (Gayer 2014b: 279). However, with the increasing presence of the Taliban in Karachi this assumption may no longer be valid. The Taliban is not interested in the status quo; it wants change at all levels, including in Karachi. Regardless of whether a grand political accord can be put together, which would assist in breaking the socio-economic dead weight of the ghettos, if action is not taken very soon in trying to deal with the sustainability of Karachi, the city could collapse from the sheer weight of its uncontrolled and unregulated urban growth. Moreover, as socio-economic conditions worsen, ethnic boundaries harden and ghettoization deepens, making it that much more difficult to make any headway on the sustainability front. And given Karachi's critical economic role in sustaining the Pakistan state, this state of affairs has now become a national security issue. So action needs to be taken today. The only glimmer of hope is that despite all the massive sustainability problems in Karachi, the city remains Pakistan's most developed, prosperous and literate city (Yusuf 2012: 26). Let us hope this can remain the case before it is too late.

References

Ahmed, K. (2012) *Sectarian War – Pakistan's Sunni-Shia Violence And its Links to the Middle East*, Oxford: Oxford University Press.

Ahmed, N. (2014) 'Pakistan Growing Urbanisation: Shifting Sands', *Dawn*, 25 August. Online. Available: www.dawn.com/news/1038256/growing-urbanisation-shifting-sands (Accessed 16 June 2014).

Ali, I. (2013) 'Be it the Year 2017 or 2022, Karachi Circular Railway's on Track', *The News*, 10 March. Online. Available: www.thenews.com.pk/Todays-News-4–164545-Be-it-the-year-2017-or-2022-Karachi-Circular-Railways-on-track (Accessed 25 July 2014).

Aligi, I. (2011) 'In a City Where 40 people Fight for 1 Seat, Mass Transit is the Solution', *The Express Tribune*, 28 February. Online. Available: http://tribune.com.pk/story/124800/in-a-city-where-40-people-fight-for-1-seat-mass-transit-is-the-solution/ (Accessed 25 July 2014).

AlSayyad, N. (2011) 'The Fundamentalist City?' in N. AlSayyad and M. Massoumi (eds.) *The Fundamentalist City?* (pp. 3–26), London: Routledge.

Bano, M. (2012) *The Rational Believer*, Cornell: Cornell University Press.

Bayat, A. (2007) 'Radical Religion and the Habitus of the Dispossessed: Does Islamic Militancy Have an Urban Ecology?' *International Journal of Urban and Regional Research*, Vol. 31, no. 3, September, 579–590.

Boivin, M. (2002) 'Karachi et ses territoires en conflit pour une relecture de la question communautaire', *Héredote*, vol. 101, 180–200.

Census of India (2011) *Provisional Population Totals*, Delhi: Government of India.

City District Government of Karachi (CDGK) (2007) 'Karachi Master Plan 2020', Karachi, January. Online. Available: www.urckarachi.org/KMP-2020-Draft%20Final%20 Report.pdf (Accessed 25 July 2014).

Craig, T. (2014) 'Karachi Residents Live in Fear as Pakistani Taliban Gains Strength', *The Washington Post*, 14 February. Online. Available: www.washingtonpost.com/news search/search.html?st=Karachi+Residents+live+in+Fear+as+Pakistani+Taliban+Gain s+Strength&submit=Submit (Accessed 22 July 2014).

Desk, W. (2013) 'Army in Karachi: Khursheed Shah Opposes MQM demand', *The Express Tribune*, 27 August. Online. Available: http://tribune.com.pk/story/595834/army-in-karachi-khursheed-shah-opposes-mqm-demand/ (Accessed 19 July 2014).

Furseth, I. (2011) 'Why in the City: Explaining Urban Fundamentalism', in N. AlSayyad and M. Massoumi (eds.) *The Fundamentalist City?* (pp. 27–50). London: Routledge.

Gayer, L. (2007) 'Guns, Slums, and 'Yellow Devils': A Genealogy of Urban Conflicts in Karachi, Pakistan', *Modern Asian Studies*, Vol. 41, No. 3, 515–544.

Gayer, L. (2014a) 'Frontline Karachi', *Newsweek*, 17 September. Online. Available: http:// newsweekpakistan.com/frontline-karachi/ (Accessed 1 October 2014).

Gayer, L. (2014b) *Karachi – Ordered Disorder and the Struggle for the City*, London: C. Hurst & Co. Ltd.

Gazdar, H., and Mallah, H.B. (2013) 'Informality and Political Violence in Karachi', *Urban Studies*, Vol. 50, No. 15, November, 3099–3115.

Husain, I. (2012) 'Demography as Destiny', *The Dawn*, 6 April. Online. Available: www. dawn.com/news/708562/demography-as-destiny (Accessed 18 July 2014).

Imtiaz, S., and Walsh, D. (2014) 'Extremists Make Inroads in Pakistan's Diverse South', *The New York Times*, 15 July. Online. Available: www.nytimes.com/2014/07/16/world/ asia/militants-in-pakistan-make-inroads-in-the-diverse-and-tolerant-south.html?mod ule=Search&mabReward=relbias%3Ar%2C%7B%221%22%3A%22RI%3A9%22% 7D&_r=0 (Accessed 20 July 2014).

Inskeep, S. (2011) *Instant City – Life and Death in Karachi*, New York: The Penguin Press.

International Crisis Group (2007) 'Pakistan: Karachi's Madrasas and Violent Extremism', *Crisis Group Asia Report*, No. 130, 29 March.

International Crisis Group (2009) 'Pakistan: The Militant Jihadi Challenge', *Crisis Group Asia Report*, No. 164, 13 March.

International Crisis Group (2014) 'Policing Urban Violence in Pakistan', *Crisis Group Asia Report*, No. 255, 23 January.

Kaleem, M., and Khan, J. (2011) 'New Flashpoints, Old Worries', *The Herald*, September, 60–61.

Khan, A. (2005) *Politics of Identity – Ethnic Nationalism and the State in Pakistan*, New Delhi: Sage.

Khan, N. (2010) *Mohajir Militancy in Pakistan*, Milton Park: Routledge.

Khan, N. (2012) 'Between Spectacle and Banality: Trajectories of Islamic Radicalism in a Karachi Neighbourhood', *International Journal of Urban and Regional Research*, Vol. 36, No 3, May, 568–584.

Khattak, D. (2014) 'Rivals Fight for Pakistani Taliban's Soul', South Asia Channel, *Foreign Policy*, 1 May. Online. Available: http://southasia.foreignpolicy.com/posts/2014/05/01/ rivals_fight_for_pakistani_taliban_s_soul (Accessed 24 July 2014).

Khuro, H., and Mooraj, A. (eds.) (2010) *Karachi – Megacity of Our Times*, 2nd edn., Oxford: Oxford University Press.

Kugelman, M. (2014a) 'Understanding Pakistan's Unstoppable Urbanization', in M. Kugelman (ed.), *Pakistan's Runaway Urbanization: What can be Done?* (pp. 1–20). Washington, DC: The Wilson Center.

Kugelman, M. (2014b) 'Will Karachi Become the Next Waziristan?' South Asia Channel, *Foreign Policy*, 5 June. Online. Available: http://southasia.foreignpolicy.com/posts/2014/06/05/will_karachi_become_the_next_waziristan (Accessed 21 July 2014).

Mallet, V., and Bokhari, F. (2014) 'Karachi Under Siege', *Financial Times*, 26 June. Online. Available:www.ft.com/intl/cms/s/0/e6042de2-fc46–11e3–98b8–00144feab7de.html?site edition=intl#axzz37a3t01NQ (Accessed 26 June 2014).

Massoumi, M. (2011) 'Fundamentalism at the Urban Frontier: The Taliban in Peshawar', in N. AlSayyad and M. Massoumi (eds.), *The Fundamentalist City?* London: Routledge, 209–233.

Nasir, S. (2014) 'Kidnapping for Ransom cases in Karachi break a 10-Year record', *The Express Tribune*, 10 June. Online. Available: http://tribune.com.pk/story/651253/kidnapping-for-ransom-in-karachi-break-a-10-year-record/ (Accessed 19 July 2014).

Nawaz, S., (2008) *Crossed Swords*, Oxford: Oxford University Press.

Rahman, S. and Dempsey, N. (2012) 'Cultural Diversity and Spacial Structure in the Indian Urban Context', *Journal of Urban Design*, Vol. 17, No. 3, August, 425–447.

Saleem, F. (2010) 'Why Karachi is Bleeding', *The News*, 21 October. Online. Available: www.thenews.com.pk/Todays-News-13–1458-Why-Karachi-is-bleeding (Accessed 18 July 2014).

Samar, A. (2014) 'Centre to Complete Rs15 bn Bus Project in Karachi: Nawaz', *The News*, 11 July. Online. Available: www.thenews.com.pk/Todays-News-13–31515-Centre-to-complete-Rs15-bn-bus-project-in-Karachi-Nawaz (Accessed 25 July 2014).

Santana, R. (2012) 'Pakistan's Largest City rocked by Wave of Violence', *Big Story*, Online. Available: http://bigstory.ap.org/article/pakistans-largest-city-rocked-wave-violence (Accessed 22 July 2014).

Santana, R. (2014) 'Police Under Attack in Pakistan's Largest City', *Big Story*, Online. Available: http://bigstory.ap.org/article/police-under-attack-pakistans-largest-city (Accessed 24 July 2014).

Siddiqi, F. H. (2012) *The Politics of Ethnicity in Pakistan*, London and New York, Routledge.

Sigal, I. (2014) 'Karachi's Killers', *South Asia Channel, Foreign Policy*, 23 June. Online. Available: http://southasia.foreignpolicy.com/posts/2014/06/23/karachi_s_killers (Accessed 24 June 2014).

Ul Hassan, S. (2013) 'The Solution of Karachi's Fiasco', *Tribune International*, 8 September. Online. Available: http://tribune-intl.com/?p=2480 (Accessed 24 July 2014).

Ur Rehman, Z. (2011) 'Karachi Militants Linked to Doctors' Slayings', *Central Asia Online*, 3 February. Online, Available: http://centralasiaonline.com/en_GB/articles/caii/features/pakistan/main/2011/02/03/feature-01 (Accessed 20 July 2014).

Ur Rehman, Z. (2014) 'Karachi: Enter TTP', *Dawn*, 9 March. Online. Available: www.dawn.com/news/1091918 (Accessed 21 July 2014).

Verkaaik, O. (1994) *A People of Migrants – Ethnicity, State and Religion in Karachi*, Amsterdam: VU University Press.

Yusuf, H. (2012) 'Conflict Dynamics in Karachi', *Peaceworks*, Report No. 82, Washington, DC: United States Institute of Peace.

Ziring, L. (2003) *Pakistan: At the Crosscurrent of History*, Oxford: Oneworld Publications.

Part III
Reflections

10 Including religion as well as gender in Indian urban planning policy

With reference to lessons from the United Kingdom

Clara Greed

Introduction

No room for religion

Modern Western town planning is a secular, scientific and humanistic profession, which has little time or space for religious issues, worship space or faith communities (Sandercock 2006). It is weak on the social aspects of urban development, especially women's needs. It is ill-equipped and set at too high a level to deal with the planning of developing world cities including Indian cities. According to Libby Porter, in many developing countries, 'the planning system exists as a kind of layer over the top of a landscape of social and spatial relations to which it bears little relation and certainly barely penetrates' (Porter 2013: 289). Planning has generally been an impersonal activity which prioritises economic development rather than the needs of the poor. Entire cities have been zoned for the convenience of the business-man, worker and commuter, all predominantly male images. The needs of women have been rendered secondary or even invisible, whilst religion has simply not been a consideration in the planners' agenda.

Conceptual perspective and religious context

Religious capital, rather than just economic capital, is increasingly being recognised as a key factor in urban development (Baker and Beaumont 2011). But much of the work has been related in the West and to its Christian heritage, and to the challenges that Islam presents to Western cities. Little attention has been given to the needs of Hindus in the United Kingdom arguably because of the smaller numbers involved, and they present a peaceful, politically non-threatening image (Peach and Gale 2003). It is estimated there are over three million Muslims, around one million Hindus and half a million Sikhs within the total UK population of 63 million people. Black Africans comprise approaching one million, whilst Afro-Caribbeans (from the British West Indies) are around half that number, and both are characterised by a preference for Pentecostal forms of Christian worship.

184 *Clara Greed*

Pentecostal churches are characterised by large gatherings and ecstatic and emotional spiritual worship. Arguably this is quite different from traditional Western white churches and has more in common with some Eastern religions. Pentecostal churches also provide social, educational and welfare services for their mainly immigrant congregations, all of which requires large premises (Kay 2000). They are also the fastest growing Christian denomination in the West and are a force to be reckoned with in many UK cities, especially in immigrant areas. The vast majority of the rest of UK population still define themselves as Christian but less than 5 per cent attend church services and their religion is separated out from their daily lives. In contrast Hindus represent over 90 per cent of the population in India, and their religion suffuses every aspect of life, whilst Christians constitute around 4 per cent, with Pentecostals comprising a small but growing subgroup in South Asia (Bergunder 2008; Burgess 2001) and across the developing world (Freeman 2014).

In the United Kingdom, it has been the Pentecostal churches' growth and demand for new worship that has put the spotlight on the planners' ignorance and hostility towards religion. This is manifested in a high level of refusal of planning applications for new church buildings. These research findings are discussed more fully in Greed (2011a) and Greed (2014). The purpose of this chapter is to identify lessons (shown in italics) that can be drawn out in respect of the negative way faith communities, which are seen as being relics from the past not key components of modernity, are dealt with in the United Kingdom. Such biases have been exported via ex-pat and Western-trained planners working in India. As urbanisation gathers pace in India, Western town-planning policies and experts are exerting increasing influence (Falk 2014). They are generally welcomed as providing modern solutions to the problems of Indian cities, because of their imagined superior knowledge. In India, there is still a respect for English town planning owing to its links to the British Empire and now the Commonwealth. But foreign-educated experts manifest little understanding of the importance of religion in Indian society and cities and are thus likely to contribute to the secularisation of Indian cities and marginalise the needs of faith communities.

Contents

In the first part of the chapter, I investigate the relationship between planners and religion which was much more positive in the past but has now become quite hostile. The origins and problems presented by the prevalence of a land use zoning mentality in planning are discussed. Next the different forms of 'capital' that are seen to drive development are discussed, highlighting the conflict between economic and religious capital. Examples are given of how religion is treated by the planners in the United Kingdom, drawing out parallels for India. In conclusion, means of changing the situation are presented, including the presentation of a 'Toolkit' (series of consciousness raising questions) that might facilitate the mainstreaming of religion into planning policy making.

Planning's changing relationship with religion

The city of god

In most ancient civilisations, cities were designed to give a high priority to religious worship and ceremony (Mumford 1965). For example in Western civilisation, Classical Greek and Roman cities were planned around a central square alongside the main temple with major roads and processional routes radiating out, and with local shrines and religious buildings in each neighbourhood. Economic and industrial activity was often relegated to outside the main city in marginal zones and large sectors of the population were seen as unclean including not only slaves and women, but also traders, shop keepers and artisans who were not allowed full citizenship rights. Subsequently within European Christendom, for centuries, cathedrals were the most prominent, and tallest, townscape features in towns and cities. Chapels and churches were central townscape elements in every settlement: a veritable 'credo scape' (a townscape shaped by belief) (Sheldrake 2007). Likewise in South Asia, some of the greatest and most ancient cities such as Harappa and Mohenjo-Daro were built around religious principles, whilst also being organised in a functional manner way ahead of their time in terms of infrastructure and drainage. Indeed most Indian cities are old, if not ancient, and their design and layout is steeped in religious significance.

As Narayanan (2015) explains, when modern planners consider religious sites and buildings, it is usually in relation to policies on tourism, culture and urban conservation, as in the case of Jaipur. Ordinary local people in areas have been designated UNESCO (United Nations Educational, Scientific, and Cultural Organization) world heritage site are likely to suffer the most, even finding they are banned from entering their ancestral settlements and temples. There is a conflict between meeting the needs of the local people and catering for the tourists in famous historical cities such as Agra, Amritsar, Jaipur and Delhi. Planners fail to see that such historical buildings still have an important religious function and perhaps because of their age and disrepair, they fail to realise they are still part of the living fabric of the city (Timothy and Olsen 2011). Planners are very keen to 'write them off' as redundant and out of date, suggesting a huge gap between the understanding of the planners and the lives of the planned. This mind-set undoubtedly has been imported from the West, where many religious buildings really are disused because society has changed, but it is totally inappropriate in India.

Lesson One: Planners prefer religious buildings to be empty and very old so they can treat them as cultural artefacts, museums and tourist attractions, rather than accepting the buildings and surrounding localities are still full of people, life and spirituality.

The Industrial Revolution, called forth a new form of town planning the West to deal with the effects of urbanisation, population growth, disease, poverty and slum housing. However, the secular and the religious ran along side-by-side, cross-fertilising each other to start with. As a result of the spread of the Protestant

186 Clara Greed

work ethic, trade, business and making money were no longer seen as 'sins' or as activities only fit for outcasts, slaves and foreigners, but signs of blessing and a person's 'election' to salvation (Tawney 1922; based on Weber 1905). Tawney's book *Religion and the Rise of Capitalism* is a much-quoted classic as if its principles apply to the whole world. But his arguments are totally inappropriate for the Indian situation. For him 'religion' only meant Christianity. He assumed that economic growth (capitalism) had its origins in the Protestant work ethic, but that capitalism would only reach its zenith as society moved on to a secular phase. He also assumed that as society urbanised, religion would decline: the complete opposite of what is happening in India (Narayanan 2015, chapter 4).

The city of man

By the early twentieth century, planning was being taken over by the UK state as a government function, and priorities changed. Rudimentary town planning acts were introduced in 1909 and 1919, which required the production of a Town Plan for each local authority area showing the land-use zonings. Patrick Geddes, a founding father of modern town planning, developed a scientific approach to planning, based on the mantra of 'survey, analysis, plan'. He promoted the need for 'order' for separation of land-uses in the name of functionality. Geddes' ideal rational city was divided into three zones: home, work and play. Master Plans were produced which divided cities into three land-use categories: employment, residential and recreational zones. (Geddes 1968/1915). What did the term 'play' include? Sport, clubs, men's leisure activities? Where was religion in this tripartite division? Was it meant to go in with 'play' and leisure? If so, it seriously devalued the importance of religion in society. But in India, religion cannot be divided off into a separate compartment as it is embedded in all places, and every aspect of life and activity.

From a gender perspective, there was also no place in Geddes' tripartite arrangement for a fourth factor, namely all the caring, home-making, childcare undertaken by women in the home, which does not count as either 'work' or 'play'. Indeed this division was a classic example of the Western 'Third place mentality' based on the experiences of men, who need some 'time out' and 'play' space, to chill out 'between work and home', but have no caring duties to undertake at home. In Geddes' view 'the home' was a haven for men to relax after work, whereas for women it was the major locus of their work. Zoning was 'justified', along with low density layouts to reduce overcrowding, in the name of public health. But, the founding fathers of planning arguably used these mechanisms to control a woman's place in the city, by increasing land-use segregation and travel distances, and thus to prevent her from transgressing spatial boundaries and moral protocols and venturing into the public realm of the city of man. Geddes saw women as inferior and in need of control and was enamoured by Freud's association of the mother principle with 'stagnation' (Bologh 1990: 14, Geddes and Thomson 1889). Such attitudes towards women undoubtedly shaped his approach to land-use zoning (Greed 1994:117–118). He was also strongly opposed to women's suffrage (Kingsley Kent 1987: 35). Women were initially barred from entering the planning and architecture professions, which were run like gentleman's clubs. Even as late as the 1950s, those women who did work in government departments were required to leave their jobs upon marriage. Few women were in a position to influence the development of modern planning, or challenge the sexist nature of land-use planning.

Christianity was as guilty as planning, as it endorsed sexism through a superficial interpretation of Scripture (1 Timothy 2 v.11–15, and I Corinthians 11 verse 5), verses which apparently forbid women to preach, teach or exert authority over men, and advised them to keep silent. As a result, women have always experienced problems being heard in traditional European churches. Women's position within Hinduism has also been somewhat challenging and vexed, as although, in theory, everyone is equal, patriarchal structures and customs tended to relegate women to second place with few women leaders (but paradoxically many goddesses). However Narayanan (2015) explains (in Chapter 7) that traditional Hindu cities accommodated women's needs for safety and security, with networks of footpaths, and respect and space for women visiting local temples. Modern cities, planned according to Western secular principles, give little seclusion or privacy forcing everyone out into public view on the new highways. Zoning and separation of land uses, has destroyed the close-knit relationship between home, workplaces and local markets, within historic neighbourhoods and increased the distances between different land uses.

Lesson Two: Not only is zoning hard on women, it gave little space for God, religion and worship either. There is no space for feelings, emotions, sex, frenzy, and ecstasy, or for messy, 'dirty' women either, in the tidy, clean soulless world of scientific planning.

When new capital cities and administrative towns were built in the Empire's territories, they were designed by architects and planners imbued with the need to impose order on perceived chaos (Richards 2014/1904). For example the famous architect Edwin Lutyens designed New Delhi as the administrative capital of India on a magnificent scale, using zoning principles. This resulted in the ordinary local people (and their gods) being strictly excluded from the city centre, and religion being artificially contained in separate buildings. The new city was not even practical as the poor people lost their access to water supply and local services (Ganashen 2000). This process continued through the twentieth century with a series of modern Five-Year Development plans being introduced from 1951 onwards. Slum settlements were either pulled down in the name of progress, with the people were relocated on the outskirts or the city, or the slum areas were completely ignored with the modern city being built around them as if they did not exist (Haynes 2013). Mumbai (Bombay) and Kolkota (Calcutta) are now world-class mega cities with enormous modern industrial and commercial extensions as well as large traditional areas of poor housing, and lack of infrastructure, which are arguably given little attention as they have no economic value in the eyes of the city planners and developers.

Lesson Three: Planners cannot cope with so-called chaos, with overlapping land uses and activities, with fluidity, extreme poverty, and complexities of human life, as found

188 *Clara Greed*

for example in many Indian cities. Instead, planners want order, separation and 'everything in its place'. So rather than valuing the 'slum' areas they are cleared, ignored, or redeveloped, thus sweeping away millions of people and their livelihoods and religions in the process.

As Narayanan (2015) explains, even the modern environmental movement and sustainability agendas (powerful Western religions in themselves!) in spite of their ostensible concern with social issues have resulted in local villagers' needs being rendered secondary to those of rural conservation. According to the Rio UN declaration (1992) sustainability had three components, environmental protection, economic development and social equity, that is Planet, Prosperity and People. Originally the sustainability agenda was part of the fight against global poverty and for social justice (Brundtland 1987). As time has gone on, the environment component has tended to predominate. This is particularly true in Britain, because the planning system has been traditionally concerned with physical land-use matters, and has been run mainly by men with little awareness of social issues. It is much easier to set 'green' environmental standards and policies that can be measured scientifically in terms of changes in land-use, the climate, and pollution and other impersonal issues, than it is to introduce complex social policies. This mentality is transferred to India by ex-pat planners.

As a result of the overwhelming environmental emphasis, local people may be banned from going into nearby forests to gather firewood as they have done since time immemorial. Western-led, 'people-less' ecological policies and wildlife protection schemes are set at too high a level to take into account the needs of the impoverished people who live in such areas. Global elite policy makers live on a different plane from those in the developing world, and their environmental sustainability policies often greatly disadvantage, impoverish and restrict the lives of ordinary people, especially women (Greed 2011b). Modern aggressive, religiously illiterate environmentalism has little connection with, or respect for, the ancient principles of taking a caring, custodial role towards the planet, which Indians have practiced for millennia, as an ethical duty which is part of Hindu Dharma (Jain 2011). Women are often seen as more religious than men, and so are the true gatekeepers of Dharma, for as it says in the Manu Smriti (Laws of Manu), 'the gods are pleased when women worship' and may listen to them more.

Lesson Four: Sustainability, wildlife, the Planet, global warming, all take precedence over, and diminish, the very real needs of the local people, especially women, and condemn them as ignorant, selfish and stupid. It would be so much better if environmental experts listened to local people, especially women, and respected their spiritual harmony with the environment.

The murky roots of zoning

Paradoxically, modern land-use zoning comprises a secularised and highly patriarchal outworking of ancient Judeo-Christian beliefs on the separation of pure and impure, male and female, good and evil. An investigation of the origins of the word 'zoning' reveals both the occult and sexist roots of this apparently scientific planning principle. Zoning had long been used to control of women's place in urban space by keeping them out of public life and civic space and within the domestic realm of house and home (Greed 1994: 70–81). In ancient Greek, the word 'zona' conveys the idea of a belt and by inference to the restriction of the 'loins' that is the control of sexuality and the production of children (the fruit of the loins), and thus is linked to the control of women's sexuality and moral pollution. Marilyn French (1992: 76) points out the Hebrew for 'prostitute' – *zonah* (harlot) – means 'she who goes out of doors', that is, she is in the wrong place and has lost her respectability. In Latin, *zonam solvere* means 'to lose the virgin zone', that is to get married or lose one's virginity or, in medieval parlance, to remove the chastity belt. It is also only a short etymological leap from *zona*, to *zana*, to *sana*, to *sanitary*, and to the obsession with sanitation and hygiene in the modern secular city. Social hygiene appeared to be more about controlling women than actual disease, especially the dirtiness (sexuality) of working-class women. Ancient, dualistic, influences were at work in the conceptualisation of modern planning. These stressed the philosophical concept of there being a split between spirit and body, between pure and impure, and the need for man's spirit to escape the perceived impurity of the body and earthly realm (Douglas 1966). One of the characteristics of religion is to make a clear division between sacred and profane, public and private, right and wrong, clean and unclean, male and female, thus imposing order on the world.

Zoning and separation principles promoted by Geddes were popular with other European planning theorists and planners. Le Corbusier drew his inspiration from ancient occult and Masonic sources, in seeking to codify and control space and women's place both within the city of man and in the layout of the home (Birkstead 2009). Although Le Corbusier stated that 'a house is a machine for living in', neither he nor his fellow members of the Modern Movement had much idea how ordinary women used their 'machine' (home) and the problems they encountered in the city of man (Greed 1994: 121–124). Le Corbusier is famed for designing Chandigarh as the capital of the Punjab in Northern India, which comprises of a low-density layout of 'functionalist' office buildings. The residential areas were designed with little reference to the realities of local people's lives and needs, or the distances they needed to walk to get around. Le Corbusier imposed a highly impractical zoning pattern on the city which bore little relationship to the needs of the local people, in respect of both the importance of religion, and the needs of women (Shrey et al. 2010).

Lesson Five: Western planners deal better with static, fixed and slowly evolving, land-use patterns through zoning. They cannot cope with large numbers of people and fluctuating situations. The less people the better, empty ordered streets are seen as better than busy streets full of animals, people, shrines, market stalls and traders.

Contemporary century priorities

By the mid-twentieth century, town planning became a major powerful function in Britain, charged with urban reconstruction after the extensive bombing of

190 *Clara Greed*

World War II. Most of the philosophical and visionary origins of planning were long forgotten. But 'work', that is the economic component of the tripartite divisions that underpinned zoning principles as outlined above, remained the most important factor. Whatever their political ideology of successive governments, the importance of economic capital remained constant. Looking across the sociological continuum, Marx put the greatest emphasis on the importance of 'capital'. Marx saw economic supremacy, and thus capitalism and capitalists, as the main agents of power within society, and an evil power at that. Marx gave no place to religious and spiritual capital within either production or consumption, relegating it to the realms of the superstructure and declared 'religion is the opium of the people'. Subsequently the founding fathers of sociology discounted religious capital as a primary force within society. Religion was generally only seen as a vehicle of the rise of capitalism (Tawney 1966), not as a source of power or as a form of real capital in its own right. Economists across the spectrum from Left to Right continue to see capital, labour, employment and business investment as key drivers of the economy.

Lesson Six: modern planning is far better at dealing with material, economic, and physical land-use matters, than with cultural, social and religious factors. Planners like things they can count. I was told as a young planning student, 'If you can't count it, it doesn't count', and so I have spent my whole life disproving this!

But studies have shown indigenous religious groups can be important agents in generating sustainable development and local economic enterprises, mainly because they can provide local leadership and organisational structures, with women having a more prominent role, without reliance on Western experts and non-governmental organisations (Freeman, 2014). In India, there is much debate about *who* actually benefits when vast amounts of foreign money and expertise are poured into development, given the curious workings of government departments, multi-national companies and undemocratic political organisations. Red tape, bureaucracy and sheer slowness can block ordinary people's attempts to improve their housing conditions, whilst planning applications from big business are fast tracked (Luce, 2011).

Lesson Seven: if the planners do not like something but have limited powers to stop it, they will seek to slow down the process by referring to technicalities in the hope that the applicants will give up exhausted in the end and that they will run out of time, energy and resources!

The war of the capitals

There has been a gradual shift in academia towards acknowledging the importance of religious, spiritual and social capital, as players alongside economic capital and political power. Weber and other less-deterministic sociologists, such as Tönnies, Durkheim and Talcott Parsons, acknowledged the role of social capital, in the form of community identity, religious tradition, social class and status, and personal 'habitas' in shaping society and economic development (Greed 2013, Greed and Johnson 2014: Chapters 8 and 14, Weber 1905), but they were still weak on women's issues (Bologh 1990). By the mid twentieth century, the importance of cultural capital was identified by Bourdieu, Lefebvre and Williams, as another key factor in shaping not only society but the nature of urban space. Religion, belief and spirituality were identified as key ingredients in the creation of culture (Williams 1981).

In recent years, both religious and spiritual capital have been identified and defined as key forces within post-secular society (O'Sullivan and Flanagan 2012). Baker takes a two pronged approach separating spiritual and religious capital (Baker 2012). He describes religious capital as the resources, beliefs, networks, sense of community and values that enrich faith groups, whereas spiritual capital is seen as the motivation, faith, spirituality that energises such religious communities. Spiritual capital is not only a resource within the church, but like economic capital, it can perform as a source of prosperity, power and change within society. But the tragedy is that its power and its people, which could contribute so much to urban regeneration and the economy, are being held back by the planners. Nowadays, there is a battle going on between the forces of the different capitals, economic, cultural, social and religious to determine the land use and physical content of our towns and cities. One is reminded of Doreen Massey, the urban geographer, as to how power groups shape urban space through 'the reproduction over space of social relations' (Massey 1984). The process of transmission is mediated, to a considerable degree, through the role of the planning profession, in determining what should be built where. The beliefs of the main urban decision-makers, including the planners, property developers and politicians are themselves shaped by the dominant world views arising from the relative power of the different capitals, and sadly nowadays religious capital is short on influence. I have already been down this path in seeking to explain why planners do not take women's needs into account, because gender is recognised as important within the subcultural values of the planning profession (Greed 1994: Chapter 1), but the explanation works as well for 'religion' which is another blind spot in their world view. Both God and Gender, Faith and Feminism, are of no relevance to many a secular scientifically trained planner.

Lesson Eight is: 'they just don't get it!' Planners often completely miss the bigger picture, especially the value, dynamism and importance of religion and culture in shaping and regenerating cities, and instead, they waste their time on trying to enforce petty regulations to prevent religious building taking place.

Planning and religion in the United Kingdom

The lack of importance given to religion within the subculture of the planning profession directly shapes the nature and priorities of planning policy. There is a lack of national policy guidance on the place of religious buildings within strategic urban land-use planning, or on how local planning authorities should deal with applications for places of worship. The situation is not consistent across the nation as some local authorities taking a more positive view than others towards the 'same' sorts of applications. A major report on the planning system's approach

192   Clara Greed

to places of worship (CAG 2008) observed that there is no national strategy or high-level governmental policy statement on this matter. Most planning authorities, at county, city and local district level, do not have a specific policy statement in their development plan documentation on places of worship.

One of the key reasons for planning applications for churches not being given adequate value is because 'religion' does not fit in the planners' terms of reference and policy priorities. Therefore applications concerning religious buildings are dealt with through a secular lens, and judged by the standards of existing categories, such industrial, commercial, and residential and leisure uses. Within the UCO (Use Classes Order) (the nation-wide land-use 'Zoning Ordinance' regulations), there is no special category for 'worship buildings and uses' rather churches come under the same designation (D1) as cinemas, dance halls and other places of public assembly, with no consideration of their different social, moral and religious role in society. Refusals are given for a range of more cultural and social reasons, such as noise, disturbance, crime, being 'out of place' and a whole variety of convenient technicalities. In fact, churches are likely to get more protection as historical, architectural or tourist features than as living congregations. One can surely see parallels with the way in which temples and shrines are 'seen' by the planners in South Asia, with the largest, oldest and emptiest being given the most attention because of their likely attraction for Western tourists.

Because of the lack of available religious premises, such as redundant church buildings or empty public buildings, many new black Pentecostal churches have resorted to applying to use empty industrial units, often on trading estates on the edge of town (Lewisham 2008). The argument always given to justify refusal is that church development will take up valuable space allocated for employment, which itself is seen as vital to the economy: even where there is no demand from businesses. In parallel, church buildings and their congregations are generally seen as obstacles to urban regeneration, plan-making and as a nuisance within the inner city. Whilst in India religious buildings and communities often find themselves marooned in city centre locations with the tides of redevelopment all around them, in the United Kingdom, faith groups are likely to find they are being pushed out to the edges of the city, alongside industrial estates, storage depots, sewage works and other unpopular land uses.

The planners still seem to have an old-fashioned attitude to what constitutes the economy, and what might create growth and urban regeneration, in which 'industry' is still given a privileged position. They do not see churches as a source of employment, regeneration or indeed of creativity, although 'creative industries' and entrepreneurial activity may arise from within the church community. In the United Kingdom, churches often provide day care facilities, education and careers guidance and undertake a host of charitable activities and positive interventions in the surrounding neighbourhood, all of which contribute to residents finding work and having the housing, education and childcare to participate in the workforce in the first place. But urban regeneration policy is so obsessed with employment and investment issues, and increasingly with achieving environmental sustainability and 'green' credentials, that planners often forget all about

Including religion and gender 193

the essential social support system needed to enable people, especially women, to get into the workforce (Greed 2005, Greed 2012). So 'church' is not seen as an engine of the economy (as Patrick Anderson a black Christian planner working at Planning Aid for London has discussed with me). Thus religious capital is not recognised as a change agent, or as a force as potentially powerful as economic capital, because it does not 'fit' into the planners' view of how the world should be.

Lesson Nine: Planners are on a different wave length and are so obsessed with achieving economic policy objectives that they underestimate the power and importance of religion to people lives and as a force for urban regeneration and economic growth.

Whilst established church congregations are tolerated by the planners, what planners like even more are empty redundant churches which are commended for their age and quality of architecture. They can be re-used as community centres, upmarket housing, art galleries, museums, and even bars and clubs, within the context of regenerating the inner city. Likewise in view of the lack of affordable housing, there is increasing moral pressure for the Church of England to release redundant churches for conversion to housing. Without a positive planned approach, research shows, there is likely to be a significant national under-provision of worship space (Smith and Parham 2010). It is hard to imagine now, but it is possible that if the current trends towards secular planning continue in India, it too will find it has a lack of worship space in the future.

Contrary to media coverage, and to the general assumption by planners that churches, especially white ones, are in terminal decline from the 1960s (Cox 1965), there has in fact been a tremendous growth in church attendance and membership in many inner city areas. Whilst the growth of the membership of black Pentecostal mega-churches runs into many thousands, Goodhew (2012) has found that that adult membership of the Anglican churches in the diocese of London has also increased 70 per cent between 1990 and 2010, and much of this growth is due to immigration. According to www.brierleyconsultancy. com, around 7,000 new churches have been started since 1980, and in the last 10 years, more new ones have started than old ones closed down. There is a very high, unmet demand for new places of worship. Likewise in India, it seems some government authorities, planners and business leaders like to give the impression that Hinduism is just a superstition that the population will grow out of when they are more 'educated' and better off, thus completely denying the existence of the divine. Indeed, religion is being increasingly marginalised in many developing countries as 'old-fashioned' 'superstitious' or 'just for old women and peasants'.

Lesson Ten: In spite of this statistical proof, planners and much of society still believe religion is in decline and subscribe to the secular values promoted by the mass media. Therefore they do not collect religious data, and so it is invisible. But religion is not neutral, and if it is ignored, it will affect people negatively and may cause tension between different religious groups. But, if it is included it will benefit, bless and regenerate cities.

It is important to develop new planning methodologies that mainstream religion into the planning process, and which are transferable to the Indian

194   *Clara Greed*

sub-continent (Greed 2005). Modern city planning in the developing world has a dangerous tendency to clear out the 'clutter' to remove the street traders, small artisans, and illegal shanty town development, and impose scientific order and mono-use zoning, resulting in many people losing their homes and jobs (Sheth 2008). Ignoring the religious dimension may also create tension between different religious groups, because of what are seen as biased policies on the demolition and provision of religious buildings for particular faith groups (Gayer and Jaffrelot 2012).

Lesson Eleven: Planners simply do not understand how religious activity interrelates to and supports other policy objectives such as employment, social welfare and housing. They never seen the link between business enterprise and religion and may have extreme contempt and snobbery towards shop keepers and small-business people.

Lesson Twelve: They simply do not see religion as a strategic planning matter (like retail or residential development) at urban, regional or national level, in spite of it having very tangible physical built environment implications regarding land use allocation, zoning and new development.

Power of prayer and planning

How can we change the situation? We need to draw on the resources and power of spiritual capital (Zohar and Marshall 2004). Why do religious planners often feel ashamed about talking about their beliefs when in the presence of other planners? Do we compartmentalise our lives into the religious and the professional? Being myself a member of two total subcultures and contradictory belief systems 'planning' and Pentecostalism, should I turn to prayer or urban policy making or some of each? Since the problems seem so intransigent and endemic within urban planning, I personally am taking a two prong approach. I continue to pray about these issues (CARE 2009) but also to seek planning solutions. As for the power of prayer, it says in the Bible, 'the fervent prayer of the righteous man (and woman) availeth much' (James 5 v.16), and 'faith is the substance of things hoped for' (Hebrew 11 v.1). 'For we wrestle not against, not just planning authorities, but principalities and powers' (Ephesians 6 v.12), so we need to 'pray without ceasing', (I Thessalonians 5 v.17). There is a long tradition of weak, powerless people, praying for a miracle as a solution to what often seem to be completely impregnable barriers and obstacles confronting their pathway. The churches need to get more involved in urban politics too, and not see such activity as 'unspiritual' or 'worldly' (Beckford 2000, Guttierez 2001, Jamoul and Willis 2008). Likewise in India there is need for more community engagement, and an emphasis on participatory planning, rather than a 'top-down' approach being imposed on people's lives and cities.

As for planning solutions, we need to adapt models previously used to integrate other so-called minority issues into planning, such as gender, to mainstreaming religion into planning. Therefore I have been adapting the 'Women and Planning' principles which we used to develop the Gender Mainstreaming Toolkit which sets out a series of questions for the planners to ask themselves (Greed

2005, Reeves 2005). Gender mainstreaming initiatives continue to be promoted at UN level (Madariaga and Roberts 2013). This time around I am adapting the gender mainstreaming toolkit to the purposes of mainstreaming 'religion' into the plan-making process, as God and Religion are often just as 'invisible' as gender is in the planning process. To do so, one must present the process in language that planners understand, using recognised mainstream methodologies which relate the process of plan making, which still boils down to the stages of 'survey, analysis and plan'. There also needs to be a greater diversity of types of people doing planning, including women, and people from ethnic and religious 'minority groups who can bring a different perspective and who may be more in touch with ordinary people and their needs (De Graft Johnson et al. 2009).

As for Lesson Thirteen (the unlucky and cruellest lesson) regarding planners and life itself: Never trust anyone. Never believe anyone, especially those who say they have your best interests at heart, until you have observed what they are really like. Never assume anything about anyone, in particular never assume experts, policy maker, planners and academics know what they are talking about or have superior knowledge to that of the ordinary people.

Appendix 10.1
Summary of the RTPI gender mainstreaming toolkit

In order to integrate women's issues into planning, one must ask the following questions at each stage of the planning process, and in respect of each aspect of policy making:

1. What organisational resources and experience is there on gender mainstreaming?
2. How is the policy team chosen and is it representative of men and women?
3. Who are perceived to be the planned?
4. How are statistics gathered, are they disaggregated by gender, and who do they include?
5. What are the key values, priorities and objectives of the plan?
6. Who is consulted and who is involved in participation?
7. How is it evaluated?
8. How is the policy implemented, managed, monitored and managed?

In order to mainstream religion into planning one needs to ask the same sort of questions. I have expanded on each initial question to give you a range of indicative questions that might asked of the planners, with some adaptation, in both Western and Developing World situations. This should not only raise consciousness, but also provide a path to recognising and planning for religious needs. I mainly refer to Christianity in this illustration, but this schema could be adapted for any main religion depending on the requirements of the locality in question.

Appendix 10.2
Proposed toolkit to mainstream religion into planning

Urban policy makers and planners should ask themselves these questions:

1. What resources and expertise are available in the planning department to carry out this process? How much knowledge and experience do planners have of religious issues? Are they scripturally illiterate? Is money available to send them on training courses? Are paid experts, ministers and consultants to be brought in? Where are they from?
2. Does the policy team include planners and community representatives who are knowledgeable about religious issues? Are there male and female? Do you only speak to the Priests and Elders? What caste, class, background do they come from? Are there representatives from different faith groups?
3. Who are perceived to be the planned? Which religious groups are included? What other religious groups and faith communities are included? Who is the plan for? Is it for the benefit of rich developers and bankers or poor local people or outsiders? Who is missing from the plan?
4. Do you have up-to-date statistics on religious affiliation, size, levels of use and location of temples, churches and mosques? Do you keep records of levels of refusal for new religious buildings or change of use? What does this tell you about demand? Do you have records of the levels of occupation and demand for historical religious buildings?
5. What are the objectives of the plan? Is economic development the primary consideration? What about social infrastructure, childcare and community facilities? What role do you envisage the church playing in this provision? Are religious buildings and faith groups seen as obstacles to redevelopment or as generators of economic and cultural renewal in their own right? Do any of your other main policy topics, such as employment, transport, housing, have implications for religious development?
6. Who is consulted over the plans? Do you make an effort to explain the planning process to people, do you give pastors, imams and other faith group leaders some training on planning law, building control and how to read plans? Are women and men, rich and poor, and all ethnic groups involved?
7. How is the plan evaluated? What are your criteria of success? Is it based on economic, social, cultural or religious satisfaction and enrichment? Have you

198   *Clara Greed*

expelled and alienated the original residents by bringing in outside developers, clearing away so-called slums, clutter, street markets and chaos, thus depriving people of their livelihoods? Does your transport policy improve pedestrian routes and public transport, or does it just knock new highways through existing settlements and restrict public transport access?

8. How is the policy implemented? Are the needs of existing businesses respected or are they replaced by national chain stores and factories? Are churches and other faith groups still involved in ongoing monitoring or have they been dropped once development has taken place? Is there still room for everyone, including God?

Think on these things!

References

Baker, C. (2012) 'Exploring Spiritual Capital: Resource for an Uncertain Future?' in O'Sullivan, M. and Flanagan, B. (eds.), *Spiritual Capital: Spirituality in Practice in Christian Perspective*, Farnham: Ashgate.

Baker, C., and Beaumont, J. (eds.) (2011) *Post-Secular Cities: Space, Theory and Practice*, London: Continuum.

Beckford, R. (2000) *Dread and Pentecostal: A Political Theology for the Black Church in Britain*, London: SPCK.

Bergunder, M. (2008) *The South Indian Pentecostal Movement in the Twentieth Century*, Cambridge: Eardmans Publishing Company.

Birkstead, J. (2009) *Le Corbusier and the Occult*, London: MIT Press.

Bologh, R. (1990) *Love or Greatness: Max Weber and Masculine Thinking: A Feminist Inquiry*, London: Unwin Hyman.

Brundtland Report (1987) *Our Common Future*, World Commission on Environment and Development, Oxford: Oxford University Press.

Burgess, S. (2001) 'Pentecostalism in India: an overview', *Asian Journal of Pentecostal Studies*, Vol. 4, No. 1, pp. 85–98.

CAG (2008) *Responding to the Needs of Faith Communities: Places of Worship: Final Report*, London: CAG (Cooperative Advisory Group) Planning Consultants.

CARE (2009) 'Making a Christian difference through prayer', *Care Prayer Guide* www.care.org.uk, London: Christian Action, Research and Education.

Cox, H. (1965) *The Secular City: Secularisation and Urbanisation in Theological Retrospect*, Harmondsworth: Penguin.

De Graft-Johnson, A., Sara, R., Gleed, F., and Brkljac, N. (2009) *Gathering and Reviewing Data on Diversity within the Construction Professions*, London: Construction Industry Council in association with University of the West of England.

Douglas, M. (1966) *Purity and Danger: An Analysis of the Concepts of Pollution and Taboo*, London: Ark.

Falk, N. (2014) 'India's urban future: achieving smarter growth', *Town and Country Planning*, Vol. 81, No. 10, October Issue, pp. 456–461.

Freeman, D. (ed.) (2014) *Pentecostalism and Development: Churches, NGOs and Social Change in Africa*, London: Palgrave Macmillan.

French, M. (1992) *The War against Women*, London: Hamish Hamilton.

Including religion and gender 199

Ganashen, P. (2000) *Planning the City: Urbanisation and Reform in Calcutta, c1800–1940.* New Delhi: Tulika Books.

Gayer, L., and Jaffrelot, C. (eds.) (2012) *Muslims in Indian Cities: Trajectories of Marginalisation,* New Delhi: Harper Collins.

Geddes, P., and Thomson, J. A. (1889) *The Evolution of Sex,* London: Scott.

Geddes, Patrick (1968, originally 1915) *Cities in Evolution: An Introduction to the Town Planning Movement and to the Study of Civics,* London: Architectural Press.

Goodhew, D. (2012) *Church Growth in Britain: 1980 to the Present,* Farnham: Ashgate.

Greed, C. (1994) *Women and Planning: Creating Gendered Realities,* London: Routledge.

Greed, C. (2005) 'Overcoming the factors inhibiting the mainstreaming of gender into spatial planning policy in the United Kingdom', *Urban Studies,* Vol. 42, No. 4, pp. 1–31.

Greed, C. (2011a) 'A Feminist Critique of the Post Secular City: God and Gender', in Baker, C. and Beaumont, J. (eds.). *Post-Secular Cities: Space, Theory and Practice,* London: Continuum.

Greed, C. (2011b) 'Planning for sustainable areas or planning for everyday life and inclusion', *Journal of Urban Design and Planning,* Vol. 164, No. DP2, June, pp. 107–119.

Greed, C. (2012) 'Planning and transport for the sustainable city or planning for people', *Journal of Urban Design and Planning,* Proceedings of the Institution of Civil Engineers, Vol. 165, No. DP4, pp. 219–229.

Greed, C. (2013) 'A Feminist Perspective on Planning Cultures: Tacit Assumptions in a Taciturn Profession', in Young, G. and Stevenson, D. (eds.), *The Ashgate Research Companion to Planning and Culture,* Farnham: Ashgate.

Greed, C. (2014) 'Pentecostals and Planning in the UK', *Pentecostalism and Development,* 8th Glopent Conference Proceedings, London: SOAS (School of Oriental and African Studies).

Greed, C., and Johnson, D. (2014) *Introducing Planning,* London: Palgrave Macmillan.

Guttierez, G. (2001) *A Theology of Liberation,* London: SCM Classics.

Haynes, D. (2013) 'The making of the hyper-industrial city in western India: the transformation of artisinal towns into middle-sized urban centres', 1930–1970, *South Asia: Journal of South Asian Studies,* Vol. 36., No. 3, pp. 336–353, Special Issue on Beyond the Colonial City, Re-evaluating the Urban History of India 1920–1970.

Jain, P. (2011) *Dharma and Ecology of Hindu Communities: Sustenance and Sustainability,* New Delhi: National Book Organisation.

Jamoul, L., and Willis, J. (2008) 'Faith in politics', *Urban Studies,* Vol. 45, No. 10, pp. 2035–2056.

Kay, W. (2000) *Pentecostals in Britain,* Carlisle: Paternoster.

Kingsley Kent, S. (1987) *Sex and Suffrage in Britain 1860–1924,* London: Routledge.

Lewisham (2008) *Report from Planning Committee (A) on Elizabeth Industrial Estate change of use of ground floor,* London: London Borough of Lewisham, Case File DE/237/C/TP, DCS Number 100–054-444, see www.planningresource.co.uk

Luce, E. (2011) *In Spite of the Gods: The Strange Rise of Modern India,* London: Abacus.

Madariaga, I. S., and Roberts, M (eds.) (2013) *Fair Shared Cities,* London: Ashgate.

Massey, D. (1984) *Spatial Divisions of Labour: Social Structures and the Geography of Production,* London: Macmillan.

Mumford, L. (1965) *The City in History,* London: Penguin.

Narayanan, Y. (2015) *Religion, Heritage and the Sustainable City: Hindus and Urbanisation in Jaipur,* London: Routledge.

O'Sullivan, M., and Flanagan, B. (eds.) (2012) *Spiritual Capital: Spirituality in Practice in Christian Perspective,* Farnham: Ashgate.

200 Clara Greed

Peach, C., and Gale R. (2003) 'Muslims, Hindus, and Sikhs in the new religious landscape of England', *Geographical Review*, Vol. 93, pp. 469–490.

Porter, L. (2013) 'Editorial: Comparison, context and finding the political in planning', *Planning Theory and Practice*, Vol. 14, No. 3, September, pp. 289–291.

Reeves, D. (2005). *Planning for Diversity: Policy and Planning in a World of Difference*. London: Routledge.

Richards, E. P. (ed.) (2014) *The Richards Report 1914: The Condition, Improvement and Town Planning of the City of Calcutta and Contiguous Areas*, London: Routledge.

Rio (1992) *Rio Declaration: United Nations Conference on the Environment at Rio De Janiero*, New York: United Nations.

Sandercock, L. (2006) 'Spirituality and the urban professions – the paradox at the heart of urban planning', *Planning Theory and Practice*, Vol. 7, No. 1, 69–75.

Sheldrake, P. (2007) 'Place the sacred: transcendence and the city', *Literature and Theology*, Vol. 21, No. 3, pp. 243–258.

Sheth, Alpen Suresh (2008) 'Generating Spatial Surplus: The Politics of Zoning in the Mumbai Metropolitan Region', *Open Access Theses*, Paper 129, www.scholarlyrepository.miami.edu/cgi/viewcontent.cgi?article=1128/

Shrey, S., Kandoi, S., and Srvastava, S. (2010) *Urban Planning in India*, SOC 477 Project at www.verenigingvanbouwkunst.nl/agenda/1003-india/india-urban_planning_in_india.pdf, Tilburg: Architectural Academy, The Netherlands.

Smith, P., and Parham, S. (2010) 'Making Space for Worship', *Planning*, 12 February 2010, see www.planningresources.co.uk

Tawney, R. (1966) *Religion and the Rise of Capitalism*, Harmondsworth: Penguin.

Timothy, D., and Olsen, D. (2011) *Tourism, Religion and Spiritual Journeys*, London: Routledge.

Weber, M. (1905, translated edition 1965) *The Protestant Ethic and the Spirit of Capitalism*, Harmonsworth: Penguin.

Williams, R. (1981) *The Sociology of Culture*, Chicago: University of Chicago Press.

Zohar, D., and Marshall, I. (2004) *Spiritual Capital: Wealth We Can Live By*, London: Bloomsbury.

11 Religion and urban policy for South Asia

Where next?

Yamini Narayanan

Introduction

The phenomenal rate of urbanisation in developing countries has left planners with little opportunity or foresight to deal with the rapid changes that it has brought on. In Asia, the industrial boom in Japan in the 1960s was followed by the creation of the four 'Asian tigers' – Taiwan, South Korea, Singapore and Hong Kong – and by the emergence of India and China as two major economic players. This brought on the beginning of an urban explosion throughout the region. With the exception of Africa, Asia has been urbanising much more rapidly than the rest of the world, and by 2020, more than one-third of the world's population will live in Asian cities (Logan 2002). As early as almost 30 years ago, the Brundtland Commission (1987: 282) had noted the grim challenge for urban sustainability in particularly in the developing cities of Asia and Africa:

> Few city governments in the developing world have the power, resources and trained staff to provide their rapidly growing populations with the land, services and facilities needed for an adequate human life: clean water, sanitation, schools and transport. The result is mushrooming illegal settlements with primitive facilities, increased overcrowding, and rampant disease linked to an unhealthy environment.

The issues of space, infrastructure and access that the Brundtland Commission noted above are far from techno-scientific urban issues that can be addressed through rationalist or management approaches. These are problems that are founded on the configurations and dynamics of power and powerlessness, and oppression as determined by identities, histories, memories and civic rituals of individuals and communities. It is in the engagement and scrutinisation of these dynamics that the strategies of sustainable cities in South Asia can be ultimately conceptualised and implemented. As Glaeser (2012: 111) writes, 'If cities are going to serve as engines of economic success, rather than places of sickness, crime and despair, the world will need better urban policies'. The construction of such policies in South Asia, we have suggested, plead for religion as one significant planning category for the analysis of, and approaches to urban issues.

202 *Yamini Narayanan*

The nine case studies in this volume strongly identified religion as an element of social justice in reinforcing or legitimising particular forms of urban social organisation, and access to space. In particular, the authors focussed on two themes as vital to consider in the conceptualisations of sustainable cities in South Asia, and where religion played an influential determining role: the making of place through history and heritage, and religion's role in creating spaces and practices of informality in cities.

Religious heritage for sustainable cities

Religion's role in placemaking through celebrations, conflicts and tensions is a recurring theme of this book. Civic life in the city is understood by the meanings generated by the religious system. Religious rituals shape the consciousness of city inhabitants and yet, the religious and cultural praxis is subject to constant change, covert and overt, as the city integrates more strongly with the global economy through tourism and capitalism (Parish 1997). Indeed, as Lazzaretti shows in this volume, conflict over the start and endpoints of a significant intra-city pilgrimage in Varanasi illustrates the powerful role of religious identities and rituals as assertion strategies, and the tensions between local and urban management's perception of religious heritage. The particular forms of social organisation through religiosities, and their utilisation in privileging and/or oppressing indeed spans beyond human citizens, raising new questions for animal liberation politics and their strong links with sustainable cities in Indian and other South Asian cities (Narayanan 2015).

Hitherto however the urban governance and policymaking in South Asia has resolutely ignored the obvious sociological, anthropological and theological influences that determine urban spaces and environments, to the extent that planning seems almost tainted by indifferences to the 'real' dynamics that matter. Bolay (2011: 76) asks with despair, 'How could a global and complex phenomenon such as urbanization in developing countries be so neglected that one cannot but observe that in developing countries, the urban situation is deteriorating on a human, environmental as well as infrastructural level?' A deep root of this neglect is the steady and fair engagement with volatile socio-cultural forces, prominently religion in South Asia, and the problems – but also opportunities – that religion can present secular governance.

The importance of *suitable* planning for developing sustainable cities in South Asia cannot be overemphasised. Modernist planning supported by the homogenising forces of globalisation imposes a uniform pattern of building and planning cities with disregard for the incredible regional and cultural variations that richly define a diversity of urban spaces. These effects are particularly damaging in cities that have a rich heritage and historical value. Zetter and Watson (2006: 3) note that 'these [homogenising] forces are commodifying the place-identity of historic urban spaces and places, at once detaching them from their continuity with locality, space and time'.

Religion and urban policy for South Asia   203

This fracture is a problem, in particular for high-profile tourism, heritage and pilgrimage cities in South Asia. Cities, including those of the Indian subcontinent, are not exempt from the serving the global economy, and promoting place-identities that encourage the national growth of their countries. Indeed, the case for historicity and religious-cultural distinctions – and their associated implications for claiming and colonising space and urban infrastructure can be made for almost all South Asian cities which can claim heritage value in varying degrees (Menon 2005), and which also impact their capacity to attract investment and grow. As Moore (2008: 57) notes, 'it could easily be argued that understanding city-image building or "re-imaging" is the key to comprehending the dynamics of city development and management in the 21st century, as the city is now, like any other commodity, being marketed and sold'. The physical nature of urban development matters intensely to economies, and Moore (2007: 97) argues that 'At a global scale, economic restructuring and physical change have gone hand-in-hand and have recently led to debates on the nature of the city and the kinds of development that we should be promoting'. These include 'entrepreneurial' methods such as the implementation of steps to attract greater investment and enable economic growth and engage in place marketing that further requires the services of marketing and other external consultants (in addition to urban planners) (Moore 2007: 97).

Yangon in Myanmar, as Ware has noted in this book, recently and cautiously opened to the world again, exemplifies how a previously dominant Buddhist place-identity was spatially marginalised, overtly or covertly, to foster the image of an inclusive, *multireligious* city. The image of cosmopolitanism was important not only to destabilise the power of a dominant social group, but also to encourage a welcoming and diverse image for international tourism. However this could cause defensive identities to arise particularly for long-term residents of a place, as marketers are interested in developing and promoting a more global sense of place and 'subject the past to a very controlled and deliberate reinterpretation' (Moore 2007: 98), thus potentially negating local memory and sense of place. In this way, 'in the reconstruction of place, some histories are privileged while others are expunged from collective memory' (Winchester et al 2003: 135), and the residents inhabiting the area for the longest period of time are the ones likely to feel most dislocated by this place reconstruction.

Jain's chapter has noted that Amritsar, a historic walled city with royal Sikh roots has adopted precisely the strategies of image-branding as a heritage city with a rich and religious sense of place. In Amritsar, Jain (2015) expresses anxieties about the incongruity of a World Heritage status and associated regulatory norms for the city which may not be aligned with matters of frameworks and practice of local faith. This approach has been criticised for its economic drawbacks (Moore 2007). Typically place marketing has aggressive competition, often within the same city as developers, construction companies and marketing consultants promote different sections of the same city for investment. Not surprisingly, built heritage is appropriated and positioned as one of the key features of promotion.

Religion and the production of informality

Religious heritage, tangible and intangible, also impact informal growth that are oftentimes faster and more widespread than regulated growth in South Asian cities. It is now well established that informality is not only associated with slums or shantytowns. Modernity's 'false dichotomy' of reinforcing categories such as 'legal' and 'criminal', 'fixed' and 'temporary' (Yiftachel 2012: 153) is too limited and narrow in its scope to adequately address even its own distinctions. The position on what is 'legal' and acceptable, and 'illegal' and undesirable constantly shifts, thus leading to the greater and ongoing production of gray space, and the creation of new colonial relations in the urban space, where neighbourhoods and even suburbs (such as the Dharavi slum in Mumbai) exist independently, largely unreliant on the services of formal urban planning such as state-provided sewerage, roads or even public transport facilities. Further, religion supports the political force necessary to enable informality. In their study of low caste Hindu and Buddhist slums in Pune city, Bhatewara and Bradley (2013) show that religion is instrumental in claiming agency and equality.

In this book, Rakistis takes this analysis further, using the highly illustrative case study of Karachi, South Asia's violent megacity. Though he does not refer to informality as a framework, it is clear that the production of sectarianism and fundamentalism required the careful utilisation of space. Ghettoisation and spatial marginalisation are a cause and outcome of fear, violence and insecurity. While these global-scale issues are beyond the scope of Karachi's urban management alone, there is no doubt that reclaiming and examining urban planning through the lens of religion and a myriad other socio-cultural lens is necessary to conceptualising of a sustainable city.

This volume additionally introduced two relevant lens through which to complicate informality in South Asia. Chakravarty examines the commonly perceived feature in Indian cities of the placement of religious structures *on* the road, rather than *along* the road as a condition of informality *produced and sustained* by formal planning. The careful colonial and postcolonial planning around Shahi Masjid on Kingsway in New Delhi collude to show the mosque as a protrusion or an incongruity onto an otherwise seemingly planned and meaningful space. Religious structures are thus carefully utilised by urban planning to destabilise particular religious groups or heighten their vulnerability, without actually altering the structure itself. Macrae (2004: 218) calls for the recognition that 'temples [or other religious structures] do not just happen; they are large, complex and expensive temple structures, the design, construction, maintenance and management of which requires a correspondingly complex organisation of social, economic and intellectual resources'. Formal planning thus choose to create informality rather than formally and seamlessly integrate layers of historicity and religious identities into producing spatial coherence.

Two, the volume goes beyond the counters of anthropocentrism to consider the spaces that animals in cities occupy and their (in)visibility as an instance of planned humancentric formality. The trafficking and slaughter of young male

Religion and urban policy for South Asia 205

calves in Vishakapatnam city under the guise of religious donations to the Simhachalam temple and the use of urban spaces and mobility resources to do so occur in zones of exception and outside the ambit or concern of formality (Narayanan 2015). In its various forms, informality can be argued to be the most common expression of urbanism in South Asian cities. The close critique of informality and the utilisation of religion in the production of informality is one of the greatest tasks for considerations of sustainable cities in South Asia.

What next? Considerations for future work

Even as this modest collection aims to address significant gaps in sustainable urban development in South Asia, it is, unsurprisingly left with a raft of important facets to this issue that need close and critical scrutiny for an expanded framing of sustainable cities in the region. This edited volume modestly offers a starting critique of selected themes, cities and countries for future works to carry forward the substantial analyses that remain to be undertaken. It would be stating the obvious to point to the need for in-depth studies on the intersections between religion and sustainable urban development across a wide range of cities across South Asia. Rather, we'd like to acknowledge the following themes that are vital and remain unaddressed in our own studies.

Gender and sustainable South Asian cities

A gaping hole is a gendered analysis of religion and urbanism in South Asian cities. In this volume, leading British feminist planner Clara Greed forewarns Indian and other South Asian planners against blindly following the inherited secularist planning profession, and taking care instead to mainstream gender into models for sustainable cities. This, she suggests, is a way of mainstreaming essential categories like religion into planning as well. Addressing issues of women's free and unhindered access to urban space and mobilities requires attention at multiple levels of legislation, infrastructural support and policymaking. However gender inequality is not hindered by policies and legislation alone but rather, by fundamental socio-cultural inequalities that allow such restrictions and barriers to exist in the first place. The role and influence of religion in determining women's participation in urban development, and the extent of the benefits that accrue to them – or not – is rarely discussed in South Asia. This presents problems for gender-equitable urban development, for with the best of intentions, legislations and policies, women cannot fully be involved in development processes because cultural and religious values and traditions that regulate their lives at a deeper level may not be consistent with secular developmental interventions.

Study of urban religion

A second significant opportunity for further study is the notion of religion in the South Asian city itself. Robert Orsi (1999: 42–43) had suggested a study of 'urban religion', or the particular religion and its associated religiosities that emerges with particular aspects of the industrialised and urbanised environment 'the dynamic engagement of religious traditions with . . . specific features of the industrialised and postindustrialised cityscapes and with the social conditions of city life'. In particular, he argued that the 'traditional cities of Asia, Meso-America and South Asia' were the ideal sites to study the palpable forms of urban religiosities. Without a critique of religion itself as a complex post-secular anthropological construct, there is a real risk of reductionism in the way that religion may be understood. The need for religion to be understood in its sociological, anthropological and, indeed, theological dimensions cannot be overstated.

The close study of religion leads to the vital insight that cities of South Asia for are indeed fundamentally planned and designed by the priests and practitioners of religion. The thousands of pilgrimage and religious cities in particular have a design rationale that is determined by religious values, rituals and logic for social hierarchies. In his study of the historic Bhaktapur city in Nepal, anthropologist Robert Levy (1997: 61) emphasised the role of religion and religiosity in contributing to the particular physical form of the city, and the social norms and privileges that directed the occupation and utilisation of the city spaces.

Hinduism in its most developed urban forms might be conceived of as a sort of symbolic machine which has the power to organize space, time, society, and people's private mental worlds on the large scale of the communal order of a 'unicultural' city. It is a kind of religion-in scale and in the uses to which it is put – which differs significantly, on the one hand, from that of simpler communities and, on the other, from that of the still larger imperial and economic orders which were to dissolve Hinduism's kinds of cities.

Cultivating intellectual curiosity and openness about religion is also useful for planners to design spaces in ecologically sustainable ways. Heritage and conservation scholars have for sometime bemoaned the loss of traditional planning knowledge in India (Heitzman 2008; Sachdev and Tillotson 2002). Classical planning and design texts like the *Vaastu Shastra* had secular and sacred priorities, encompassing the totality of human existence, and took into account highly localised geographical, climatic and other realities of place. In arguing for sustainable development models to earnestly consider older frameworks, of sustainability as it were, such as the *Vaastu Shastras*, Patra (2009: 247) writes: 'Traditional views are very important for a calculated modern scientific development, for they remind us the negative side of certain achievements and give useful insight to create a balance between humans and nature'.

Crucially, the traditional models remind us that religious conceptions of space may be understood dramatically differently from secularist, techno-scientific notions of space. An aspect of religiosity and urban space that may be especially confounding to the urban planner may be the notion of 'otherworldly space' such as 'planetary' space which Hindus for instance, believe exerts a profound influence on the realities of their everyday lives (Ambroise 1982). These understandings of otherworldly space extend to beyond the physical manifestations of urban space and this in turn influences the nature of the built environment.

Religion and urban policy for South Asia 207

Ultimately, the city epitomises the near-totality of humans' construction of their *habitus*. Religion brings to all aspects of human life, including the built environment where human life is produced and reproduced. Paraphrasing Finnish city planner Seppo Kjellberg, Gorringe (2002: 2) pleads for the purpose theology in urban planning as 'a science of reconciliation, promoting interdisciplinary dialogue, bringing all concerned with questions of the built environment together, but offering as its own perspective an understanding of the overall purpose of humankind with creation'. Reconciliation 'as the vivifying and revolutionary action of God within human community seeking the realisation of life in all its fullness for all people' (p. 2) is possible when the city is built, constructed, negotiated and shared such that humans can fully achieve a sense of awareness that guides them to their rightful role and place in the universe. Gorringe (2002: 26) writes, 'If God is a-spatial . . . in asking about the grounding of space in God, we are asking about the possibility of ultimate redemption for what we have made of the world'. We need to explore the points of intersection and difference between theology and urbanisms, to develop planning frameworks that work as urban planning theologies that fulfil sacred, secular and spiritual needs of humankind.

Museumfication as a condition of informality

In this book, Matti, Bastin and Ware addressed how religious and cultural artefacts in the city foreground identity and sense of place for the city. The use of culture in planning is usually implemented with a view to support the preservation and visibility of certain sections, ethnicities and their traditions to promote tourism. This can result in the museumfication or the artificial preservation of particular parts, practices and heritage of some parts of the city, and the simultaneous decay of some others. However the risk of museumfication of parts of city through the use of religious heritage in privileging sections of the dominant or the 'elite' community to the disadvantage of the reading of other histories, memories or meanings needs to be carefully examined as a planning concern. Museumfication can be especially a significant problem in old historic cores or walled cities (Narayanan 2015), of which there are thousands in South Asia.

Museumfication assumes particular importance in the hierarchical caste-based societies of South Asia. Hancock (2002) notes for instance that the ways that history, culture and identity are discussed and represented in the public intellectual life of Chennai city centres around a Hindu elite and upper-caste version of history and heritage. She refers to the Tamil cultural theme park Dakshina Chitra (comparable to the Rajasthani cultural theme park Choki Dani) where traditional Tamil crafts, dances and music are celebrated onsite. Dakshina Chitra harks liberally to Gandhian visions of the idyllic ruralism as celebrated by upper-caste Tami Brahmins, in the representations of small-scale and low-density village settlements, even in the midst of the city. The park is a contrast to the monuments and sites that were used by the Dravidian movement in the late 19th century, which sought to honour and foreground non-Brahmin Tamil poets, philosophers and leaders as representatives of the authentic Tamil culture (in

208 *Yamini Narayanan*

contrast to the Brahmins who were seen as Indo-Aryan invaders from the north), and to counter British colonialism (Hancock 2002). The modern Tamil state's conception of Dakshina Chitra carefully veers away from Dravidian expressionism and is instead represented in a way most accessible to upwardly mobile Tamil upper-caste Brahmin elites, and to 'an English-speaking global audience familiar with transcultural discourses of 'heritage' and with Eurowestern conventions of historiography and museology' (Hancock 2002: 696).

These issues particularly become a problem as several South Asian cities with iconic historical value actively pursue World Heritage status. Kathmandu and Bhaktapur cities in Nepal illustrate clearly the tensions between with tourism on the one hand, and urban rights of the citizens on the other. In Amritsar, Jain emphasises the need for religious heritage to be living, and meaningful in localised, everyday ways rather than as visual icons to a floating tourist population. Religious heritage in particular affords planning the opportunity to exercise creativity and innovation in revival of place, and to subvert museumfication. The anthropological aspects of cultural and religious museumfication in South Asian cities can provide valuable insight into the conceptualisation of spatially and socially equitable cities in South Asia.

Trans-species planning and sustainable cities

Cities are the nerve centres of neoliberal development. In the last few decades, the sustainable development meta-narrative has underpinned much of the philosophical and strategic approaches underpinning global development. In its growth-driven utilisation of nature and emphasis on an efficiency-driven paradigm in development, sustainable development is also arguably a process rife with violence, even as it claims lofty aims of ecological and social justice. In cities, sustainable development prioritises human-centred development, is fundamentally anthropocentric and does not extend its scope across species.

Lost in such analyses have been the utilisation and exploitation of animals to aid neoliberal growth and capitalist development. Animals have, amazingly, fallen between the cracks of 'not quite being nature' and 'not quite being human' in development discourse more broadly and in urban narratives in particular, in spite of their strong presence in South Asian cities. They been almost entirely neglected as a vital consideration from the perspective of rights, justice and equality. A major research need thus is the development of post-human frameworks to analyse the connections between animals/religion/development/violence in cities, and explore how in the case of domesticated animals in particular in South Asia, religion as well as sustainable development are deployed to utilise animals for urban and capitalist growth.

The violence inherent in current development practices cannot be fully dismantled unless violence to animals in the name of religion and progress is eliminated. As a starting point, animals must be made visible in their role in sustaining urban development, and identities and cultures in South Asian cities through their human-designated roles as religious icons, as well as religious and economic

Religion and urban policy for South Asia 209

resources. There is a growing need – even and especially for South Asian planners – to find ways of mainstreaming recognition and respect for nonhuman sentience through reinterpreting key religious scriptures, rituals and values through post-human perspectives. These projects can form the vital foundation for human *and* animal rights and welfare in the cities of this region.

References

Ambroise, Yvon. 1982. The Hindu Concept of Space and Time Structuring the Day to Day Life of Man. *Social Compass* 29 (4): 335–348.

Bhatewara, Zara, and Tamsin Bradley. 2013. 'The people know they need religion in order to develop': Religion's Capacity to Inspire People in Pune's Slums. *The European Journal of Development Research* 25 (2): 288–304.

Bolay, Jean-Claude. 2011. What sustainable development for the cities of the South? Urban issues for a third millennium. *International Journal of Urban Sustainable Development* 4 (1): 76–93.

Glaeser, Edward, L. 2012. The Challenge of Urban Policy. *Journal of Policy Analysis and Management* 31 (1): 111–122.

Gorringe, Tim. 2002. *A Theology of the Built Environment*. Cambridge: Cambridge University Press.

Hancock, Mary. 2002. Subjects of heritage in urban southern India. *Environment and Planning D: Society and Space* 20: 693–717.

Heitzman, James. 2008. Middle Towns to Middle Cities in South Asia, 1800–2000. *Journal of Urban History* 35 (1): 15–38.

Levy, Robert. 1997. The power of space in a traditional Hindu city. *International Journal of Hindu Studies* 1 (1): 55–71.

Logan, W.S., ed. 2002. *The 'Disappearing' Asian City: Protecting Asia's Urban Heritage in a Globalizing World*. Oxford and New York: Oxford University Press.

Macrae, Graeme. 2004. Who knows how to build a temple? Religious and secular, tradition and innovation, in contemporary South Indian sacred architecture. *South Asia: Journal of South Asian Studies* 27 (2): 217–243.

Menon, A.G.K. 2005. 'Heritage Conservation and Urban Development: Beyond the Monument'. In *Heritage Conservation and Urban Development* (pp. 1–7), ed. Rajeshwari Tandon. New Delhi: INTACH.

Moore, Niamh. 2008. *Dublin Docklands Reinvented: The Post-Industrial Regeneration of a European City Quarter*. Dublin: Four Courts Press.

Narayanan, Yamini. 2015. *Religion, Heritage and the Sustainable City: Hinduism and Urbanisation in Jaipur*. Oxford: Routledge.

Orsi, Robert. 1999. 'Introduction: crossing the city line'. In *Gods of the city: religion and the American urban landscape*, ed. Robert Orsi. Bloomington and Indianapolis: Indiana University Press.

Parish, Steven, M. 1997. Goddesses Dancing in the City: Hinduism in an Urban Incarnation: A Review Article. *International Journal of Hindu Studies* 1 (3): 441–484.

Patra, Reena. 2009. Vaastu Shastra: Towards Sustainable Development. *Sustainable Development* 17: 244–256.

Sachdev, Vibhuti, and Giles Tillotson. 2002. *Building Jaipur: The Making of an Indian City*. London: Reaktion Books Ltd.

Winchester, Hilary P. M., Lily Kong, and Kevin Dunn. 2003. *Landscapes: Ways of Imagining the World*. Harlow Pearson/Prentice Hall.

210 Yamini Narayanan

Yiftachel, Oren. 2012. 'Critical Theory and 'Gray Space'': Mobilization of the colonized'. In *Cities for People, Not for Profit: Critical Urban Theory and The Right to the City* (pp. 150–170), eds. Neil Brenner, Peter Marcuse and Margit Mayer. Oxford and New York: Routledge.

Zetter, Roger, and Georgia Butina Watson. 2006. 'Designing Sustainable Cities'. In *Designing Sustainable Cities in the Developing World* (pp. 3–18), eds. Roger Zetter and Georgia Butina Watson. Aldershot: Ashgate.

Index

Note: Italicized page numbers indicate a figure on the corresponding page. Page numbers in bold indicate a table on the corresponding page.

Abu'l Fazl shrine 46, 51–4, *54*, 57
Afghanistan 1, 50, 58, 164; *see also* Kabul (old city) religious heritage
Ahle Sunnat Wal Jamaat (The Organisation of the Followers of the Tradition-ASWJ) 170
Albanese, Catherine 156
All Karachi Trade Association 173
Amar Das, Guru 69
American Baptists 35
Amritsar, India *see* Sikhism in Amritsar, India
Ancient Monuments Preservation Act (1904) 121
Andhra Pradesh Prohibition of Cow Slaughter and Animal Preservation Act (1977) 153
Andhra Pradesh state in India 145–6, 149
Anglican Christianity 102
animal rights activists 148, 149, 158
anthropocentrism 204
anti-religious modernisation 58
a priori notions 97
Archaeological Survey of India 123
architectural existentialism 136
Arjun Dev, Guru 69
Auliya, Nizamuddin 11
Auliya Mosque 119, 127, *127*, *128*
Awami National Party (ANP) 167, 177

Barelwi Islamic jurisprudence school of thought 170
Bastin, Rohan 19
Bengal Code (1810) 123
Bengali Sunni Jaime Mosque 29, 38

Bhagvad Gita (Hindu text) 147
Bhaktapur city in Nepal 206
Bhutto, Banazir 166–7
British East India Company 122
British India 40
Brundtland Commission 201
Buddha Jayanthi Chaithya 105–6, 107
Buddhist temples 145, 153
bull-calf trafficking in Simhachalam Temple, Visakhapatnam: cattle as pillars of Hindu civilisation 146–9; conclusion 157–9; informality in developing cities 154–7; introduction 143–6; male calf donation 149–54, *151*, *152*
Burman-Buddhist nationalism in Myanmar: conclusion 41–2; downtown Yangon 28–31, *29*, *30*; post-1852 38–40; identiy, integration, and power 37–41; laying out urban grid 32–4; marginalisation of 28, 41, 42; overview 18, 27–8, 40–1; town planning and religious space 36–7; town planning and urban grid 34–5; urban planning 37–8; war and reconstruction 31–7

capitalism 11, 190
Catholic Cathedral 37
Central Public Works Department (2013) 123
Chakrabarty, Dipesh 139
Chakravarty, Surijit 19
Chandanaotsavam festival 149
Chaudhery, Amit 148
Chinese immigrant groups 40
Christian heritage the West 183–4

212 Index

Christopher, Anthony 124
Church of England 193
Cities in Evolution (Geddes) 7
Citizen Police Liaison Committee 167
City District Government of Karachi (CDGK) 175
Coburn, Noah 48
Cold War 119, 120
Colombo, Sri Lanka: conclusion 110–11; introduction 97–8; overview 98–103, **99**; population snap shot 103–5; religious institutions 105–8; Tamil Hindus in 106, 108–10
Colombo Vel Festival 109
commodification of high-value animals 157
communist ideology in Kabul 57
community-led development 36
Compassion Unlimited Plus Action 149
contested space, reshaping pilgrimage routes: alternative traces for 91–2; introduction 80–1; multi-faceted heritage 84–6; sustainability and heritage 82–4; tradition and bureaucracy 88–91; various visions for 86–8
Convention for the Safeguarding of Intangible Cultural Heritage (2003) 10
cultural heritage research 83
Curzon, George Nathaniel 121

Dakshina Chitra theme park 207
Daly, Herman 156
darshan of Shringar Gauri 89–90
de Noronha, Constantino de Sa 101
Deobandi Sunni school of thought 169
Devatagaha Mosque 103
developing country analogue 120
developmental secularism 98
Dharavi slum settlement in Mumbai 148
dual development strategies 68
Duncan, James 102
Dutch East India Company 100
Dutch Reformed Church 101

entrepreneurialism 119–21
essentialism of the "passive poor" 136
ethnic extremism in Karachi, Pakistan: conclusion 176–7; ghettoisation 172–3; inter-ethnic violence 166–9, 168; inter-sectarian violence 169–70; introduction 162–3; *Muhajirs* migrants 17, 163–4, 166; police force needs

173–4; political accord needs 174–5; setting for 163–6; stabilization of 173–6; sustainability needs 175–6
European Christendom 185
exceptional places in New Deli *132*, *132–5*, *133*, *134*, *135*

Fabricius, Daniel 136
First Anglo–Burmese War 31
Five-Year Development plans 187
formal-normative framework 120
French, Marilyn 189
Freud, Sigmund 186

Gandhi, Ajay 2–3
Gandhi, Indira 73
Gandhi, Mahatma 146, 147–8
Gangaramaya Temple 102
Ganguly, Suparna Baksi 150
Geddes, Patrick 7, 186, 189
gender and South Asian cities 205
Gender Mainstreaming Toolkit 194–5, 196
gentrification 2, 6
Geyer, H.S. 10
ghettoisation: India 16, 19; introduction 6; Karachi 172–3; South Asia 204
Gobindgarh Fort 71
Godhra carnage in Ahmedabad 4
Golden Temple complex at Amritsar, India *see* Sikhism in Amritsar
Granth Sahib, Guru 69
Greater Visakapatnam Municipal Corporation (GVMC) 146, 154
Greed, Clara 19
Green Line Bus Project 176
Gupta, Narayani 122
Gupta ji, Uma Shankar 87, 89
Gurudwara Reform Movement 72–3

Hargobind, Guru 69, 70
Hart, Keith 119
Heitzman, James 14
hierarchy, defined 16
Hinduism: cattle as pillars of Hindu civilisation 146–9; sentience and 19; in sustainable cities 154–5; Tamil Hindus 106, 108–10; urban planning and 206; utilization of symbols, rituals and histories 11; women's position within 187
Hindutva associations 84
Historic Urban Landscape 75

Index   213

Hokkien Kheng Hock Keong Chinese temple 29–30
hook-swinging 109
Hosagrahar, Jyoti 122
HRIDAY (Heritage Rejuvenation Development and Augmentation Yojana) scheme 69, 74–5, 77
human-animal conflicts 157
Human Rights Commission 165

ICLEI (International Council for Local Environmental Initiatives) 78
illegal slaughterhouses 158
Immanuel Baptist Church 29
India 4, 16, 19, 35; *see also* religion and gender in Indian urban planning; religious structures on traffic lanes in New Delhi; Sikhism in Amritsar
Indian immigrant groups 40
Indian Ocean spice trade 100–1
Indian Tamils 104
Indo-European languages 104
Industrial Revolution 185–6
informality: in developing cities 154–7; as disjuncture and exception 135–8; museumfication and informality 207–8; negative definitions of informality 119–21; religious cities and 204–5; religious structures on traffic lanes 118, 119; tensions of 144
institutionalisation of Sikhism 72–3
Intangible Cultural Heritage (ICH) 83
inter-ethnic violence 166–9, *168*
International Crisis Group 170
inter-sectarian violence 169–70
Irwin Road Mosque, Baba Kharak Singh Marg 118, 127, 129–30
Islamisation program 169

Jai Gopal Karodia Foundation 153
Jain, Shikha 19
Jain temples 145
Jallian Wala Bagh massacre (1919) 72
Jamaat-i-Islami 169
Japanese International Cooperation Agency (JICA) 176
Judeo-Christian beliefs 188
Juneja, Monica 131

Kabul (old city) religious heritage: conclusion 62–3, *63*; history of 49, 49–51; introduction 46–8, *47*; mapping urban heritage 48–9; sense of place and

51–5, *53, 54*; urban planning 55–62, *59, 60, 61*
Karachi *see* ethnic extremism in Karachi
Karachi City Commission (KCC) 175
Karpatri ji, Svami 87
Kashikandha text 86
Kashi Pradakshina Darshan Yatra Samiti (KPDYS) 80–1, 87, 89, 92
Kashi Vishvanath Trust (KVT) 81, 88
Kataragama Deviyo 108
Katra (neighbourhood/residential cluster) 70, 71
Kavadi dancing 109
Kennedy, Jackie 162
Khalsa College at Amritsar 72
Khan, Ayub 162
Kirti Sri Rajasimha 101–2
Kjellberg, Seppo 207
Kong, Lily 97–8
Kudva, Neema 118
Kumbh melas 67
Kyaik Than Karo Pagoda 33, 36, 38

land-use zoning 186
Larson, Gerald 10
Lashkar-e-Jhanvi (LeJ) 169
Lazzaretti, Vera 19
Le Corbusier (architect) 189
Levy, Robert 206
Liberation Tigers of Tamil Eelam 100
Local Intelligence Unit (LIU) 89
local theories of dwelling 82
Lutyens, Edwin 187

Madras Regulation 7 (1817) 123
male calf donation 149–54, *151, 152*
marginalisation: Buddhist Burman people 28, 41, 42; poor urban areas in Karachi 172; South Asia 14–18
Marshall, John 121–2
Matti, Stephanie 18
meaning-making devices 13
militarization of space in Delhi 122
Ministry of Tourism 75
Ministry of Urban Development 75
modernist planning 118
Modern Movement 189
Muhajirs migrants 17, 163–4, 166
multireligious cities 203
multi-species diversity 158
Municipal Corporations Act (1835) 35
Murad Khani district *see* Kabul (old city) religious heritage

214 *Index*

museumfication and informality 207–8
Muslims: Islamisation program 169;
    population changes in Karachi 163–4;
    Qizilbash Muslims 46, 50–5; Shi'a
    Muslims 46, 52
Muttahida Quami Movement (United
    National Movement – MQM) 166–7,
    175, 177
Myanmar *see* Burman-Buddhist
    nationalism in Myanmar

Nanak, Guru 69
Nasrin, Taslima 4
neoliberal age/neoliberalism 4–6, 137,
    138, 144
New Friends Colony 68
Nightingale, Carl 124

Orientalist imagination 86
Orsi, Robert 205–6
'otherworldly space' notion 206

Pakistan *see* ethnic extremism in
    Karachi
Pakistan Peoples Party (PPP) 167, 177
parikramas, defined 85
Parish, Steven 5
Partition (1947) 163, 165
Partition holocaust (1947) 4
Pashtuns 167
"passive poor" 136
Patel, Sujata 11
Pentecostalism 194
People for Animals-Gurgaon 148
Peoples Peace Committee (PAC) 167
Perlman Principles 8
place-identity 9, 38, 42, 202–3
Planning Aid for London 193
political space for religious structures
    121–4
politicization of pilgrimage 84
Portuguese Catholics 107, 110
Portuguese territories 101
PRASAD (Pilgrimage Rejuvenation and
    Spiritual Augmentation Drive) 75, 77
pre-colonial Indian medieval cities 35
pre-industrial cities 67–8
private sector development 120
Protestant work ethic 185–6
Public Health Act (1848) 35
Punjab towns 122

Qizilbash Muslims 46, 50–5

Rakisits, Claude 19
Ramdas, Guru 69
Reformation Committee for a
    Development Plan for the Pancakroshi
    Yatra Circuit 85–6
religion and gender in Indian urban
    planning: belief and spirituality,
    importance of 190–1; contemporary
    priorities 189–90; Gender
    Mainstreaming Toolkit 194–5, 196;
    introduction 183–4; mainstreaming
    religion into 197–8; power of prayer and
    planning 194–5; relationship between
    184–6; United Kingdom *vs.* 191–4;
    urban planning 186–8; zoning concerns
    186, 188–9
Religion and the Rise of Capitalism
    (Tawney) 186
religion and urban policy for South Asia:
    future of 205–9; gender and 205;
    introduction 201–5; museumfication
    and informality 207–8; production
    of informality 204–5; for sustainable
    cities 202–3; trans-species planning and
    sustainable cities 208–9; urban religion
    studies 205–7
Religious Endowments Act (1863) 123
religious fundamentalism 4, 19
religious heritage 12, 91
religious structures on traffic lanes in
    New Delhi: Auliya Mosque 127, *127*,
    128; concluding comments 138–9;
    exceptional places *132*, 132–5, *133*,
    134, *135*; framework of analysis
    118–19; general observations 130–2;
    informality as disjuncture and exception
    135–8; introduction 117–18; Irwin
    Road Mosque 127, 129–30; negative
    definitions of informality 119–21;
    origins of 124–30; political space
    121–4; Shahi Masjid Zabta Ganj,
    Rajpath 124–6, *125*, *126*
Rio UN declaration (1992) 188
road junction shrines 106–7
Roberts, Nicholas 124
Roman Catholic shrines 107
Roy, Ananya 118, 137, 138, 144
Royal Commission on the State of Large
    Towns (1844–1845) 35
rural syndrome 68

sacrality 10, 13
Saivite Hindu 104

Index 215

Sanyal, Bishwapriya 118
Second Anglo–Burmese War 31
Seddiqi, Seddiq 48
segregation concerns 39, 58
self-determination 144
sense of place notion 82–3
sexism 187
Shahi Masjid Zabta Ganj, Rajpath 118, 124–6, *125*, *126*
Shahr-e-Nau (New City) district in Kabul 56
Sharif, Nawaz 167, 175
Shi'a Muslims 46, 52
Shiromani Gurdwara Prabandhak Committee (SGPC) 72–3
Shivananda Sarasvati, Dandi Svami 87
Shrine of the Golden Temple (Sri Harmander Sahib) 69
Shringar Gauri 89–90
Sikhism in Amritsar, India: conclusion 76–8; global and national agenda 73–6; golden period of 71; institutionalisation of 72–3; introduction 67–9; rebuilding of 70–1; Sikhism in 68, 69–70
Simhachalam temple 149
Singh, Ranjit 71, 72
Singh Sabha Movement 72
Sinhala Buddhism 97, 98, 100–1, 104, 106, 108
Sipahe Mohammed Pakistan (SMP) 170
Sipah-e-Sahaba Pakistan (The Army of the Companions of the Prophet-Pakistan-SSP) 169–70
socio-cultural inequalities 205
socio-spatial justice 9
South Asia: introduction 1–3; marginalisation and violence 14–18; in neoliberal age 4–6; in sustainable cities 6–10; urban histories and heritage 10–14; *see also* religion and urban policy for South Asia
South Asian Association for Regional Cooperation (SAARC) 3
Soviet Union 56–7
spatial fragmentation 17
Suez Canal opening 103
Sunni Afghanistan 50
Sunni Tajiks 51
Sunni Tehrik (the Sunni Movement-ST) 170
sustainable cities: components of 188; contested space and 82–4; development agenda 118, 121; engagement with

informality 155; Hindu religion and 154–5; historic cities as 67; new conceptions of 137; religion heritage for 202–3; South Asia 6–10; trans-species planning and 208–9; urban development 37–8
Sustainable Development Priorities for South Asia report 17

Taliban 58, 170–1
Tamil Hindus 106, 108–10
Tamil Nadu Religious and Charitable Endowments Department 153
Tamils 100, 104, 207–8
Taylor, Bron 156
Tehreek-e-Insaf party (PTI) 169
Tehreek-e-Islami 170
Tehreek-i-Taliban Pakistan (TTP) 170–1
Tehrik Nifaz-e-Fiqh Jafria (TJP) 170
Thayet Taw Monastery 33
Timur Shah 49–50
Tooth Relic festival 102
topography issues 67
trans-regional pilgrimage 85
trans-species planning and sustainable cities 208–9
Treaty of Yandabo 31
Turquoise Mountain 47, 48, 60–3

UNESCO (United Nations Educational, Scientific, and Cultural Organization) 74–6, 185
UNESCO/UN-HABITAT Toolkit 76
United Kingdom (UK) *see* religion and gender in Indian urban planning
urban governance 8
urban histories and heritage 10–14
urban planning/urbanism: India 186–8; introduction 5, 11; Israel 15; lack of in Karachi 162; sustainability of 37–8; zoning concerns 186, 188–9
urban regeneration policy 192–3
urban religion studies 205–7

Varanasi Development Authority 86
Visakapatnam Urban Development Authority (VUDA) 146
Visakha Society for the Care and Protection of Animals (VSPCA) 150
Vishaka Urban Development Authority (VUDA) 153
Vyas ji, Kedarnath 87, 89
Vyas Pith (Well of Knowledge) 87–9

216 Index

Wadiwel, Dinesh 158
Ware, Anthony 18
Watson, Vanessa 136
Well of Knowledge 80
women's suffrage 187
World Heritage Centre 74
World Heritage status 75, 203, 208
World Monuments Fund Watch List 59
World War II 190

Yangon Heritage Trust 27
Yangon/Rangoon *see* Burman-Buddhist
nationalism in Myanmar
yatras, defined 85, 86
Yiftachel, Oren 15

Zain al-Abedin shrine 53
Zia-ul-Haq 169
zoning concerns 186, 188–9